Lawyers, Clients & Narrative

Lawyers, Clients & Narrative

A Framework for Law Students and Practitioners

Carolyn Grose

PROFESSOR OF LAW AND DIRECTOR OF SKILLS INTEGRATION
MITCHELL HAMLINE SCHOOL OF LAW

Margaret E. Johnson

PROFESSOR OF LAW, DIRECTOR OF THE BRONFEIN FAMILY LAW CLINIC
AND CO-DIRECTOR OF THE CENTER ON APPLIED FEMINISM
UNIVERSITY OF BALTIMORE SCHOOL OF LAW

CAROLINA ACADEMIC PRESS
Durham, North Carolina

Library of Congress Cataloging-in-Publication Data

Names: Grose, Carolyn, author. | Johnson, Margaret E., (Law teacher), author.
Title: Lawyers, clients & narrative : a framework for law students and
    practitioners / Carolyn Grose and Margaret E. Johnson.
Other titles: Lawyers, clients and narrative
Description: Durham, North Carolina : Carolina Academic Press, [2017] |
    Includes bibliographical references and index.
Identifiers: LCCN 2017024286 | ISBN 9781531003845 (alk. paper)
Subjects: LCSH: Practice of law--United States. | Law--Vocational
    guidance--United States. | Lawyers--Training of--United States. | Attorney
    and client--United States.
Classification: LCC KF300 .G76 2017 | DDC 340.023/73--dc23
LC record available at https://lccn.loc.gov/2017024286

e-ISBN 978-1-53100-385-2

CAROLINA ACADEMIC PRESS, LLC
700 Kent Street
Durham, North Carolina 27701
Telephone (919) 489-7486
Fax (919) 493-5668
www.cap-press.com

Printed in the United States of America
2018 Printing

To Matt, Max and Maya
for being so supportive and loving.
—Margaret

To my parents, Claudia and Peter Grose,
for their enduring curiosity and encouragement.
—Carolyn

Contents

Acknowledgments

This book has been a labor of love, aided along the way by countless colleagues, mentors, students and friends. Mitchell Hamline School of Law (MHSL) and Dean Mark Gordon supported Carolyn with summer research fellowships; and Roger Haydock, Jim Hilbert, Ann Juergens, Peter Knapp, Kate Kruse and Dean Raths, in particular, contributed ideas and experience to chapters throughout the book. University of Baltimore School of Law (UB) and Dean Ron Weich supported Margaret with a summer research fellowship and sabbatical leave to write this book. And UB's current and former clinical faculty supported and inspired us in our narrative journey, especially Jaime Lee, Leigh Goodmark (U. Md.), Michele Gilman and Jenn Kim (Cardozo).

In addition, thanks to our readers and editors—Elizabeth Cooper (Fordham), Michele Gilman (UB), Peter Knapp (MHSL), Binny Miller (WCL), Sarah Paoletti (Penn), Laurie Morin (UDC David A. Clarke School of Law) and Shanta Trivedi (UB); research assistants—Kathleen Seifert, Jennifer Mahan and Elizabeth "Addie" Crawford; UB law librarians—including Bijal Shah, Adeen Postar and Savanna Nolan; and workshop participants at MHSL, UB, UDC LLM program and University of Pennsylvania. Thanks also to the Clinical Law Review Writers' Workshop and the AALS Clinical Conference for allowing us to workshop portions of the book two years in a row! And thanks to our patient and creative students (at UB, MHSL, Georgetown and WCL) who have used narrative and storytelling to represent clients, and taught us more and more about its power as a tool for effective lawyering. Margaret wants to give thanks to Carolyn for this fun and amazing opportunity to collaborate. Carolyn wants to thank Margaret for launching us on this incredible journey—and keeping us on track till the last cite was checked!

Finally, we list below particular people or resources who helped shape different pieces of each chapter. Thanks to all of you for your generosity and wisdom.

Chapter One: We are indebted to those with whom we have taught storytelling and lawyering, from whom we learned so much, and with whom we developed many of the lessons shared here. First and foremost is Ann Shalleck (WCL) with whom we taught early in our teaching careers and whose work in this area is an inspiration. In addition, thanks to Nancy Cook, Diane Weinroth (WCL), Vivian Hamilton (William & Mary), Matt Fraidin (UDC), Leigh Goodmark, Binny Miller, Deborah Epstein (Georgetown) and Rachel Camp (Georgetown).

Chapter Two: We thank Roger Haydock, Ann Juergens and Peter Knapp for their guidance and materials on self-evaluation in a required course.

Chapter Three: Thanks to Ann Shalleck and Diane Weinroth and the rest of the Women and the Law Clinic crew who provided the foundation for the Evaluation and Reflection exercise at the end of this chapter.

Chapter Four: We are grateful to Michelle Jacobs (Florida) for bringing the importance of cross-cultural competency to the forefront in clinical teaching, and Susan Bryant (CUNY) and Jean Koh Peters (Yale) for providing teaching resources for clinicians to help our students grapple with and learn about these important lawyering issues. Also thanks to Deborah Epstein for creating a practical exercise to build students' ability to reflect on their identity and their collaborations. And to Liz Keyes (UB) for sharing her experience and ideas for these two subjects with us. We thank Deborah Epstein, Sophie Sparrow (UNH) and Rachel Camp for their work in the area of collaboration. And finally, we thank Kim Grose Moore (Carolyn's sister) for enlightening us with her research and ideas, especially as to cross-cultural competency and collaboration.

Chapter Five: Thanks to Laura Rovner (Denver), Marty Guggenheim (NYU), and Jean Koh Peters, who, along with Margaret, created the *Derrico* hypothetical for the 2011 AALS Conference on Clinical Education; and to Ann Shalleck who introduced us to the terms "narrative probing" and "narrative listening."

Chapter Six: We thank Ann Juergens for the Judge Wapner example. The family of this "son of a tailor" was actually her client!

Chapter Seven: Thanks to Peter Knapp, Ann Juergens and Roger Haydock for their creation, with Carolyn, of the tort simulation we use in this chapter. Thanks to Jaime Lee and Bernice Grant (Penn) and Amy Dillard (UB) for their ideas regarding fact investigation and transactional lawyering and criminal lawyering respectively.

Chapter Eight: Thanks to Alison Korn (UCLA) for sharing her adaptation of Joy Radice (Tenn) and Paula Schaefer's (Tenn) presentation at the 2013 Southern Clinical Conference entitled "Integrating Negotiation into the 1L Curriculum." The Jack Donaghy clips and exercise came from them.

Chapter Nine: The landlord-tenant hypothetical comes from Mitchell Hamline School of Law's first-year Lawyering course. Thanks to Dean Raths and, before him, Mehmet Konar-Steenberg and Deborah Schmedemann for the excellent material.

Chapter Ten: We thank Peter Knapp for introducing us to the *Picket Fences* example and analysis.

Chapter Eleven: Thanks to Andrew Krouse, formerly of MHSL, for the "IRAC" paragraph example.

Chapter Twelve: We thank Elizabeth Cooper and Marcy Karin (UDC) who shared legislative advocacy ideas and materials with us.

Final Notes: Any analysis of others' creative work, such as that in *Serial*, is the opinion of Professors Carolyn Grose and Margaret Johnson, and not necessarily those of the authors of the other creative work. Professors Grose and Johnson provide opinions in this text that are the product of their legal and teaching expertise and experience. Also, the authors have chosen, for editorial reasons and without presumptions about gender identity, to use she/her when referring to or describing lawyers or law students; and he/him for all other characters—e.g., clients, judges, witnesses, etc.

Introduction

I. Introduction

"Lawyers are storytellers." "The law is all about storytelling." "To be a good lawyer, you have to be a good storyteller." These phrases appear throughout popular, scholarly and academic literature about our profession, so much so that students and new lawyers might well feel that although they have done well in law school and passed the bar, they might not, after all, have what it takes to succeed in their chosen profession. They are lawyers or soon-to-be lawyers, not experts in storytelling!

This book is for those law students and new lawyers who want to develop more fully as effective legal professionals by learning how to hear, tell, construct and deconstruct stories. Built around concrete lawyering skills and values, and using examples of storytelling from popular media, this book is a comprehensive examination of how to lawyer using narrative.

This is the first legal education text that systematically addresses lawyering and narrative across the broad array of lawyers' skills and values specifically for law students in experiential-based courses. Each chapter is built around at least one such skill or value, providing examples of storytelling from the media, and specific exercises to teach lawyering through narrative. One tool we will use from popular culture to explore story construction, narrative, and storytelling techniques is Season One of the podcast *Serial*, which is described as "one story told week by week." Through twelve installments, the podcast explores the alibi of Adnan Syed, a high school kid convicted of murdering his ex-girlfriend Hae Min Lin on an afternoon in 1999. We recommend you listen to the *Serial* podcast as you work on your narrative and storytelling through this book. All episodes are available for free at serialpodcast.org.

By the end of this book, we hope you will understand how the full range of lawyering fits with narrative and storytelling. After working through this book, chapter by chapter, you will be able to identify narrative components and the choices to be made in constructing stories. And you will learn to implement those choices when you conduct interviews; engage in legal counseling, negotiation, fact investigation and planning; develop case and project theories; and practice oral and written advocacy. In addition, you will be able to use narrative theory to engage in critical reflection and professional development, to explore questions of justice and multi-cultural competency, and to practice creative and effective problem-solving. We hope, in short, that you will feel that you do indeed have what it takes to succeed in your chosen profession!

II. Lawyering Practice and Narrative

Lawyers perform a range of activities that the American Bar Association and legal education categorize as "skills and values."[1] Lawyering skills include activities such as: client, witness and stakeholder interviewing; legal counseling; legal research and analysis; fact investigation, development and analysis; negotiation and other alternative dispute resolution methods; oral and written advocacy; advising entities, groups or individuals regarding various kinds of legal compliance; legislative advocacy; community organizing; drafting of pleadings, motions, contracts and other non-litigation legal documents; engaging in discovery and other pre-trial activities; planning for and conducting trial skills; and creating business entities.[2]

To perform these skills successfully, lawyers need to be effective listeners and creative problem-solvers. We need to be able to collaborate effectively, and engage in critical self-reflection and evaluation. We must be open to examining and challenging assumptions we and those we interact with hold. We must be curious, critical thinkers, able to identify and resolve ethical issues professionally. We must be cross-culturally competent, and pursue justice, whatever form that

---

1. Robert MacCrate, Esq. and the American Bar Association Section of Legal Education and Admissions to the Bar, Legal Education and Professional Development—An Educational Continuum: Report of the Task Force on Law Schools and the Profession: Narrowing the Gap 138–141 (1992), http://www.american bar.org/content/dam/aba/publications/misc/legal_education/2013_legal_education_and_ professional_development_maccrate_report).authcheckdam.pdf (hereinafter "MacCrate Report").

2. Alicia Alvarez and Paul R. Tremblay, Introduction To Transactional Lawyering Practice 7–9 (2013).

may take. Most of all, we lawyers need to make intentional choices about how to develop, maintain, and exercise all of these skills and values.[3]

So what does all of this have to do with narrative and storytelling, and this book? Remember, "Lawyers are storytellers." "The law is all about storytelling." "To be a good lawyer, you have to be a good storyteller." Trials and other kinds of advocacy, and legal counseling and problem-solving are examples of the ways in which narrative and storytelling are embedded in the lawyering skills and values described above.

A. Trials and Advocacy

Because good stories depend on an understandable and compelling ordering of facts, they are great tools for legal persuasion and advocacy. Cases go to trial because there are factual disputes, not legal ones. If the dispute is purely legal, the matter would be decided on a motion to dismiss or a motion for summary judgment. Trials, therefore, seek resolution of battling narratives. A judge or jury is asked to decide whose version of the facts — whose rendition and explanation of "what happened" — is the most persuasive and compelling. The facts themselves don't win the trial — it is the choices the lawyer makes about how to order and use those facts that makes a story compelling enough to persuade the decision maker. Such choices might include which facts to highlight, and which to leave in the background; what character traits to emphasize and deemphasize; which details to use to appeal to the decision maker's emotions in a way that helps your story; and which to leave out so as to avoid a negative emotional reaction. When we construct a compelling story to achieve the client's goal then we are able to persuade the decision maker to see the facts the way we want him to see them and to resolve the dispute in a way that favors our clients.

Episode Two of *Serial*, Season One, provides a really good example of dueling factual narratives, and how they might or might not be persuasive to a decision maker. The parties created these narratives from the same broad set of facts (events and people) and applied them to the same criminal law. Yet they are different narratives, and whichever one is believed by the jury will prevail.

As laid out in Episode Ten, at the trial of Adnan Syed, the prosecutor described the defendant as a Pakistani male enraged about his loss of control over his ex-girlfriend, Hae Min Lee, after they had broken up. The prosecu-

---

3. The MacCrate Report includes a few other skills (communication and law practice management) and values (competent representation; justice, fairness and morality; improve profession; professional development). MacCrate, *supra* note 1, at 138–141.

tion's narrative played into "masterplots"—stories that already exist in main-stream culture, often built around stereotypes,[4] that capture an audience's imagination as familiar and compelling narratives. Here, the prosecutor's story was of an immigrant (despite the fact that Adnan was not an immigrant at all) from a non-western country (Pakistan). This narrative played into anti-immigrant fears, including those regarding Pakistanis because of the so-called "War on Terror." The prosecution's narrative also played into the masterplot of domestic violence, as seen in the O. J. Simpson case,[5] where a male partner is shunned by the female partner, and then uses physical violence to harm or control her.

The defense in the Adnan Syed case, meanwhile, presented a narrative based on a different masterplot—this time the one about a corrupt and/or inept police department. Interestingly, this is the same masterplot that the O. J. Simpson defense team used to great effect in gaining Simpson's acquittal.[6] Here, the defense claimed the prosecution had the wrong guy, that Adnan Syed was not the murderer,[7] and suggesting that the police and prosecutor had overlooked clues that could exonerate Adnan. Which of these two narratives won the day? *Serial* leaves the impression that the prosecution successfully convicted Adnan in part because its narrative was more persuasive and effectively presented, and because the defense failed to construct the best narrative it could have. Two narratives, based on the same set of facts, with wildly different results: lawyers' choices about narrative construction matter!

B. Legal Counseling and Problem-Solving

Although most of popular culture focuses on lawyers in litigation, where narrative and storytelling are critically important, a large percentage of all

---

4. Stefan H. Krieger & Richard K. Neumann, Jr., Essential Lawyering Skills: Interviewing, Counseling, Negotiation And Persuasive Fact Analysis 133–34 (4th ed. 2011) (discussing script schemas, akin to stock stories, that play into the audience's understanding of predefined events, groups, or personality types); Anthony G. Amsterdam & Jerome Bruner, Minding The Law 121–122 (2002) (discussing masterplots, what they call stock scripts).

5. *People of the State of California v. Orenthall James Simpson,* Superior Court of the State of California for the County of Los Angeles, Case No. BA097211 (1995). Trial transcripts can be found at http://edition.cnn.com/US/OJ/trial/.

6. http://edition.cnn.com/US/OJ/trial/.

7. The defense did not identify who the murderer was. Of course, legally the defense does not have the burden of proof in a criminal trial and only needs to show there is reasonable doubt that the prosecution's case is correct.

lawyers engage in lots of other forms of lawyering.[8] For one thing, most cases do not in fact go to trial. In criminal cases, 97% of federal cases and 94% of state cases are resolved without a trial.[9] It is estimated that 80–92% of all civil cases settle.[10] In addition, a large number of all lawyers perform transactional work as well as or instead of litigation work.[11] And narrative and stories can help with all of these.

For instance, in legal counseling, lawyers must help a client identify the issue he is facing and his goals in resolving it. Then the lawyer must work with the client to identify legal and non-legal options that could potentially address the issue consistent with the applicable legal framework. The lawyer works with the client to evaluate potential options based on the client's goals by thinking through the legal and non-legal consequences. Finally, the client needs to make a decision.

How can narrative and stories help with this? As we will explore in Chapters One and Two, narratives describe a character's steady state, or status quo, and a problem that disrupts that steady state. The plot of the narrative is propelled by the character's efforts to resolve the problem. By requiring attention to both the qualities of a character's steady state and the characteristics of the problem disrupting that steady state, narrative helps the lawyer focus on the client, the client's problem and the client's hopes for resolution. Through narrative, lawyer and client can clarify that problem and identify potential solutions that are consistent with the client's goals for resolution.[12]

III. Structure of This Book

Chapters One and Two of this book provide a primer on basic narrative theory, including narrative components, and how to construct a narrative. Chapter One provides you with the vocabulary and tools to construct your legal narratives with your client. These elements are malleable by you, as Chapter

---

8. Ruthe Catolico Ashley, *Creating the Ideal Lawyer*, http://www.americanbar.org/content/newsletter/publications/new_lawyer_home/ideal.html.

9. Erica Goode, *Stronger Hand for Judges in the 'Bazaar' of Plea Deals* (March 22, 2012), http://www.nytimes.com/2012/03/23/us/stronger-hand-for-judges-after-rulings-on-plea-deals.html?_r=0.

10. Jonathan Glater, *Study Finds Settling Better than Going to Trial* (August 7, 2008), http://www.nytimes.com/2008/08/08/business/08law.html.

11. Kenneth N. Klee, *Teaching Transactional Law*, 27 CAL. BANKR. J. 295 (2004).

12. Don't worry! Chapter One goes into detail regarding the components of a narrative, including these elements of characters, events, including setting, masterplots, and closure, involving steady state, problem and resolution.

Two discusses, but first you need to know what they are and the purposes they serve. With this knowledge you can then make informed choices about how to construct your narratives to achieve your clients' or other lawyering goals.

Chapters Three and Four focus on general legal skills and values, such as collaboration, cross-cultural competency, critical reflection and professionalism. These chapters will help you integrate narrative into your lawyering to enhance your performance in these areas. In addition, these chapters show how increasing your multicultural competency, for example, will increase your narrative competency and make your lawyering more effective.

The remaining chapters teach you how to use narrative theory and storytelling across a range of specific lawyering skills and values, including interviewing, case and project theory development, fact investigation, legal counseling, negotiation, and oral and written advocacy. All lawyers practice these skills, whether they focus on litigation, transactional practice, legislative advocacy or community organizing.

Compelling narratives should begin with a "well-told promise" that the narrative will be worth the audience's time.[13] Season One of *Serial* begins with its storyteller's explanation that "For the last year, I've spent every working day trying to figure out where a high school kid was for an hour after school one day in 1999, or, if you want to get technical about it, and apparently I do, where a high school kid was for twenty-one minutes after school one day in 1999." These opening lines compel us to keep listening—over the course of twelve episodes—to learn everything we can about Adnan Syed and those twenty-one minutes. While perhaps not quite as compelling as a missing twenty-one minutes and a teenage homicide, we hope that our promise that this book will teach you how to be better lawyers is well told enough to keep you reading through to the end.

---

13. Andrew Stanton, *The Clues to a Great Story (March 2012)*, http://www.ted.com/playlists/62/how_to_tell_a_story (Stanton is the screenwriter for the successful Pixar movies Toy Story, Finding Nemo and Wall-E).

Lawyers, Clients & Narrative

Chapter 1

Story and Narrative Basics

I. Introduction

Where better to begin a book aimed at lawyering, stories and narrative than to give you the basic components and choices that turn life events into narratives and stories? This chapter introduces the various elements and structural components of a narrative: these are the tools to help you both to construct a narrative with your clients as well as to hear narratives and decipher the stories embedded in them that your clients and others tell you.

II. *Serial*

This chapter will focus on the following episodes of *Serial*, Season One (hereafter referred to as *Serial*) at www.serialpodcast.org: Episode One, Episode Two, Episode Three (from beginning to 17:00), Episode Ten (beginning at 8:30), and Episode Twelve. If you haven't done so already, we ask that you listen to these portions of *Serial*.

III. Story and Narrative Defined

Before getting more deeply into how narrative and story make lawyering more effective and interesting, let's agree on some terms, particularly *story* and *narrative*, because they really do mean different things. And though at first blush, this distinction might seem very technical, as we work our way through this chapter, we hope these terms and their meanings become much more accessible.

Simply put: story is "what is told" and narrative is "how the story is transmitted."[1] Story is the events that transpire (what is told) and narrative is the representation of those events (how the story is transmitted).[2] Let's turn to a basic fairy tale, "Little Red Riding Hood."[3] In Little Red Riding Hood the *story* is the events that happened to Little Red Riding Hood as she walked through the woods, and the *narrative* is how these events are represented to the reader.

Let's consider the concept of time. *Story*, the happening of events, is bound by the laws of time and as such, can only move through time from the beginning to the middle and to the end.[4] Think again of Little Red Riding Hood. The *story*—bound by time—follows a forward progression sequence of events:

1. Little Red Riding Hood walked through the woods to get food to her sickly grandmother.
2. As she walked, a disguised wolf told her to pick flowers.
3. She stops and picks flowers.
4. The wolf goes ahead to the grandmother's house.
5. The wolf eats the old woman and puts on her clothes.
6. When Little Red Riding Hood appears, the wolf tricks her and then eats her.[5]

That is the *story* as it happened in the world—bound by time, it occurs in chronological order.

Now let's compare *narrative*. Because a *narrative* is how the story is constructed or represented, it is not bound by the story's order or time.[6] Indeed, one scholar suggests that *narrative* is how we organize our "understanding of time."[7] The ordering of events and the passage of time in the narrative are within the author's control. Indeed, as we will see later in the book, these are

---

1. Routledge Encyclopedia of Narrative Theory 566 (David Herman, et al. eds., 2005) (emphasis and internal citations omitted). It is important to note that this Encyclopedia along with other Narrative Theory text refer to what we are calling "narrative" as "discourse" or "narrative discourse." For accessibility reasons, we have chosen to stick to two terms, narrative and story. See also Monika Fludernik, An Introduction to Narratology 21 (2009).

2. H. Porter Abbott, The Cambridge Introduction to Narrative 13 (2d ed. 2008) (providing the example that " 'my dog has fleas' " is not a narrative because there is no event or action, but "my dog was bitten by a flea' " is a telling of an event and hence, a narrative).

3. Charles Perrault, *Little Red Riding Hood*, http://www.pitt.edu/~dash/perrault02.html.

4. Abbott, *supra* note 2, at 238 (emphasis omitted).

5. There are lots of versions to this story. This one is the original story by Charles Perrault, *supra* note 3.

6. Abbott, *supra* note 2, at 237–238.

7. Abbott, *supra* note 2, at 3 (emphasis omitted).

choices a lawyer (as the constructor of a narrative with her client) must make in order to present the narrative effectively.

Going back to Little Red Riding Hood, one recent narrative of this story is the animated movie *Hoodwinked!* That narrative does not begin with Little Red Riding Hood taking her walk in the woods to her grandmother's house. Instead, the *narrative* begins with the girl being attacked by the wolf at her grandmother's house, and then goes back in time to tell what happened.[8] The chronological *story* describing the events that happened in the world is transformed (by the screenwriter and director) into a *narrative* that plays with time and place and structure.

These concepts apply to our lawyering just as much as they do to Little Red Riding Hood. Our client's *story* is the events that took place in his life that caused him to come looking for legal help. Multiple *narratives* emerge from this *story*. First, there is the *narrative* the client presents to the lawyer—his account of "what happened." Then multiple *narratives* evolve over the course of the lawyer-client relationship as the lawyer works with the client to represent— orally and in writing—the events that happened to the client. As one narrative theorist explains, "we never see a story directly, but instead always pick it up *through* the narrative discourse."[9]

Consider this description: "When I woke up I packed two loaded guns and ski mask, drove to the bank, robbed it, and was back in time for dinner."[10] That is a narrative about a bank robbery. Here is another description of those same events: "He loved that old familiar, yet always strangely new, sensation of being someone else inside his ski mask, a pistol in each hand, watching the frightened teller count out a cool million. Nothing like it to wake a guy up. Nothing like it to give him a good appetite."[11] The audience reading or listening to these narratives has to discern the actual time and ordering of events, thereby constructing what we call "the story."[12] The audience will construct a very different *story* after hearing the first narrative—an antiseptic listing of events— than from the second narrative, which focuses on the thrill of the crime. And that is the power of narrative: the constructor/author/teller can take the same series of events and make choices about such components as order and detail and time (we will get into all that in a minute), resulting in very different interpretations by the audience.

---

8. Hoodwinked! (The Weinstein Company 2006).
9. Abbott, *supra* note 2, at 20.
10. Abbott, *supra* note 2, at 16.
11. Abbott, *supra* note 2.
12. Abbott, *supra* note 2, at 17.

IV. Why Narrative and Story?

So why are we teaching you about narrative and story to help you learn about and improve your lawyering?

- Because when you are in court and giving your opening statement, you are presenting a narrative that you and your client constructed.
- Because when you are meeting with an opposing party and trying to mediate a dispute between the parties, you and your client are constructing narratives.
- Because when you are engaging in estate planning, you and your client are constructing potential narratives about the future.
- And because when you are meeting with a small business about drafting its articles of incorporation, you and the business are constructing a narrative.

How does narrative help with these endeavors? Again, the answer is simple: story and narrative are how people communicate with themselves and with each other. Because everyone—lawyers, clients, judges, witnesses, police officers, civil servants, children, refugees, everyone—understands the world through story, when we as lawyers use narrative intentionally, we communicate more effectively.

Narrative helps lawyers be more persuasive by explaining why events happen the way they do, why people are trying to achieve a goal, and what the cause and effect of different obstacles are in trying to reach the goal. These people, or characters, are interesting to audiences because they show human agency, goal-driven action and problem-solving.[13] And audiences root for (or against) characters in the narrative. So narrative helps lawyers relay what happened, and use the facts and the law to create an emotional connection to the legal problem that persuades the decision maker or other audience to find in the lawyer's client's favor.[14]

Narrative makes lawyers better problem-solvers. When lawyers engage with narrative, they are more successful at defining a client's problem, understanding how that problem disrupted the client's steady state, and generating ideas that might resolve the problem. Finally, narrative helps lawyers listen to the client's narrative and reflect upon and gain understanding about why the client constructed his own narrative the way he did.

---

13. ANTHONY G. AMSTERDAM & JEROME BRUNER, MINDING THE LAW 30 (2002) (emphasis added).

14. *Id.* at 110.

The power of narrative to your lawyering is that it can help you control how your audience constructs the story to be discerned from your narrative. To be effective, your narrative has to be *compelling*. It has to make your reader or listener keep reading or listening. It has to engage your audience in wanting to reconstruct the story from the narrative. By making smart choices about the components of your narrative, you can make it compelling and believable. By making smart choices, you can help ensure that your audience will construct the story you intend. By making smart choices, you can help ensure that your audience interprets a visual story, a mental image of what happened, that will make it all the more compelling and memorable.[15]

V. You Are Already a Narrative and Story Expert

As a lawyer, your job is often to facilitate problem-solving or to teach the court or another arbiter about your client's conflict and how best to resolve it. Providing well-constructed narratives will help you do your lawyering. And the best part is, you already know how to construct narratives. No doubt you have been telling stories for most of your life. As a society, we are accustomed to understanding the happenings of the world through narratives that help us to discern stories (the chronological sequence of events involving characters and things). We are also familiar with conveying information to others by constructing narratives.

Think back to Dr. Seuss's classic *And to Think That I Saw It on Mulberry Street*.[16] There, the young boy regularly crafted richly detailed, fantastical stories about the many things he "saw" on his walk back from school, including a Raja riding an elephant with two giraffes astride pulling a military band and an old man in a small house, while the Mayor looked on and an airplane threw down confetti. His story is compelling because of the characters and details he provides. From his narrative, we construct the story of a parade of the exciting creatures he saw on the way home from school. But also from his narrative, we construct the story that this boy wants to tell the best and most fantastical story. He wants to beat other storytellers. In the end, the boy changes his narrative to one involving only a simple horse-drawn cart walking down Mulberry Street. From this new narrative, we construct the story of a boy who wants to abide by his father's edict to tell a true—even if more boring—story of what he saw on his way home from school.

---

15. Routledge Encyclopedia of Narrative Theory, *supra* note 1, at 347.
16. Dr. Seuss, And to Think That I Saw It on Mulberry Street (1989).

We have been hearing stories and using stories to understand the world since childhood. One study reported that among blue-collar white families in Baltimore, mothers with preschool children told one narrative every seven minutes.[17] This rate of storytelling and story-listening is probably not uncommon across all U.S. families. And our media engagement, from television, to movies, to gaming, to podcasts, has only increased our exposure to and engagement with storytelling and listening.

So you have expertise just from living and creating, hearing, and experiencing stories. That expertise was probably honed in school, one way or another. In grade school you might have studied the various elements of a story to learn how to read and write narratives. You have read literature and participated in classroom discussions of storytelling elements such as the characters, plot and setting. And if you were an English major in college, you might have studied literary criticism and narrative theory. But fear not! For our purposes, the elementary school study of stories will provide a solid enough foundation in the tools of story and narrative.

To be able to tell compelling and persuasive narratives on behalf of your client, to be able to listen to narratives told by your client or others and gain insight into all the information contained therein, you will need to understand narrative theory—the choices that create meaning and impact from narrative construction and deconstruction. In the next section, we explain the various components of a narrative and the choices available for constructing narratives using those components. Making choices of whether and how you and your client include these various components is a key to good lawyering.

VI. The Components of a Compelling Narrative[18]

Compelling narratives have certain common elements. For each element there are many choices to be made about the construction of your narrative.

---

17. Amsterdam & Bruner, *supra* note 13, at 114.

18. There are lots of wonderful books on narratology that identify components of narrative. Each provides a slightly different list of components. For instance, Philip Meyer relies on Amsterdam's five components for legal storytelling: scene, cast and character, plot, time frame and human plight. Philip N. Meyer, Storytelling for Lawyers (2014). We rely on H. Porter Abbott's list of components, and have expanded upon it using others' work. Abbott's list is streamlined, manageable, and clear to use as a rubric for lawyers' legally constructed narrative.

Take a moment and think. Did you tell a narrative or were you told a narrative today by a family member, friend or colleague? Do you remember it? Why? Was the narrative compelling and believable? Why or why not? Use this insight to help you explore the parts of an effective narrative.

A. *Characters and Other Entities*

Entities are essential to narrative because they either cause events to happen or events happen to them. The term "entities" includes human or human-like characters and non-human things and is a broader term than characters. Characters are those entities that have human qualities and "act with *intention*."[19] If there are no entities, there are no events.[20] Because our study of narrative is with the goal of lawyering, we will focus on *characters* primarily.

Narratives include human-like *characters* with agency, motivations, emotions and beliefs.[21] Andrew Stanton of Pixar tells us that compelling characters should "have a spine" and an "itch they want to scratch."[22] This is because cognitive science shows us that people are goal-directed and try to figure out other people's goals to assist in achieving their own goals.[23] Characters in a narrative are central as they make the action happen in order to resolve the trouble and restore the steady state or transform it. For instance, in *Finding Nemo*,[24] Marlin, a father clown fish who is separated from his son Nemo, spends the movie searching the ocean to find his son despite his fears of the unknown waters. Marlin's overcoming of his fears to find his son is emotional and compelling. The cognitive science tells us that "emotion determines the meaning of everything" and, therefore, compelling narratives need to be based on emotion.[25]

---

19. ABBOTT, *supra* note 2, at 19.

20. ABBOTT, *supra* note 2, at 19.

21. AMSTERDAM & BRUNER, *supra* note 13, at 113–14. As Amsterdam and Bruner suggest, there are narratologists who may take issues with this list, but for our purposes it should suffice to provide common terminology to provide the foundation for lawyering choices in constructing effective stories. *Id.* at 114. *See also* MEYER, *supra* note 18, at 4–5 (listing story elements as scene, cast and character, plot, time frame and human plight).

22. Andrew Stanton, *The Clues to a Great Story*, TED (Mar. 2012), http://www.ted.com/talks/andrew_stanton_the_clues_to_a_great_story/transcript?language=en.

23. LISA CRON, WIRED FOR STORY: THE WRITER'S GUIDE TO USING BRAIN SCIENCE TO HOOK READERS FROM THE VERY FIRST SENTENCE 65–83 (2012).

24. FINDING NEMO (Walt Disney Pictures 2003).

25. CRON, *supra* note 23, at 44–64.

Characters can be anything with human-like qualities, so they can be people, animals, even places, depending on the story. Not every character is given the same emphasis as the main ones, who are the stars or protagonists. Supporting characters help make the narrative happen. And minor characters are those who add the necessary details to the background of the narrative.[26] Who becomes central to the story and who recedes into the background is a choice we as narrative constructors have. For each character, we need to also define their characteristic traits, motivations, intentions, emotions and beliefs as well as their will to self-determine and self-direct their lives (a.k.a. their agency).

Marian Winnick,[27] the memoirist, provides this useful checklist to review as we construct our characters in order to ensure they will be memorable:

1. Main characters are *likeable* so audience roots for them to succeed.
2. Main characters have *likeable* traits.
3. Main characters have *some flaws* that are usually forgivable but act to give them depth. For instance, Leslie Knope (played by Amy Poehler) in *Parks and Recreation*[28] is committed but she is also naïve.
4. Bad actor characters have *some positive* traits. For instance, Walter White (played by Bryan Cranston) in *Breaking Bad*[29] was manufacturing and dealing methamphetamine and therefore would normally be considered a bad guy with such traits as criminal and dangerous. However, he began the business in order to leave his disabled son and wife with money as he was diagnosed with terminal cancer, so he also had traits of being generous, compassionate and responsible. Here we learn his psychological motivation that gives us more context and hence understanding of what would otherwise be seen as bad actions.

In constructing or deconstructing characters in narratives, we need to develop or discern a character's human qualities (traits) and a character's acts (agency) with intention. This is critical for our legal narrative because courts, opposing counsel, and other stakeholders will make decisions based on their inferences of who did what to whom, who caused the legal problem, and who should be responsible for the legal problem. These inferences from the narratives we construct with our clients are based on our depiction of the char-

---

26. Marion Winik, Presentation at the University of Baltimore School of Law (2016).
27. Marion Winik, http://www.marionwinik.com (last visited Dec. 31, 2016).
28. Parks and Recreation (NBC 2009–2015).
29. Breaking Bad (AMC 2008–2013).

acters and how they exercised their free will or agency in making choices relating to the events at issue in the narrative.[30]

Serial—Characters [31]

Let's go back to *Serial*, Season One (hereinafter *Serial*),[32] to further examine the characters in that narrative. Please listen to Episode One before continuing with this chapter. As you listen to Episode One, focus on Adnan Syed. How do the traits for Adnan shift depending on whether Rabia Chaudry, the state's prosecutor or Sarah Koenig is the storyteller presenting the narrative? Given that Sarah's goal is to find out whether Adnan or Jay is lying (see 11:55 of Episode One), do Sarah's descriptions of Adnan position the listener to believe Adnan or Jay? How so?

How do the characters' traits affect the listener's understanding of the narrative? How do these traits affect the narrative's believability?

Sarah Koenig identifies that Rabia and her brother Saad present the narrative that Adnan is a typical teen. And because he is typical, he can't be a murderer. In Episode One at 4:30, Sarah reports that in addition to being Hae's ex-boyfriend, Adnan is a "good kid, an especially good kid, smart, kind, goofy, handsome." Rabia states that Adnan was the "the community's golden child, honor roll student, volunteer EMT, on the football team, star of track, homecoming king, led prayers at the Mosque." Rabia insists that people were shocked when Adnan was arrested. While Sarah corrects these facts to some degree (Adnan was paid for his EMT work, he was on the track team, but not a star, he played football, he did lead prayers, and was the prince of prom, not homecoming king) the facts are pretty much those one would believe to be inconsistent with a murderer. As Sarah relates, Adnan was an "incredibly likable and well-liked kid." At the original airing of *Serial*, Adnan is 32 years old. As Sarah describes him, he is larger and "properly bearded." But, he has "big eyes like a dairy cow," making Sarah question whether Adnan could in fact have killed Hae. ("Idiotic, I know," she chided herself for her own superficial bias.) Adnan professes his innocence and says he had "nothing to do with Hae's murder and

---

30. MEYER, *supra* note 18, at 73 (2014).

31. STEPHEN ELLMANN, ET AL., *Narrative Theory and Narrative Practices, in* LAWYERS AND CLIENTS: CRITICAL ISSUES IN INTERVIEWING AND COUNSELING 160–164 (2009) (this contains a very useful discussion of Characters and Motives.) Also, in AMSTERDAM & BRUNER, *supra* note 13, at 113, they explain that a bare bones discussion of narrative includes a "*cast of human-like characters,* beings capable of *willing their own actions, forming intentions, holding beliefs, having feelings.*"

32. *Serial,* https://serialpodcast.org/season-one.

doesn't know who did." Yes, Adnan admits he loved Hae, but when she broke up with him, he got over her and was not obsessed with her. He held no ill will towards Hae. He had no motivation to kill her. And Sarah describes that he is "adamant and staunch" about his innocence.

On the other hand, the state prosecutor, who was trying to convict Adnan for Hae's murder, provided the following traits: Adnan was born in the United States, but his parents were Pakistani and conservative Muslims. He was not allowed to drink, smoke or date. But Adnan lied to his family and his Mosque and did date and smoke marijuana. Having risked everything to secretly date Hae, when she broke up with him, Adnan was driven to murder her. Adnan was duplicitous and a liar.

By making the character of Adnan in this narrative complex with lots of traits, we can see him as a person and understand his strengths and weaknesses. By providing more positive than negative traits, Sarah may be trying to present a narrative more sympathetic to Adnan, at least in this first episode, and therefore, has described traits for a character that meet her narrative's goal. Sarah describes Adnan as very likeable, so we root for him to be innocent (and for Sarah to show he isn't lying). He has flaws, for sure, but they make him more likeable because those flaws are forgivable—dating and using drugs like a typical teen.[33]

Sarah Koenig is also a character in her constructed narrative. She certainly has a spine and an itch she wants to scratch, using Stanton's instructions for character development. Accordingly, she too is a compelling character, for whom we want to keep listening to see if she is able to achieve her goal of figuring out who is lying, Adnan or Jay.

B. Events

In narrative, there are the necessary "constituent events," which are "the events that drive the story forward and that lead to other events."[34] And there are the "supplementary events" that occur, but if they were deleted, the story would still move forward.[35] In addition to the selection of which events to include in the narrative, we will consider the timeline of events, how we order

---

33. Again, we need to note that Sarah insists on saying Adnan is a typical "American" teen as if somehow a Pakistani American teen isn't typical but only non-Pakistani or white teens are. We will discuss these issues in her narrative in Chapter Four, when we discuss cross-cultural competency.

34. ABBOTT, *supra* note 2, at 22.

35. ABBOTT, supra note 2, at 22–23.

the events in our narrative, the narrative time of the events, and the setting for the events. The sequence of events is called the plot.[36]

Although the narrative can be ordered differently in time, as discussed above, the audience will infer a story that has a chronological ordering. Therefore, a narrative will have a beginning, middle, and end that may differ from the story's beginning, middle, and end. Which events are included and how they are ordered in the construction of narrative are choices. Often narratives are ordered chronologically because it is an easy way to organize and to listen to a story. There may be good reasons to do this to provide context.

Another option would be to start the narrative with the problem[37] occurring in the narrative and then go back to describe what was happening before the problem. This can put a spotlight on a problem that is disrupting the client's situation, or the so-called steady state.[38] It can highlight the cause of the problem as well. For instance, in a child custody case, a lawyer may want to begin with a moment on the timeline that was the most meaningful to the kid or parent regarding their relationship. The lawyer can describe that moment as if a camera were on its zoom lens—focusing on it as the steady state of the parent/child relationship—and then the story can entail the "wide-angle"[39] lens of describing the entire relationship including the problem that has occurred causing the child custody issue.

Events are constructed in narrative time, not real world time. Therefore, "[i]f an event matters, we dwell on it; we take longer to tell it than it could ever take to happen…."[40] Events are usually located in a setting or story world that is developed to lend credibility and interest in the narrative.

Serial—Events

Events: In *Serial,* the constituent events are what Adnan was doing on January 13, 1999, the date of Hae's murder, what Jay was doing on January 13, 1999, and the way in which Adnan was pursued by the police and prosecuted. The supplementary events—those that do not drive the podcast's narrative forward, but do add interest and complexity—include how the

---

36. Meyer, *supra* note 18, at 11–13. The basic components of plot, according to Meyer, are the (a) regular course of events, or steady state, that gets disrupted by a (b) problem, that is either created by or able to be addressed by human action, and (c) that human tries to address the problem, (d) resulting in the restoration of the old steady state or a new one, and (e) ends with a lesson learned, or moral.

37. See description of "problem" and "steady state" later in this chapter.

38. Amsterdam & Bruner, *supra* note 13.

39. Kim Lane Scheppele, *Foreward: Telling Stories*, 87 Mich. L. Rev. 2073, 2075 (1989).

40. Amsterdam & Bruner, *supra* note 13, at 124.

Innocence Project operates at the University of Virginia Law School.[41] The focus on *Serial*, as Sarah Koenig states at the beginning, is "for the last year, I've spent every working day trying to figure out where a high school kid was for an hour after school one day in 1999, or if you want to get technical about it, and apparently I do, where a high school kid was for twenty-one minutes after school one day in 1999." With this beginning, Koenig unfolds a story of a teen boy, now a man, who is imprisoned for having killed his ex-girlfriend — Hae Min Lee — during those twenty-one minutes. He claims he did not do it, but cannot remember what he was doing during the time she was killed.

Timeline: In Episode Five, Koenig and her producer Dana Chivvis try to recreate the timeline of that afternoon of January 13, 1999. How did Koenig construct a timeline? Why was a timeline important to construct? (For more information on constructing the timeline, visit serialpodcast.org/maps/time lines-january-13-1999.)

Setting: In *Serial* Episode Three, Koenig, Chivvis, and Justin George, a *Baltimore Sun* reporter, visit Leakin Park and the place where Hae Min Lee's body was discovered. How did the descriptions of the Park and the location of Hae Min Lee's body help you to understand the story? Would the audience have gotten as clear a description of the Park or the location of Hae Min Lee's body without Koenig and the others travelling to Leakin Park themselves? Why or why not?

C. Rhetoric, Persuasion and Communication

Rhetoric involves all the elements that lead to how we interpret and find meaning in the narrative.[42] Amsterdam and Bruner suggest that "[r]hetorical narratives use a story rather than a set of propositional assertions to prove something persuasively."[43] This persuasion results from both the author's careful construction as well as the audience's interpretation. The important pieces of the rhetorical power of narrative are (1) causation, (2) normalization, (3) masterplot, and (4) closure.[44]

---

41. See *Serial* Episode 7, https://serialpodcast.org/season-one/7/the-opposite-of-the-prosecution (featuring University of Virginia Innocence Project Clinic).

42. ABBOTT, *supra* note 2, at 40.

43. AMSTERDAM & BRUNER, *supra* note 13, at 134. This persuasion is "more powerful than just as a device for convincing people to *do* something. It is the means ... by which a story shapes reality." *Id.* at 135. Amsterdam and Bruner say the rhetorical power of narrative comes from "value-laden" stories, "tailoring a story to suit an audience," conventionality, and believability. *Id.* at 135–139. These ideas are embedded as well in the structure of narrative we use in this chapter that are taken from Abbott.

44. ABBOTT, *supra* note 2, at 40–41.

1. Causation

As Abbot explains, people are wired to look for causation in the transpiring of events.[45] In constructing a narrative, then, the author sequences events in a way to explain the cause and effect.[46] For instance, in the popular television series *How I Met Your Mother*, each episode is the father telling his two children the story of how he met their mother, and hence how they came to be born. In each episode, the father constructs a narrative that the children interpret to try to discover the cause (the meeting of their parents) that had the effect (their being born). The show lasted nine seasons, throughout all of which, the audience along with the children try to guess which person in the narrative is their mother. The causation of their birth (the father meeting the mother) is finally disclosed in the final episodes of the series, thereby concluding the narrative.[47]

The interpretation of cause and effect is an important piece of our lawyering as we will discuss further in Chapter Six regarding Case and Project Theory.

Serial—Causation

Causation is in the *Serial* podcast as well. For instance, Adnan states in Episode One (21:40), "I had no reason to kill Hae." In other words, there needs to be a motive (cause) for there to be a murder (an effect). And in the final episode (Episode Twelve, 35:50), Koenig and her producers agree that Hae Min Lee was murdered one month after she broke up with Adnan and he was over it, so had no motive to commit murder. Adnan's defense counsel (and Koenig) suggest this lack of a causal connection between Adnan and Hae Min Lee's death, thereby undermining the prosecution's narrative that he committed the crime.

2. Normalization

Narrative coherence and the ordering of events, including cause and effect sequences, provide a sense of "normal" to which people are drawn.[48] Indeed, some scholars suggest that "our need for narrative form is so strong that we don't really believe something is true unless we can see it as a story."[49] Thus, a narrative that is internally consistent (makes sense from beginning to end) AND externally consistent (makes sense with the audience's understanding of

---

45. ABBOTT, *supra* note 2, at 41. See also CRON, *supra* note 23, at 144–165.

46. ABBOTT, *supra* note 2, at 41.

47. How I Met Your Mother (CBS 2005–2014).

48. ABBOTT, *supra* note 2, at 44–45.

49. ABBOTT, *supra* note 2, at 44.

how the world works) is a more believable narrative.[50] Cognitive science shows us that our brains will fight randomness and instead organize information into "meaningful patterns," which help to predict the next event.[51]

A narrative that tells of a person entering a home and closing a wet, dripping umbrella while exclaiming, "I just walked through a fire!" would not fit with our sense of normal. To be externally consistent, she should have burnt clothes, not a dripping wet umbrella, or be coughing from the smoke. To make this narrative conform with our understanding of the world, we may interpret the story as her walking through a fire just as the firefighters doused the area with a fire hose. If that is not what the narrative constructor (the storyteller) wants us to believe, she needs to provide additional information to explain what appears to be an external inconsistency in the narrative.

Serial—Normalization

Turning to *Serial*, Sarah Koenig constructs a narrative that normalizes Adnan Syed so we do not find his proclamation of innocence internally or externally consistent. As discussed above, Koenig begins the series by stating "for the last year, I've spent every working day trying to figure out where a high school kid was for an hour after school one day in 1999, or if you want to get technical about it, and apparently I do, where a high school kid was for twenty-one minutes after school one day in 1999." The fact that Adnan can't account for twenty-one minutes of his time that afternoon could undermine his claim of innocence. But Koenig chooses to frame that fact with contextual information about how people remember things, and shows that Adnan's inability to recall those particular twenty-one minutes actually normalizes him: none of us can recall what we did last week or month, let alone a particular twenty-one minutes! By normalizing him, she invites her audience to empathize with Adnan and see him not as a convicted murderer, but as one of us.

Koenig could have chosen to begin the *Serial* story talking about Adnan being in prison for 16 years, or by describing his size, or his beard, or his Muslim faith. Any of those choices would have been a different narrative about Adnan because those choices could play into an internally and externally consistent story of a guilty person, especially for audiences who are biased against those who are incarcerated, Muslim, large, and bearded. Instead, Koenig as

---

50. David Chavkin, Clinical Legal Education: A Text for Law School Clinics (2002); Amsterdam & Bruner, *supra* note 13.

51. Cron, *supra* note 23, at 185–199.

storyteller seems to further a goal of minimizing what would be wrongful bias against him in determining his innocence and thereby positions Adnan in a more favorable light with the listener.[52]

3. Masterplot

Masterplots "are stories that we tell over and over in myriad forms and that connect vitally with our deepest values, wishes, and fears."[53] David and Goliath is a masterplot that contains the constituent events of a young, small man being able to conquer a menacing large giant. This narrative resonates with values of justice and good triumphing over evil, smarts and merit over non-smarts. Masterplots have "enormous emotional capital that can be drawn on in constructing a narrative,"[54] lending credibility to that narrative.[55] Another way to describe these narratives is "stock scripts" or "stock stories."[56]

---

52. A choice to construct a narrative around anticipated biases rather than to confront them may undermine justice goals of challenging and eradicating prejudices and biases. Indeed, Koenig's storytelling in *Serial* raises questions of prejudice and bias and a lack of cultural competency. Much has been written about this flaw of *Serial*. Anita Sinha, *There Is Nothing Casual About Prejudice: The Popular Podcast 'Serial' and the Notion of Implicit Bias*, The Huffington Post (Dec. 13, 2014), http://www.huffingtonpost.com/anita-sinha/there-is-nothing-casual-a_b_6311000.html (critiquing Koenig's dismissal of discriminatory racial, cultural and religious bias by the jurors and failure to understand the power of implicit bias and its effects on people's decision-making); Jay Caspian Kang, *White Reporter Privilege*, The Awl (Nov. 13, 2014), http://www.theawl.com/2014/11/serial-and-white-reporter-privilege (identifying race, culture and ethnic discriminatory judgments made by storyteller Koenig and her omission of the impact of Adnan's identities, such as his religion and race, on his criminal case); Soraya Roberts, *Thoughts on Race, Journalism, and "Serial,"* Bitch Media (Nov. 20, 2014), http://bitchmagazine.org/post/thoughts-on-race-journalism-and-serial (questioning the claim of white privilege bias in Koenig's reporting, but acknowledging reporter's privilege, and that "it's the job of good reporters of all races to recognize what they don't know and what assumptions they're bringing to the story."); Conor Friedersdorf, *The Backlash Against Serial—and Why It's Wrong*, The Atlantic (Dec. 3, 2014), http://www.theatlantic.com/politics/archive/2014/12/unpacking-the-social-justice-critique-of-serial/383071/ (responding to the critique that *Serial's* "narrator and producer stands accused of exemplifying white privilege, stereotyping Asian Americans and Muslims, racism against blacks, and making 'people of color' cringe."); Steve Rousseau, *Why Was This a Story—Success and "Serial" Backlash*, Digg (Nov. 19, 2014), http://digg.com/2014/serial-podcast-backlash. *Serial* is a worthy subject of study because it shows us the range of narrative construction and also provides lots of fodder for deconstruction and critique.

53. ABBOTT, *supra* note 2, at 46.

54. ABBOTT, *supra* note 2, at 46.

55. ABBOTT, *supra* note 2.

56. AMSTERDAM & BRUNER, *supra* note 13, at 121.

A modern example of such a narrative is being told by protesters against the police shooting of Michael Brown in Ferguson, Missouri, and Freddie Gray's death in police custody in Baltimore, Maryland: anti-Black racism permeates our society and is state-sponsored.[57] Importantly, masterplots as narratives compel us because they are familiar but also because they embed a value or moral that we believe is good and hence compels audiences to root for the character trying to adhere to the value or moral (or against the character working against the value or moral).[58]

Within masterplots, there are recurring characters, called "types." For instance, in the masterplot of state-sponsored anti-Black racism, there are types, including the prison system disproportionately populated by black men and the racist white police officers.[59] In a masterplot about domestic violence, there are two types—the passive female victim and the abusive male perpetrator.[60]

Masterplots create compelling narratives that seem familiar to audiences, with characters that audiences expect to see, and know to root for, or against. They can be challenging as well, however, because in real life, heroes are not always the ones trying to land the sling shot rock, and police officers are not necessarily the villains. Indeed, masterplots are so ingrained in our culture that they shape our understanding of how the world works. Decision makers may find it difficult to interpret facts in a way to counter a masterplot. Narratives that rely on some aspects of a masterplot may hold an audience's interest because they ask us to consider what happens if the masterplot veers from the expected.[61] In this interest lies the understanding that masterplots endure despite past violations to them.[62] As such, masterplots contain their power in narrative.

Serial—Masterplot

The prosecution in the Adnan Syed trial used two masterplots to convince the jury that he was guilty of killing Hae Lee. The first one we heard in Episode

---

57. Alicia Garza, A HerStory of the #BlackLivesMatter Movement, Black Lives Matter, http://blacklivesmatter.com/herstory/.

58. AMSTERDAM & BRUNER, *supra* note 13, at 113–14. As Amsterdam and Burner suggest, there are narratologists who may take issues with this list, but for our purposes it should suffice to provide common terminology to provide the foundation for discussing lawyering choices in constructing effective stories. *Id.* at 114. *See also* MEYER, *supra* note 18, at 4–5 (listing story elements as scene, cast and character, plot, time frame and human plight).

59. MICHELLE ALEXANDER, THE NEW JIM CROW: MASS INCARCERATION IN THE AGE OF COLORBLINDNESS (2010).

60. ABBOTT, *supra* note 2, at 49.

61. AMSTERDAM & BRUNER, *supra* note 13, at 122.

62. AMSTERDAM & BRUNER, *supra* note 13, at 112.

One (9:30–10:20) when Rabia and Saad discuss how the prosecutor painted Adnan as a familiar villain: a dangerous, foreign Muslim man who, in a fit of jealous rage, kills his ex-girlfriend with his own hands. This "type" was created by the prosecution's distortion of Adnan's ethnicity and religion as a Pakistani-American Muslim man.[63] This masterplot develops further during Adnan's bail hearing (Episode Ten around 8:30), where the prosecution describes murders committed by Pakistani men of their ex-girlfriends as honor killings.

Please listen to Episode Two of *Serial* now. What was the second masterplot that the prosecution used to convince the jury that Adnan was guilty of murdering Hae?

4. Closure

Narrative scholars agree that what drives narrative is conflict.[64] And therefore, what ends narrative, often, is resolution of the conflict.[65] Bottom line: "Stories go somewhere. They have an end."[66] So how do we achieve closure in a way that makes the narrative compelling?

Let's start by understanding the conflict and its resolution. Conflict is generally introduced in a narrative through a disruption to a character's "steady state." The steady state is the normal state or status quo of the character's life. If there were no disruption, the steady state would continue into the future. What makes a narrative go is the introduction of a problem that can be addressed by human agency.[67]

In *Finding Nemo*, the steady state is Nemo living happily at the Great Barrier Reef with his father Marlin. Nemo is captured by scuba divers who take him to live in a dentist office aquarium. This is the problem. The steady state—Nemo's and his father's normal life—is disrupted, and the remainder of the movie is about trying to resolve that problem. Closure is achieved when the father succeeds in locating and reuniting with Nemo and returning with him to their home in the Great Barrier Reef.[68] Now there is a new steady state.

How the steady state and disruption are defined in the narrative can affect the audience's interpretation of cause and effect. This interpretation is very important because the law often seeks to determine who is responsible for the

---

63. For more discussion of the use of type and stereotypes in *Serial*, see Chapter Four discussing cross-cultural competency.

64. ABBOTT, *supra* note 2, at 55.

65. ABBOTT, *supra* note 2, at 56.

66. AMSTERDAM & BRUNER, *supra* note 13, at 127.

67. AMSTERDAM & BRUNER, *supra* note 13, at 113–14.

68. Finding Nemo, *supra* note 24.

disruption in a character's steady state, and seeks resolution that will prevent such a disruption from occurring again. Depending on how the legal storyteller defines/describes the steady state and disruption, closure might look very different to different audiences.

It is also possible that a narrative does not close but is nonetheless meaningful or satisfying.[69] Closure happens, according to Abbott, when "expectations are fulfilled [or violated] or questions answered [and enlightenment gained]."[70] It is important to understand that closure "can refer to more than the resolution of a story's central conflict. It has to do with a broad range of expectations and uncertainties that arise during the course of a narrative and that part of us, at least, hopes to resolve, or close."[71]

We can see this concept of closure embedded in the guidance offered by Andrew Stanton, who wrote the Pixar hits *Finding Nemo*, *Toy Story* and *Wall-E*, for creating good, compelling stories. Stanton states that compelling stories need to (1) have a beginning that provides a promise that the story is worth your time; (2) let the audience solve the problem that holds the audience's attention; (3) feature a character that has an itch that needs to be scratched; (4) create drama and anticipation with the uncertainty of what will happen; and (5) develop themes that involve values in which we believe.[72]

Serial—Closure

Listen to Episode Twelve of *Serial*. Is there closure? What is it? Were your expectations met or violated? Were your questions answered or not? How does the closure, or lack thereof, leave the audience? On reflection, was the suspense of whether or not Adnan killed Hae, this lack of closure, compelling to you as a listener of the narrative? Why or why not?

VII. Additional Considerations—Action, Reflection and Stakes

The *Serial* producers themselves provide guidance on how to construct a good narrative: First, there must be action, motion where one thing happens and then another and then another.[73] Second, there has to be reflection, where

---

69. Abbott, *supra* note 2, at 57.

70. Abbott, *supra* note 2, at 58–61.

71. Abbott, *supra* note 2, at 57.

72. Andrew Stanton, *supra* note 22.

73. *Serial*, https://serialpodcast.org/season-one.

the audience gets inside the head of the character experiencing the action and the character says something the audience can connect to, making the experience relatable. [74] And third, there have to be stakes—a question or problem that keeps the audience listening to figure out if it will be answered or resolved.[75]

Throughout the course of this chapter, we have identified the action of *Serial* and the stakes, or the question that Sarah Koenig is trying to answer—that is whether Adnan killed Hae. But what about reflection? Can you identify moments of reflection in Episode One? What are they? How do these moments make the narrative compelling for you?

VIII. Narratives and Storytelling Are Not Dirty Words[76]

The power of narratives comes not from "verifiability but from verisimilitude."[77] This means that narratives are able to captivate and persuade if they are "true enough," even if they are not provably true.[78]

A. Ethical Narratives

At first blush, you may feel uncomfortable thinking of narrative as manipulation, spinning the truth, or even telling falsehoods and violating the Rules of Professional Conduct. To understand the power of narrative and why making choices in the construction of narrative is important to ethical lawyering, we have to go back to the beginning of this chapter and the difference between *events* that happen, *narrative,* and *story.* These help us understand the concept of *truth.*

In the documentary *Stories We Tell,* Academy Award Nominee Sarah Polly investigates a story about her mother by interviewing members of her family. Multiple family members describe the same events, but "[e]ach of the inter-

---

74. *Serial,* https://serialpodcast.org/season-one.

75. *Serial,* https://serialpodcast.org/season-one.

76. Binny Miller, *Telling Stories About Cases and Clients: The Ethics of Narrative,* 14 Geo. J. Leg. Ethics 1 (2000) (article on ethics, case theory and storytelling) and Stefan H. Krieger & Richard K. Neumann Jr., Essential Lawyering Skills: Interviewing, Counseling, Negotiation, and Persuasive Fact Analysis (4th ed. 2011).

77. Amsterdam & Bruner, *supra* note 13, at 30.

78. Amsterdam & Bruner, *supra* note 13, at 30.

viewees has a slightly different perspective, influenced by their own place in the story, and out of their mouths the story becomes entirely different."[79]

This range of narratives about the same set of events is known as the "Rashomon Effect," based on the Kurosawa film *Rashomon*, in which four different people relate four different versions of a murder they all witnessed.[80] It probably seems obvious that multiple perspectives lead to multiple interpretations of the same facts, generating multiple different narratives. Because events are interpreted differently in this way, there really is no such thing as one objective "truth."[81] An example of multiple narratives relaying the same events exists not only within *Serial* with the different narratives of the prosecution and Adnan, but also between the *Serial* podcast and Chaudry's own podcast, *Undisclosed*, about Adnan's wrongful conviction.[82]

B. *Narrative and Justice*

Constructed narratives can have many pitfalls. For instance, narratives in their attempts to persuade audiences with preconceived views may reify stereotypes with masterplots and types.[83] Yet understanding this is the first step in "guarding against its perils."[84] We will discuss in Chapters Three and Four how narrative construction can help improve our cross-culturally com-

---

79. Wesley Emblidge, *"Stories We Tell" Review: Storytelling From Multiple Perspectives*, The Tam News On Line (May 8, 2013), http://thetamnews.org/2013/05/stories-we-tell-review-storytelling-from-multiple-perspectives/.

80. Chavkin, *supra* note 50; Ryûnosuke Akutagawa, In A Grove (1922).

81. This is different from intentionally constructing a false narrative that conflicts with the actual events. For example, in her novel *Gone Girl* [SPOILER ALERT!], Gillian Flynn presents conflicting stories between the wife's diary and the husband's narration. The author resolves the conflict in the end with the disclosure that one of the narratives was intentionally created to be false.

82. *Undisclosed*, http://undisclosed-podcast.com/about/. See also Rabia Chaudry, Adnan's Story: The Search for Truth and Justice After Serial (2016).

83. Amsterdam & Bruner, *supra* note 13, at 113. Telling a story that does not fit the master plot is hard. Matthew I. Fraidin, *Changing the Prevailing Narrative in Child Welfare Cases, in* Representing Parents in Child Welfare Cases (2015); Leigh Goodmark, *When Is a Battered Woman not a Battered Woman? When She Fights Back*, 20 Yale J.L. & Feminism 75 (2008); Elizabeth Keyes, *Beyond Saints and Sinners: Discretion and the Need for New Narratives in the U.S. Immigration System*, 26 Geo. Immigr. L. J. 207 (2012); Lucie E. White, *Subordination, Rhetorical Survival Skills and Sunday Shoes, Notes on the Hearing of Mrs. G*, in Clinical Anthology: Readings for Live Client Clinics (1997); Deborah Epstein, et al., The Clinic Seminar (2014).

84. Amsterdam & Bruner, *supra* note 13, at 113.

petent lawyering and guard against relying on stereotypes that might undermine justice missions.

Lawyering involves constructing narratives that fit with legal elements to win in an adversarial system, or to further a client's goals in a transaction. When constructed without intention and awareness of the narrative elements and their effects, legal narratives can be overly simplistic and fail to provide the context that could result in a just outcome, not simply a legally determined outcome.[85] In the next few chapters, we explore ways to use narrative and storytelling in the context of client-centered lawyering and lawyering driven by justice outcomes. Indeed, when constructed with intention and awareness of narrative elements and their effects, narrative can further lawyering justice missions by overturning power structures through the telling of powerful counter-stories.[86]

IX. Conclusion

This chapter has defined narrative and story. We have identified narrative components and how they are constructed in popular culture narratives to compel, persuade, engage, and communicate with the audience. We have also discussed the control that lawyers have over a narrative, because a narrative represents our understanding of a story. Lawyers must be able to use a story to create a persuasive, emotional, and compelling narrative. This chapter also explored the elements of a compelling narrative. The next chapter takes these narrative basics and discusses how you and your client can choose to employ these components in constructing narratives. As explained and demonstrated in the next chapter, constructing narratives with your client is all about making intentional choices that further your client's goals. Subsequent chapters will explore the use of narrative elements across lawyering activities.

---

85. AMSTERDAM & BRUNER, *supra* note 13, at 118.

86. Richard Delgado, *Storytelling for Oppositionists and Others: A Plea for Narrative*, 87 MICH. L. REV. 2411 (1988); Scheppele, *supra* note 39, at 2075.

Chapter 2

Constructing Stories and Client-Centered Lawyering

I. Introduction

Now that you understand the power of stories and their essential characteristics, you might be saying, "Yes, we get it that story and narrative are essential; now how can we use them to make us better lawyers?" That theory in action is the actual craft of constructing stories, based on choices made with intention and reflection by the lawyer and her client.

II. Constructing Legal Stories

We use the term "Narrative Theory" to describe the study of story *construction*, which is different from—though clearly related to—story *telling*. Construction is the act of building: putting together the elements that will comprise the narrative and then writing it down.[1] Performance of the narrative—reading it, telling it, enacting it—comes later.

Narrative theory studies that process of construction by asking: Once I know the elements of story and narrative, what choices must I make about those elements? What process do I go through to make those choices? By choosing what goes into the narrative, what have I left out? How is the narrative different as a result of those choices? Have those choices been made intentionally or reflexively? What factors influence me in making those choices?

---

1. We use the term "author" here to refer to the person who puts the story together and writes it down—the story constructor. The storyteller might continue the process of construction, but many of the choices have already been made by the time the story gets told or read or enacted.

Narrative theory involves discussions about what stories are and what makes a narrative "good" (persuasive, compelling, goal-oriented), both substantively (the "what" of the narrative) and technically (the "how" of the narrative). The storytelling practice involves constructing and deconstructing stories and narratives, focusing on their elements—both the "what" and the "how"—and on the choices that resulted in the narrative's substance and structure.

Narrative theory and storytelling practice lead to an understanding that we, as lawyers, are constructors of narratives, and, as such, we need to make intentional choices about that construction. In order to do so, we must recognize audience and context as both the engines and frames of effective persuasion; and we must recognize thorough and complex fact gathering as the engines and frames of effective legal counseling.

Lawyering that relies on this kind of narrative theory and storytelling practice both starts from the premise and leads to the realization that "The Law" is made up of a set of narratives that have been adopted by decision makers, and that those narratives have been constructed by none other than lawyers. As you arrive at this conclusion, you begin to recognize the power and responsibility you hold as narrative constructors: you realize that you are makers of "The Law."[2]

Narrative theory is an exploration and elaboration of the idea that the law is made up of narratives that are constructed by lawyers, clients, and decision makers. Each one of these narratives consists of distinct and identifiable elements, both substantive and technical, and each one of these elements is the product of choices made—consciously or not—by the narrative's constructor.[3] Storytelling itself is the craft that puts this theory into practice—the act of constructing the narrative's elements and the choices the storyteller makes in the process, and then the actual telling of the narrative.

Thinking about the practice of law as a practice of constructed storytelling gives us the opportunity to look behind and between and over and under the black letter rules that comprise "The Law."[4] In those interstices, we find facts and language and structure and ideas that go well beyond the holding of an opinion or the mandate of a statute.[5] By viewing the law through a narrative lens, we discover not only "how law is found but how it is made."[6]

---

2. *See* Carolyn Grose, *Of Victims, Villains and Fairy Godmothers: Regnant Tales of Predatory Lending*, 2 Ne. U. L.J. 97 (2010).

3. *Id.*

4. Anthony G. Amsterdam and Jerome S. Bruner, Minding the Law (2000).

5. Law's Stories: Narrative and Rhetoric in the Law (Peter Brooks and Paul Gewirtz eds., 1996).

6. *Id.*

Cultural psychologist Jerome Bruner describes the act of storytelling as so instinctive, so intuitive, as to render an explanation of how we do it close to impossible: "We stumble when we try to explain, to ourselves or to some dubious other, what makes something a story rather than, say, an argument or a recipe."[7] And yet, if we are to be effective storytellers—the kind who explain not only how law is found, but also how it is made—we must be able to overcome this asymmetry between doing and understanding what we do.[8] We must be able to describe—if only to ourselves, so we can do it again—what goes into the making of a narrative.

Lawyers are particular kinds of storytellers, influenced by variables unique to our role as tellers of our clients' narratives. In that role, as makers of legal arguments, we decide in consultation with our client what narrative to tell and how to tell it "guided by some vision of *what matters*."[9] Put another way, in order to figure out what narrative to tell and how to tell it, the lawyer must weigh three substantive factors, the same factors that make up the theory of the case or project (which we explore in Chapter Six of this book): the law, the facts and the client's goals.[10] In addition, of course, the lawyer must consider contextual factors, e.g., the audience, the forum, availability of resources, personality of the client, and potential supporting or detracting characters in the narrative. The lawyer must also take into consideration particular cultural norms and values in deciding among different narratives and ways of telling them. And finally, the lawyer must consider factors personal to him in determining what constructed story to tell and how to tell it: is he comfortable in a courtroom, can he pull off a humorous narrative, does he do better in a more formal or less formal setting, does the client's situation raise personal moral or ethical concerns, etc.

Thus, narratives are not "recipes for stringing together a set of 'hard facts.'"[11] Rather storytellers *construct* the facts and construct the narratives by sorting through what is out there and figuring out both what to say and how to say it, based on the storyteller's own perspective about "what matters."[12] Because a

---

7. JEROME BRUNER, MAKING STORIES: LAW, LITERATURE, LIFE 3–4 (2003).

8. *Id.* at 7.

9. AMSTERDAM & BRUNER, *supra* note 4.

10. Binny Miller has written extensively about the construction of case theory, which is the incorporation of law and facts and client goals into a story that can be used to drive a case or an organizing campaign, etc. Binny Miller, *Give Them Back Their Lives: Recognizing Client Narrative in Case Theory*, 93 MICH. L. REV. 485 (1994).

11. AMSTERDAM & BRUNER, *supra* note 4, at 111.

12. *Id.* at 116.

set of events—a "story"—can be organized into multiple alternative narratives, the choice among them depends on perspective, circumstances, and interpretive frameworks. And those choices are governed by what we care about. Thus the "fabric of narrative reflects the shape of our concerns."[13]

For lawyers, figuring out "what matters" is a complex and nuanced process.[14] When we choose what narrative to tell and how to tell it, we must work hard and with awareness to reconcile and balance these various facets of "what matters." What lawyers must appreciate is that when we choose to tell a particular narrative in a certain way, we are shaping future narratives. If the narrative we present is persuasive, then other stories will be shaped to fit that "winning" narrative. This process reifies what the legal system recognizes as actionable harms, essentially making law. When constructed and told without contextual awareness or intention, therefore, such narratives might make very bad law: e.g., women really being harassed at work quit their jobs; women really being beaten leave their husbands.

An inquiry into the client's narrative context would involve learning about her steady state, which Jerome Bruner and Anthony Amsterdam describe as a state "grounded in the legitimate ordinariness of things."[15] That is, what did the client's day look like? What did it feel like? What characters, animate or inanimate, filled her day? What did she do and not do regularly? What was her life like before the trouble began?

The trouble, of course, describes the reasons for the client's visit to the lawyer. Something happened to disrupt her "legitimate ordinariness." What was it? Who was it? What happened? The trouble, then, involves much more than just the client's "legal" issue. To fully understand why the client has come to the lawyer, the lawyer must come to be familiar with the multiple layers of the client's steady state, and how and why it has been disrupted by the trouble she describes.

---

13. AMSTERDAM & BRUNER, *supra* note 4, at 124.

14. Depending on the kind of relationship the lawyer has with the client, and the kind of lawyer she is, the client might play a significant role in helping to choose and craft the narrative the lawyer tells on his behalf; or he might take a more background role. *See, e.g.* Carolyn Grose, *"Once Upon a Time, In a Land Far, Far Away …": Lawyers and Clients Telling Stories About Ethics (and Everything Else)* 20 HASTINGS WOMEN'S L.J.163 (2009). GERALD LOPEZ, REBELLIOUS LAWYERING: ONE CHICANO'S VISION OF PROGRESSIVE LAW PRACTICE (1992); Lucie E. White, *Subordination, Rhetorical Survival Skills, and Sunday Shoes: Notes on the Hearing of Mrs. G.*, 38 BUFF. L. REV. 1 (1990); Ascanio Piomelli, *Appreciating Collaborative Lawyering*, 6 CLIN. L. REV. 427 (2000).

15. AMSTERDAM & BRUNER, *supra* note 4.

The lawyer must also inquire into and come to understand what efforts at redress the client has made or would like to make. How can the trouble be resolved? How does the client want it to be resolved? Does she want to return to the steady state, or does she seek some kind of transformation? Finally, does the client's story carry with it a message, a moral for the client, for the story's characters, for the lawyer, for the system in which the client's situation arises?

Thus, storytelling is a way to understand persuasion, for instance. We persuade by presenting narratives that decision makers believe and adopt. Part of why narrative theory is so compelling is that stories and narrative are elemental to human interaction — we recognize and react to them instinctively.[16] And storytelling is a way to help solve problems — once a trouble is defined, it changes what facts come into focus and thereby what legal elements are necessary to resolve the trouble.

So our suggestion that lawyers use narrative theory in our practice is not a suggestion that lawyers do anything radically different, just that we harness what we are already doing in some systematic and intentional way. If as we are listening to our client, something does not make sense, or we find ourselves wondering about the absence or presence of a particular character, or we imagine how we might feel in a similar situation, a narrative theory approach suggests that we recognize those reactions as important clues to help guide our ongoing pursuit of the client's narrative; and it suggests that we use these clues to work with the client to construct a narrative that will engage the decision maker's curiosity and compassion without triggering his disbelief or dismissal.

This is, of course, distinct from letting a lawyer's own values and judgment guide that process, which is exactly what happens when we do not recognize our own reactions to the client's narrative as just that: our own reactions. Instead, narrative theory is a tool for lawyers to use to harness our natural curiosity. Imagination and common sense are valuable tools as listeners and storytellers, and such tools need to be used critically — with intention and awareness of the choices underlying the narrative's construction — so as not to result in the lawyer's voice dominating or overwhelming the client's, and so as not to result in the adoption of narratives — the making of law — the lawyer did not anticipate or intend.[17]

---

16. Steve Johansen & Ruth Ann Robbins, 2nd Applied Legal Storytelling Conference, *This is Your Brain on Story* (July 2009, Lewis & Clark Law School, Portland, OR).

17. Grose, *supra* note 2.

III. Narrative Theory, Normative Theory and Lawyering

One more thing before we move into the nitty-gritty of each lawyering skill. As we explored in Chapter One, narrative theory identifies choices that a storyteller makes about the content and structure of a story (what we have called the "what" and the "how" of a story). But it does not tell us HOW to make those choices. It identifies the elements of a story, but does not tell us what the story IS. The law provides some boundary—lawyers can't just tell any story. But lawyers also need some kind of normative theory to guide our choices. One normative theory that guides us—and most clinical teachers and practitioners—is client-centered lawyering. Another is justice and professionalism. We explore these theories in this chapter.

Before we do, let's remember that narrative theory is not the only technique lawyers need to master in order to be competent client-centered professionals devoted to justice. Indeed, narrative theory itself is enhanced by the practice of cross-cultural competency and critical reflection. Chapter Four examines the goal and methods of practicing Cross-Cultural Competency; Chapter Three explores the essential lawyering tool of Self-Critique—Critical Reflection and Self-Evaluation. When lawyers are guided by the normative theories of client-centeredness and a commitment to professionalism and justice, and practice techniques of cross-cultural competency and critical reflection in making their narrative theory choices, they are more likely to develop contextually rich narratives likely to achieve their clients' complex and nuanced goals. Thus any practice of narrative theory must be accompanied by the normative theories and practices described in this section and those in Chapters Three and Four.

A. Client-Centered Lawyering

Client-centered lawyering is lawyering that is focused on the client and driven by her goals. The client is the decision maker in her case.[18] There are many benefits to client-centered lawyering, such as the recognition that because the legal problem facing the client is his, having the decision driven by his goals permits him greater satisfaction with the short and long-term outcomes of the decision.

---

18. DAVID A. BINDER, ET AL., LAWYERS AS COUNSELORS: A CLIENT-CENTERED APPROACH 318–321 (3d ed. 2012).

Similarly, the client will be more invested in making and sticking to the decision if he is supported in his agency to make it. Further, client-centered counseling recognizes that the client is the expert in his life and in the best position to know what satisfies him based on his context and values. Finally, the lawyer-client relationship is more egalitarian and collaborative, and more likely to comport with professional responsibility norms that require an attorney to decide on the means of the representation (in consultation with the client) while permitting the client to control the ends of the representation.

Because client-centered lawyering requires the lawyer's understanding of the client's goals and values, it is important that the lawyer inquire and listen as well as understand and empathize with the client. An understanding of narrative theory helps lawyers do all of these things. When interviewing a client, if a lawyer listens to the client's narrative, and pays attention to how he defines the steady state and the problem as well as who are important characters affecting the problem or resolution, the lawyer can learn what the client's goals and values are through the choices the client makes in constructing the narrative.[19] Such careful listening, for instance, can override a lawyer's assumption about what the problem is that the client is trying to solve and instead focus on the client's true issue.

Such an approach places the client in the center of the inquiry and requires the lawyer and client to engage actively in dialogue and problem-solving. It allows the lawyer and client to arrive at solutions together that both respond to the particular client's needs and attend to the moral and ethical concerns the lawyer, the client and society might have. By using a critically reflective, intentional process of inquiry around ethical concerns, the lawyer must focus on this particular client in the context of the client's life and the client's legal and non-legal needs in this particular situation. By widening the frame in this way and focusing on the client's whole story—not just his legal case—the lawyer is much better able not only to resolve whatever ethical or other conflicts may arise, but maybe even to avoid them altogether.

Attention to the client's narrative might include, but is certainly not limited to, a consideration of what kind of case he has, what system he's up against, or his relative power. An exploration of this kind of context entails a widening of the frame of the client's legal problem: an investigation into its history, a consideration of where the client is socially and culturally situated, and an understanding of the web of relationships involved in the problem.

---

19. Stephen Ellman, et al., *Narrative Theory and Narrative Practices*, in Lawyers and Clients: Critical Issues in Interviewing and Counseling (2009).

How stories help with empathy and understanding of the actual person sitting with the lawyer, the client, and not some assumed client or story is demonstrated powerfully in Chimamanda Ngozi Adichie's TED Talk "The Danger of the Single Story."[20] We recommend you watch it here: http://www.ted. com/talks/chimamanda_adichie_the_danger_of_a_single_story. In her talk, Adichie provides multiple examples of how assuming one knows THE story about another person—fairytale characters, her family's houseboy's family, herself—rather than asking questions, impedes the person holding onto the single story from truly listening and learning from the person about who they are, what their goals are, what they want to achieve, and what their obstacles might be. This is the danger of the single story, as Adichie relates. It is also a danger for lawyers because a lawyer cannot achieve the benefits of client-centered lawyering without engaging with the client's narrative rather than only the lawyer's.

B. Professionalism

In addition to attention and loyalty to the client, lawyers must also be attentive to notions of professionalism and justice. During law school, you should begin to develop a sense of yourselves as independent professionals with responsibilities for your work product, environment, and reputation. Also, you should understand the importance of facts and context, and the relationship between facts and law; the contours of the lawyer-client relationship, and the different role(s) you might play within that relationship; and how to recognize and construct narratives within and outside that relationship that serve to further your clients' goals. We will explore these goals in this part of the chapter.

When asked for a quick rundown of her professional obligations, a lawyer will probably answer automatically that she owes her client a duty of confidentiality and zealous advocacy, and that she owes the tribunal a duty of candor. Those are the basic tenets of the lawyer's Code of Professional Conduct, also called the "Model Rules" of Professional Responsibility.[21]

And while it is true that lawyers are guided by those state and model codes, we suggest that the system of ethical regulation is best interpreted to allow

---

20. Chimamanda Ngozi Adichie, The Danger of a Single Story (2009), http://www.ted.com/talks/chimamanda_adichie_the_danger_of_a_single_story; Chimamanda Ngozi Adichie, The Danger of a Single Story (2009), http://www.ted.com/talks/chimamanda_adichie_the_danger_of_a_single_story/transcript.

21. MODEL RULES OF PROF'L CONDUCT (2016).

room for the attorney to consider and incorporate the client's narrative context. There is a whole school of scholars who propose that the lawyer's ethical obligations be "analyzed with a paramount focus on achieving justice,"[22] and that the lawyer's fidelity be not to "their own moral principles, but ... to the moral principles inherent in the law."[23] Susan Carle looks to the context of the parties' respective power.[24] She explains that "[i]n the context of representing powerful clients, lawyers' incentive is to do too much for their clients; in the context of clients lacking substantial resources, lawyers' incentive is to do too little."[25] She suggests, therefore, that the relative power of the individuals or entities involved in a particular situation might justify contextual application of ethical rules.

This call to context builds on traditional client-centered theory, which demands that lawyers attend to their clients and work together with them to identify and achieve the goals of the representation. It also expands on that theory by suggesting that lawyers, and the system that regulates them, should work to hear their clients' narratives for what they are: unique and particular narratives comprised of legal and non-legal elements that are fluid and evolving, not static or unchanging. As Kate Kruse remarks, "[c]lients come to lawyers, not to get answers to routine legal questions, but to get help solving problems that are deeply embedded within particular contexts."[26]

Because our system of ethical regulation must provide some measure of predictability, uniformity, and enforceability, the Rules of Professional Conduct themselves cannot be written to address with particularity the unique and specific problems inherent in our clients' stories. But they can be read to do so. The lawyer has—and should exercise—discretion to enter into meaningful dialogue with her client about his particular context. She can work with him to determine how his concerns fit in to the regulatory system and how the regulatory system can be interpreted to respond to his concerns. If the lawyer is able to do this authentically—through critical reflection and collaboration with her client—the lawyer and client together will be able to construct and present a narrative that meets the needs of the client, the third parties, and the legal system.

---

22. Susan D. Carle, *Power as a Factor in Lawyers' Ethical Deliberation*, 35 Hofstra L. Rev. 115, 116 (2006)

23. Katherine R. Kruse, *Lawyers, Justice and the Challenge of Moral Pluralism*, 90 Minn. L. Rev. 389, 430 (2005).

24. Carle, *supra* note 22, at 119.

25. Carle, *supra* note 22, at 119.

26. Katherine R. Kruse, *Fortress in the Sand: The Plural Values of Client-Centered Representation*, 12 Clinical L. Rev. 369, 374 (2006).

C. *The Sisters: An Example*

Consider the situation of two elderly sisters, Lillian and Ellie, who want a lawyer to create an estate plan for them.[27] The lawyer knows about the rules about dual representation and confidentiality and dutifully drafts a waiver explaining those rules and the potential conflicts they are designed to protect against.[28] He prepares to present the waiver to each of the sisters and counsel each of them separately about the risks associated with having him represent them both. The problem is, neither of the sisters will agree to meet with him without the other sister present. What options does the lawyer have? Does he have to decline to represent either? Does he pick only one to represent? Does he proceed without any further action?

The Rules don't guide the lawyer in this situation, but narrative does. Using the narrative elements as a map, the lawyer can do further information gathering from his potential client(s). He might explore whether there really is a conflict between Lillian's interests and Ellie's. What are their actual financial resources? What kind of relationship do they have, not just on paper, but in reality? What is Lillian's interest in having the lawyer draft the will for Ellie? What is Ellie's interest in the same? Are there other people who might need to be involved in these conversations? Are there other interests that might be at stake? The lawyer might also wonder if there are reasons not to try to separate the two women, even for a brief period.

The lawyer might offer his expertise on their rights to zealous advocacy, which, as described above, would involve individual meetings and waivers. But the lawyer must be open to the possibility that neither sister really wants that. By the same token, the lawyer's own understanding of his role as advocate might need to shift, challenging the assumption of the lawyer-client dyad and making room for the possibility that he actually could, consistent with his duty to provide zealous advocacy, represent both sisters at the same time. Can the sisters work together with the lawyer, as one client, to fashion a relationship that protects all three of them, in light of how each individual self-identifies? The lawyer's job, in this case, might be to round up all the interested "parties," legal and otherwise, so that whatever decisions he and the sisters end up making incorporate and address those multiple interests, both now and for the foreseeable future. This framework also provides the potential for long-lasting, comprehensive, and satisfying solutions for both lawyer and client or clients.

---

27. This scenario comes from Grose, *supra* note 14, at 169–172.

28. *See* Model Rules of Prof'l Conduct Rules 1.6, 1.7 and 1.8 (2016).

This attention to the client's narrative allows for the complexity of client contexts by giving the lawyer discretion to inquire into and incorporate the multiplicity of client's stories. If lawyers, under the system of ethical regulation, are able to make judgments based on the full frame of their clients' lives, those judgments are more likely to be "good" judgments for the lawyer, for the client, for the judicial system, and for society—such judgments respond to the problems of real people in real life situations. As Phyllis Goldfarb describes, "ethics becomes a sustained practice of empirical attention and reflection on the actions of people in actual situations ... The better our context-sensitive empiricism, the better our moral deliberations, and the more precise the articulation of our ethical principles will be."[29]

IV. Exercise

So let's give you an exercise to help you apply this narrative theory to construct a legal story. Here is a very short video produced by National Geographic. Please watch it. https://www.youtube.com/watch?v=AgJXXo97D4c

When you have finished watching, write a description of what you just saw. Not word for word, or all the details—just tell the *narrative* of what you just saw: Who are the characters, what are the events, what is the causation for the events, what is the normalization of the events, are there any masterplots, and what is the closure (including steady state, problem and resolution)?

Now watch the video again, but this time, imagine you are the client-centered lawyer *for the accused*. Write the narrative of what you saw, as if you were the client-centered lawyer for the accused. Same questions: Who are the characters, what are the events, what is the causation for the events, what is the normalization of the events, are there any masterplots, and what is the closure (including steady state, problem and resolution)?

Now watch the video a third time, but this time, you are the client-centered lawyer *for the accuser* (the prosecution). Write the narrative of what you saw as if you were the prosecution. Same questions: Who are the characters, what are the events, what is the causation for the events, what is the normalization of the events, are there any masterplots, and what is the closure (including steady state, problem and resolution)?

Now go through all three narratives you have written and identify similarities and differences. In what way were the three narratives similar? How was each

---

29. Phyllis Goldfarb, *A Theory-Practice Spiral: The Ethics of Feminism and Clinical Education*, 75 Minn. L. Rev. 1599, 1698 (1991).

narrative different from the other two? By identifying these similarities and differences, you are able to identify the *choices* you made in each narrative. Why did you make those choices? What were your goals in telling each narrative and how does each choice you made further or hinder those goals? How did being client-centered affect your narratives? How did attention to your client's narrative context affect your narratives?

V. Conclusion

We can anticipate the reaction we always get to suggestions that we use more theory in our practice: "how can I possibly do all this? I don't have time; I can barely get the client's facts out in the first interview, let alone do all this narrative theory stuff." But the reality is that lawyers do all this anyway; we just do not know we are doing it, and are therefore not doing it as intentionally, and as effectively, as we could be. If we do not understand the choices we make and make them intentionally, we will fail in our effort to persuade the decision maker, or we will persuade the decision maker to act in a way that ultimately does not benefit our client, or future clients. All of which to say: using narrative theory is a way to understand that we are making these choices and helps us make them intentionally, which, in turns leads us to become better lawyers.

Law is made through the telling and believing of narratives. Thus, all lawyering involves some kind of persuasion, and all persuasion involves some kind of storytelling. In order to be effective professionals, therefore, lawyers need to know how to construct and present narratives. That means we need to recognize narratives as constructed, and we need to recognize ourselves as constructors of narrative. As we saw with Sarah Koenig's choices about how to begin the story in *Serial*, when made intentionally, these choices can be — are — very powerful tools in constructing compelling narratives. Since what we as lawyers do is construct and tell narratives, learning how to identify and make these choices is very important.

Chapter 3

Critical Reflection

I. Introduction

Critical reflection is crucial for lawyers in two ways: challenging the lawyer's assumptions so they don't end up controlling the lawyering, and providing the lawyer with tools to constantly improve and understand her lawyering across all contexts and issues. We explore both of these aspects of critical reflection, and how narrative theory helps, in this chapter.

II. What Is Critical Reflection?

As always, we start with a definition of terms. We use the term "critical reflection" to describe the method that guides our extraction of theory from practice, and the application of practice to theory. Critical reflection pushes us to generalize from the specific and transfer our learning beyond that specific. We need to engage in critical reflection in order to uncover the assumptions through which we tend to pass all information that comes our way, including how we define and categorize people seeking our legal assistance.

Through critical reflection, the lawyer self-consciously situates herself within the particular context in which she is operating. Specifically, she recognizes that she, as a lawyer, is someone with (relative) power in the legal system. She knows its rules and how to use them.

Through critical reflection, the lawyer further comes to understand and evaluate her power and ability to act, and recognizes that she operates **in relation to** the other characters involved the legal system in general, and in the particular case or project she is involved in. Those other characters could be the other people involved: the judge, the other lawyers, the witnesses, the government agency, the opposing party, or the client. In addition, the lawyer understands and evaluates her power in relation to the relevant rules, rituals, and practices of the particular system.

Through critical reflection, the lawyer recognizes that although she might have relative power, she does not have absolute power to function in the legal system. Critical reflection helps her identify both her power and any limitations on that power: her gender, for example; her proficiency in English; her size and physical presence; her age; her experience; her familiarity with the law firm's conference room, the courtroom or the judge. She learns to notice which, if any of these kinds of things, prevents her from moving freely among the various pieces of the system.

Critical reflection also helps the lawyer identify the power of the other characters to move freely within the system, and the impediments on their ability to do so. For example, a judge's power rests in the judge's ability to interpret the law and make the rules; but is that power unimpeded? What kinds of things might restrain a judge's power?

And what about the other lawyers—are there things that might undermine their power to operate freely in the system? Are these things related to the particular case—e.g., bad law, bad facts, bad witnesses? Or are they systemic—e.g., gender, race, language, etc.?

And of course, critical reflection guides the lawyer to consider the relative power or lack of power that her client has. What are the client's sources of power, and what impediments are there to his exercise of that power? Again, the lawyer, through critical reflection, considers the impact that race, gender, age, etc. might have on the client's relative power; but are there other sources of or impediments to a client's power?

Critical reflection, to put it another way, helps the lawyer see the forest AND the trees AND the relationship between them.

On a practical level, critical reflection often means asking questions: given what I know about the judge's source of power and my client's source of power, how will the judge apply the statute to my client's situation, and why? Are there things about the jury that might affect how it might react to my client's appearance on the stand? Are there any reasons, other than strategic, that the opposing attorney is unpleasant in negotiation? Why am I having such a hard time connecting with my client?

Critical reflection also means looking for answers about what the client actually wants and cares about. As we described in earlier chapters, and explore more deeply in Chapter Four, lawyers must attend carefully to what the client is asking of us, practicing exercises such as "methodological doubt and belief" to accept what he tells us as his truth, even if it doesn't make sense with what we know as our truth.Through that process, the lawyer might come to a better understanding of what brings her client to her and, as a result, might be better able to resolve any issues that arise in the course of the representation.

The result of all this critical reflection—all of these questions and answers— is that the lawyer has a better grasp on what choices she has, and how to make those choices, consistent with what she knows about the law, the legal system, the client, the client's system, etc. Critical reflection, therefore, makes lawyers more intentional and effective practitioners.

III. Challenging Assumptions

Narrative theory helps with critical reflection. As we explored in earlier chapters, attending to the narrative elements in a client's situation— characters, events, causation, normalization, masterplots, closure—allows lawyers to harness our natural curiosity. Imagination and common sense are valuable tools for listeners and storytellers, but such tools need to be used critically—with intention and awareness of the choices that might underlie the narrative's construction.

In order to be effective client-centered lawyers, we need to be consciously and vigilantly aware of what we bring to our representation of clients. We need to attend to the unstated values that underlie legal norms and rules, as well as our own personal norms. We need to make explicit to ourselves the lenses we use to see the world, and how those lenses affect how we see our clients. If we don't engage in critical reflection, we risk letting our own values and judgment guide our lawyering, and we fail to recognize our own reactions to a client's story as just that: our own reactions.

This is particularly important when lawyers represent clients whose personal narratives do not conform to the masterplots that decision makers and other audiences expect to hear. In such cases, lawyers must attend carefully to their clients' different realities. The lawyer's goal, though, is not to arrive at some submerged, alternate reality, but rather to create the space for the client to speak by examining whatever is inhibiting the lawyer from hearing. The most important element in representation is not portraying the "other" with verisimilitude (what really happened, what the client's story *really* is, finding out and telling the "truth"), but rather to engage in critical reflection to undertake a collaborative process with the client to construct a narrative that rings true to his experience and meets his goals.

A. Lawyering without Critical Reflection

Without critical reflection, it is virtually impossible for the lawyer to know—to see, to hear, to understand—her clients. Too often, lawyers unconsciously rely on their knowledge of and familiarity with the tools of their craft—language and rituals of the law—and skip over the necessary step of attempting to see and hear their client. The narrative they present to the audience outside the relationship, therefore, is at best, a distorted version of the client's story, and at worst the lawyer's own version of what she thinks the client's story is or should be. In neither case is the client himself able to speak or be heard.

The challenge deepens for lawyers who seek to represent clients who are marginalized from mainstream American society. Those clients are oppressed not only by the system in which they are trying to operate but also by their lawyers' inability to see and hear them as needed to portray them adequately within that system. More than just telling a wrong or incomplete narrative about the client, the lawyer's attempts to portray the marginalized client's voice without critical reflection further marginalizes the client by keeping his voice outside the dominant legal discourse.

As we explored in Chapter One, human beings constantly seek to "normalize" the stories of those around us. We all pass stories through our own pre-existing screen of "knowledge" about how people act. Because the stories of those outside the dominant discourse often conflict with that pre-existing "knowledge," a tension arises between what the insiders "know" about the outsiders and what the outsiders' narratives are describing. Confronted with this tension, insiders often choose not to question their own version of reality (what they "know" is "true"), but instead to recast the outsider's narrative into terms and language that make it consistent with the insiders' understanding of reality.

As we have seen, the problem of trying to hear the narratives of particular clients is that our assumptions about people and how they act, who they are, and what they need, prevent us from being able to hear the actual person standing before us. Moreover, our attempts to "translate" a person's narrative into language that we can hear further silence him because those very attempts take place against this backdrop of pre-understanding and assumption.

B. Example of Critical Reflection in Action

Several years ago, Professor Grose supervised a team of student attorneys who represented a transgender client. Understanding gender identity in a legal system that has static notions of both gender and identity necessitated constant critical reflection regarding the students' (well-intentioned) assumptions and judgments. Their attempts to navigate the legal system provided a valuable opportunity to unpack and challenge the assumptions that drive the "regime of truth" about gender and sexual identity.

In grappling with their case, these students came face to face with their pre-understanding about gender: that it just "was." They had to challenge their confusion because of the dissonance between the client's gender identification (female) and the client's physical appearance (male). They weren't sure what pronoun to use, for example, or even what name. When the client asked what to wear to court, the students found themselves at a loss: was the client asking what many clients who haven't had experience with the legal system often ask, i.e., "should I dress up?" Or was the client asking if she should dress "as a woman"?

When pushed to explore their confusion more closely, to engage in critical reflection, the students realized that the masterplots of gender—what makes someone "him" or "her" based on appearance, manner, or cultural norms—were interfering with their representation of their particular client. The students came to understand further that counter narratives to masterplots are complicated and require time and energy to construct: "We ... learned that it can take a while to get a story out—that it can take many, many sessions. Sometimes, we just asked the wrong questions and didn't think to follow up.... With our next client, we were able to learn to let the story come out over several visits and to keep listening and following up to get out the entire story."

We will explore throughout this book the idea that all narratives—masterplots, counter narratives, background narratives, and the outsider or insider narratives—are constructed. Moreover, and perhaps more important, lawyers play a huge role in the construction of these stories with the client, and with this role comes enormous power and responsibility. Lawyers can either use this power and responsibility to construct narratives based on what has come before, essentially ratifying what have become the masterplot legal narratives, or they can critically reflect on those masterplots and whether they work for a particular client. Having so situated themselves in relation to this system of narratives, lawyers can work with their clients to construct new narratives that both reflect the clients' own, if constructed, reality, and can be heard by the legal system.

If we notice what we bring to the representation—both our assumptions and our expertise—we are able to hear our client's particular narrative and work with him to construct a new narrative that both rings true for him and can be heard and believed by the legal decision maker. In this way, critical reflection is a skill that makes us better lawyers for all our clients.

C. Self-Critique

What does all this mean for you as students or new lawyers?

Attorneys practicing in different legal contexts share a common complaint: we get little helpful feedback on our professional performance, whether in a private setting to improve client interviewing or counseling techniques, or in a more public setting to work on techniques in trials or community group meetings. Even if some performance review and ongoing skills development training are available, they are most often reserved for the first months of practice when basic skills are learned and are then abandoned even as attorneys attempt to develop more sophisticated skills.

It is important, therefore, for you to develop the powerful tool of constructive self-critique: the ability to evaluate and learn from your own performance so that you can continually improve your skills, and be comfortable thinking about the broader questions that your daily practices raise for you. While we cannot accompany you into practice to continue to work with you to help improve your skills, we can "teach you to fish," by helping you to develop self-critique as an important skill in itself.

As we have been exploring in this chapter, critical reflection is intentional thinking about what one does as a lawyer and how society operates. Critical **self-reflection** involves articulating observations about one's experience in order to develop insights that may serve as the bases for future actions. Self-reflection is an essential part of learning from experience.

Self-evaluation is a particular kind of self-reflection. It involves comparing one's performance to standards, including those set by the student attorney or lawyer, the professor or senior lawyers, and/or other student attorneys or lawyers. With self-evaluation, a lawyer actively engages in goal-setting and strategic planning before each lawyering activity and then employs comprehensive and rigorous self-critique of her performance of that activity.

An effective **self-critique**—the kind that will help you continue to develop as an effective legal professional—includes both self-evaluation and self-reflection. Thus, the process of self-critique includes: (1) an assessment or evaluation of the strategies used to reach each goal, and an assessment or evaluation of the outcomes—expected or not—of each strategy used (or not used!); and (2) a critical reflection on what you learned from the particular performance, how you will apply what you learned to change particular behavior the next time, why those changes matter, and how the discrete decisions you make in your activities as a lawyer often raise broader questions about yourself, your client, the law, legal institutions, and society.

The first part—assessment or evaluation—includes identification and description of your goals for the particular performance you are evaluating, so it includes a description of the strategies and techniques you used to achieve those goals and an assessment of whether those strategies worked. In other words, did you accomplish what you set out to do by employing those particular techniques? The assessment or evaluation piece of the self-critique is a report: 1) of what you wanted to accomplish, 2) what you did to accomplish it, and 3) whether you succeeded.

The second part—critical reflection—is the WHY? Why did a particular technique work or not work? Why did you feel a certain way at a certain point? Why do you think the client didn't respond to that particular line of questioning the way you thought he would? Or why did the judge accept or not accept the particular argument you made? From the answers to those "why" questions come the "lessons learned" for next time: What would you do differently—or the same—next time, and why? Those "why" questions can also help you explore the relationship between the particular things that happened and larger questions involving the legal and social context within which the client's situation developed and your activity as a lawyer occurred.

IV. Exercise: Self-Critique in Action

Please select one activity you've engaged in—an interview, a class project, a meeting with your supervisor, etc.—and prepare a *personal essay* describing, evaluating and reflecting upon this event. Keep the two pieces of the essay, evaluation and reflection, separate, either on separate pages, or just clearly marked as distinct from one another, so the processes themselves remain distinct in your minds.

The questions that follow are suggestions for the subject matter your self-evaluation and reflection might address. **Remember, this is just a list of suggestions, some of which may not be at all relevant to the particular activity you're evaluating and assessing.** In order for this to be an effective tool, your evaluation and reflection should be driven by your own personal experience of the activity, not by some list that we give you.

The goal of this exercise is not to come up with a perfect blueprint for a particular lawyering activity. No such thing exists. Rather, the point of this exercise is to help you identify tools you have to continue to grow as a competent and critically reflective professional. All of these questions and topics guide you to reflect on your own experience, your own values, your own norms, and your own place in the legal system. As you go through the questions, draw on the ideas we have explored in this book so far. Push yourself to ask questions about yourself as a constructor of narrative, and to see your client as a constructor of his own narrative.

A. Self-Evaluation

Goal Implementation: What were my goals? How well did I accomplish my goals? What methods did I use for accomplishing my goals? Did they work?

Preparation: In light of the activity, was my preparation adequate? Did I use elements of narrative to guide my planning?

Emotions: How did I feel at the beginning of the session, during the session, at the end, and why? Was I nervous, calm, annoyed, angry? What effect did my feelings have on the session? How did the other person or people feel at the beginning, during and at the end of the session?

Atmosphere: What was the atmosphere like? Open? Tense? Comfortable? How, if at all, did the atmosphere affect what I did? How did my own behavior or demeanor affect the atmosphere? How, if at all, did the setting contribute to the atmosphere?

Listening and Asking Questions: Was I a good listener? Who did most of the talking? Did I use silence, passive listening, active listening and other techniques to encourage communication? What sorts of questions did I ask? What were the results? Did I consider the narrative elements of **character and traits, events, causation, normalization, masterplots and closure** to guide my questioning? Did I use those same elements to guide my listening?

Information: What kinds of information did I get? In what areas would I like to find out more? Are there areas where I am uncertain? Was I able to clarify any of these uncertainties during the session? Did I attend to the narrative elements of the client's story? Which ones? Which ones didn't I use? Why?

Law: Do I understand the law as it applies to the situation? What problems did I find in analyzing the law? What role did the law play in the discussion? Should it have played more of a role? Less? Was I able to explain the law effectively? What problems did I find in explaining the law?

Structure: Did there seem to be a structure to the session? How did it begin? How did it progress? Did it seem to move in an understandable direction? Did it seem to take unanticipated turns? What seemed to determine the structure and direction of the activity? How did the session end? Was there an understanding of what was going to happen next? Did the structure facilitate or impede rapport-building, information-gathering, meeting my goals?

Conflicts: Were there conflicts? Were such conflicts explicit? How were they addressed? Whether or not they were addressed, how did they affect the activity?

Ethical Issues: Did any arise? What did I do?

General: What was the best part of the session? What was the worst part of the session?

B. Self-Reflection

This is the *why* part. Pick one or two issues from your description of the activity, and reflect on what you learned about yourself as a lawyer, your relationship with the other people involved in the event, your skills, your place and/or your client's place in the legal and social system in which this is occurring.

What did you learn from your activity and how will you apply what you learned next time you conduct such an activity? Be specific in your reflection. The questions that follow are just suggestions, and although they are segregated into categories, those categories, too, are just suggestions. There are no bright lines between the categories, and they often overlap. In order for this to be an effective learning tool, you need to choose an experience that resonates for you personally and reflect on it in a way that helps you move along in your own development as an attorney.

Preparation: What should I or could I have done to make the activity more effective? Did I have preconceptions about the client or the law or the case or the project or the facts or the legal system or myself? Did those preconceptions affect the activity? How? Why did I have those preconceptions? How can I identify those preconceptions next time? How can I anticipate the effect they might have on the activity? Would attention to narrative elements have helped me prepare more effectively? How would I use narrative theory to help me prepare next time?

Goals: If I was successful in achieving my goals, why? If I was less than successful in achieving my goals, why? Should the goals have been different? Why? What influenced how I determined what my goals were? Did I rely on any assumptions about the client in order to achieve those goals? Were those assumptions correct? How did those assumptions impact my ability to achieve my goals? Would attending to narrative elements before and during the session have helped me achieve my goals? Why?

Emotions: Why did I feel the way I did? In what ways did emotions affect the activity?

Listening and Asking Questions: What does it mean to be a good listener? How can I tell if I am listening well? Did I use any tools to challenge my own

assumptions about the client's story? How did the choice of questions, formation, etc. affect the answers I got? How did the questions affect the rapport?
Emotions?

Information: Have I grasped the situation from multiple perspectives?
What helped me understand the situation from other perspectives? If there
are gaps between my understanding and other understandings—of the facts,
the options, the goals—why is that? Could I have done something differently
to close that gap? Should I have done something differently to close that gap?
Why?

Law: If I didn't understand how the law operates in my client's case, why is
that? If I wasn't able to explain it, why is that? Did I understand the law
differently after seeing how it operated in my client's life? Did the law seem fair?
Just?

Structure: If the structure of the activity worked to help achieve my goals,
why? If not, why not? How will I plan to structure the activity next time? Why?

Conflicts: Were there any conflicts between myself and my client, or another
person? Why were there conflicts? Could they have been the result of perceived
or actual differences in (or attitudes about) race, gender, sexual orientation,
ethnicity, class, age or other factors? Did I use normalization techniques that
might have created or added to the conflicts? Could I have anticipated those
conflicts? How? Am I happy with how I handled them? Why or why not? Could
I have handled them differently? What will I do differently the next time? Why?

Ethical Issues: Why did they come up? Could I have anticipated them? Am
I happy with how I handled them? Why or why not? Could I have handled
them differently?

General: What contributed to the successes of the session? Were they because
of me, the client, the situation? How can they be repeated? What contributed
to the problems in the session? How can they be avoided?

V. How Do Narrative Theory and Self-Critique Work Together?

Narrative theory works with the process of self-critique (and vice versa) to
help lawyers be and stay effective practitioners. By stopping and asking yourself
the self-critique questions outlined above, you push yourself to dig deeper into
the narrative elements of your and your client's situation. For example, you
may start by identifying the characters in your client's narrative as simply the
ones he describes as being "important" to the narrative. And they may indeed
be important to the narrative. But maybe there are other characters who are

also important. If you engage in critical reflection, ask yourself what lens you might be looking through as you seek to gather information—you might find that you identify more or different characters, and/or you might explore and identify different traits of those characters.

If narrative theory provides a chart for gathering information, the process of self-critique makes that chart three dimensional by creating a depth of exploration below each of the narrative elements. To put it another way, self-critique without narrative theory is a deep, narrow dive into your client's situation and your lawyering; narrative theory without self-critique is a wide, shallow dive into your client's situation and your lawyering. Put together, you have a chance at both depth and width of information and connection with your client and a greater understanding of your lawyering.

Chapter 4

Cross-Cultural Competency and Collaboration

I. Introduction

Before we dive into specific lawyering skills and values, like interviewing, counseling, and advocacy, we want to explore how narrative can contribute to your practice of general skills and values that you will use across all aspects of lawyering. In this chapter, we focus on two important lawyering skills and values: cross-cultural competency[1] and collaboration. Each of these involve the skills of deep critique, including critical reflection and evaluation, that we discussed in the previous chapter. We will first discuss cross-cultural competency and then collaboration. In each section below we define the skill and value, identify why it is necessary to lawyering, and then provide concrete examples for how to practice and develop cross-cultural competency and effective collaboration.

II. Cross-Cultural Competency

A. *What Is Cross-Cultural Competency?*

To understand cross-cultural competency, we start by defining and exploring each component part: culture, cross-cultural, and cross-cultural competency.

---

1. ALICIA ALVAREZ AND PAUL R. TREMBLAY, INTRODUCTION TO TRANSACTIONAL LAWYER-ING PRACTICE 211 (2013) (clients' satisfaction with services was higher when service providers were "sensitive to cross-cultural issues.").

1. Culture

Culture is a complex word encompassing many different facets of who we are. It covers the various social groups to which we belong or feel a part of based on their shared norms, values, ideas, experiences or identity characteristics.[2] In other words, culture "refers not only to the superficial features of a person, such as his appearance, but also refers to a person's personal identity, language, thoughts, communications, actions, customs, beliefs, values, and institutions, which often are specific to ethnic, racial, religious, geographic, or social groups."[3]

We all are composed of intersecting cultures because we belong to multiple cultural groups at the same time.[4] And our membership in many cultures that intersect make each of us the unique person we are. As a lawyer, you are part of a legal culture. And within that legal culture, there are many micro-cultures (based on such things as practice areas, practice location, practice orientation, to name a few), some to which you belong and others you do not. In addition to your vocation or professional culture, you may feel part of cultures and micro-cultures based on your race, ethnicity, gender, gender identity, sexual orientation, religion, disability and/or family status. In addition, your education-level, class and geographic location may be culturally significant to you. And while we may have a clear view of our cultural identities, society may have similar or different cultural identities that it ascribes to us based on such things as our vocation, personal appearance or experience.

And, of course, all of the above holds true for your client as well, and for the opposing party, decision maker, and other stakeholders.

2. Cross-Cultural

Cross-cultural means that we are in a relationship or relating to someone across or among similar or different cultures. Accordingly, your representation

---

2. ALVAREZ & TREMBLAY, supra note 1, at 208; Aastha Madaan, *Cultural Competency and the Practice of Law in the 21st Century*, 30 PROBATE & PROPERTY (2016), http://www.americanbar.org/publications/probate_property_magazine_2012/2016/march_april_2016/2016_aba_rpte_pp_v30_2_article_madaan_cultural_competency_and_the_practice_of_law_in_the_21st_century.html; National Institutes of Health, *Cultural Respect*, https://www.nih.gov/institutes-nih/nih-office-director/office-communications-public-liaison/clear-communication/cultural-respect.

3. National Institutes of Health, *Cultural Respect*, https://www.nih.gov/institutes-nih/nih-office-director/office-communications-public-liaison/clear-communication/cultural-respect.

4. ALVAREZ AND TREMBLAY, *supra* note 1, at 209 (2013); Kimberlé Crenshaw, *Mapping the Margins: Intersectionality, Identity Politics, and Violence Against Women of Color*, 43 STAN. L. REV. 1241, 1242 (1991).

of a client will involve a cross-cultural relationship. So too will your and your client's relationship with a decision maker, such as a judge, government agency officer or corporate board. Similarly, there will be cross-cultural relationships with interpreters, mediators, partners on a legislative advocacy project and other stakeholders in a community-based project.

When we are engaged in cross-cultural professional relationships, our relationship building and/or communication may be impeded or assisted in various ways based on differences and similarities between our cultures.

3. Cross-Cultural Competency

Cross-Cultural competency is a practice that recognizes that each person is situated in her own cultures and that relating among people or building relationships requires both this recognition, and then reflection to ensure that one's own cultures do not impede one's ability to build rapport with, communicate with, listen to and understand another person.

Our cultures, if unexamined, will affect our relationships because our cultures affect our understanding and communication. Practicing cross-cultural competency helps us communicate and understand what is communicated to us with a recognition of our cultural situations and that of our clients. The practice of cross-cultural competency is not grounded in stereotypes about our and/or our clients' cultures. Rather it is grounded in our being self-reflective and intentional about the role cultures may play in our relationships. As such, competency will enhance lawyering, and a lack of competency will impede it. This sounds difficult and important, and it is. This practice will require making ourselves vulnerable, and sometimes making mistakes, as we practice how best to be cross-culturally competent. To engage in the practice requires being non-judgmental of one's self as one continues to grow in one's competency.

B. What Does Cross-Cultural Competency (or Lack Thereof) Look Like?

Here are two examples of situations involving cross-cultural relationships. In the first, the obvious cultural differences—and tensions—among the various players were not acknowledged or addressed as part of the solution to the problem presented. In the second, the cultural differences were not only recognized and articulated, they were, in fact, an intentional part of one side's strategy. Consider how addressing cultural differences and similarities were a part of the events in these two stories. What was effective about the approaches to cultural differences and similarities, and what was not effective? Also, consider whether either approach raised ethical or justice issues and if so, how could they have been better addressed.

1. Cross-Cultural Relationships between Medical Service Provider and Patient

Anne Fadiman's *The Spirit Catches You and You Fall Down*[5] describes a Hmong immigrant family with a young daughter who suffered from grand mal seizures. The parents sought medical treatment for their daughter, and initially complied with their doctors' treatment plan. However, over time, the parents became concerned about the over-medicalization of their daughter, and stopped complying with the prescribed medical treatment. Their daughter continued to have seizures.

The doctors, concerned about the child's well-being, had the child removed from her family, which caused the child and her parents enormous emotional pain. The parents agreed to provide the prescribed medication, and the child was returned to her parents. Once home, the child had a seizure that would not end, so her parents took her to the hospital. There, the girl went into septic shock. Although the hospital ended up controlling both the seizure and the shock, the girl suffered severe brain damage. She returned home with her parents, where she continued to live, free from seizures, but in a permanent vegetative state. The doctors—surprised that she continued to live at all—blamed the girl's health problems on her parents' failure to follow the prescribed medical treatment.

The child's parents saw the entire situation differently. They believed that the seizures were a spiritual gift—and when "the spirit catches you … you fall down." The parents made the decisions they did because while they could tolerate some medical treatment, they felt that too many interventions were harmful to the child. Indeed, many in the Hmong community avoided the hospital for similar reasons. The parents believed the better approach was to address the situation by having a Hmong healer work with the child, while the family also protected her from any physical harm during her seizures. When the child suffered permanent brain damage in the hospital, the parents had the Hmong healer visit and treat her there.

In the story, Fadiman does not portray either the doctors or the parents as bad or good. Rather, the reader sees both sets of individuals acting in accordance with

_____

5. Ann Fadiman, The Spirit Catches You and You Fall Down: A Hmong Child, Her American Doctors, and the Collision of Two Cultures (2012); Melvin Konner, *Take Only as Directed*, N.Y. Times, Oct. 19, 1997, https://www.nytimes.com/books/97/10/19/reviews/971019.19konnert.html.

their culture and beliefs. The disturbing outcome for the child seems attributable to poor communication and a lack of understanding between the two sets of individuals—one group believing in medicine and science and the other group believing in the spirit and spiritual healing. Both groups—the parents and the doctors—are portrayed as people trying to do their best in this situation. The reader is left with the sense that cross-cultural competency among the two groups could have diminished the harm from the events and created a better outcome.[6]

2. Cross-Cultural Understanding between Decision Maker and Lawyer

The documentary *O.J.: Made in America* [7] offers an example of the use of cross-cultural knowledge in the legal context. In 1995, O. J. Simpson, an African American college and pro football star, was prosecuted in Los Angeles for the murder of his wife, Nicole Brown Simpson, and her friend, Ronald Goldman, both white. The film explores how the racialized context of the trial against O. J. Simpson played a critical role in the jury's decision to acquit him.

In 1992, three years before the O. J. Simpson trial, Los Angeles had been rocked by another racially charged trial—that of three white police officers who had been caught on videotape brutally beating Rodney King, an African American man. Despite that graphic video, the three white officers were found not guilty. Protests and riots broke out in Los Angeles and all over the country at what many saw as a racist miscarriage of justice by the Los Angeles police department and prosecutors.

O. J. Simpson's defense team had worked on race discrimination cases prior to taking on Simpson's case, and were connected to the black community in L.A. The jury for O. J.'s criminal trial was composed of nine Blacks, two Whites, and one Hispanic. The defense team knew that many blacks in L.A. were incensed by the injustice of the Rodney King beating verdict and they intentionally sought to portray Simpson's prosecution as another racist targeting of a black man by L.A. police and prosecutors. To do this, the defense focused on Simpson's race, and that of the main police investigator, Mark

---

6. Again, the doctors were doing the best they could. They studied Hmong culture to increase their understanding of the parents. Some additional actions the doctors could have taken would have been to ask open-ended questions to the parents about their understanding of their daughter's condition, the meaning of the condition to them, their goals for medical treatment of the child and other options besides medicine. Further, listening and understanding the narrative provided by the parents about their child's condition could have provided insight for the doctors.

7. O.J.: Made in America, ESPN, http://espn.go.com/30for30/ojsimpsonmadeinamerica/.

Fuhrman, who was white. Simpson's defense case theory was based on their belief that the jury's prevailing cultural understanding was focused on race, and specifically, that white police officers set up black men and get away with it.

And it worked. The jury found Simpson not guilty of the murders of Nicole Brown Simpson and Ronald Goldman. As reported in the documentary, "[t]he roar of the crowd lining the street outside the courtroom when the not-guilty verdict is announced on October 3, 1995, is so raucous that it frightens the police horses. Meanwhile, the released jurors high-five one another, and a few of them reportedly say, 'That was payback for Rodney King.' A community activist, Danny Bakewell, says, 'Now you know how it feels.'"[8]

C. The Importance of Cross-Cultural Competency to Lawyering

Lawyering is a profession based in and on relationships that require the lawyer, client and others to communicate with and understand each other. It is essential, therefore, that good lawyers have an understanding of their own

---

8. John Walters, *The Craziest Moments and Quotes from O.J.: Made in America*, Newsweek, June 24, 2016, http://www.newsweek.com/craziest-moments-and-quotes-oj-made-america-474222. Watch O.J.: Made in America here: http://espn.go.com/30for30/ojsimpson madeinamerica/. Another example of being attuned to cross-cultural issues also comes from the O. J. case. The defense lawyers, knowing that the majority black jury would sympathize with O. J. if he were seen as black and of their culture, staged O. J.'s home for the jury's inspection of the home to include photographs of O. J. with other blacks rather than the regular photos he had of him with white people. Carl Douglas, one of O. J.'s defense lawyers explained, "O. J.'s legal team took down numerous photos of O. J. with his white friends and replaced them with photos of O. J. and African-Americans inside his home. They even took a Norman Rockwell print of a young African-American girl from Johnnie Cochran's office [one of the lead defense attorneys] and set it at the top of a stairway. 'If we had had a Latin jury, we would have had a picture of him in a sombrero!' Douglas boasts. 'There would have been a mariachi band out front! We would have had a piñata at the top of the staircase!'" John Walters, *The Craziest Moments and Quotes from O.J.: Made in America*, Newsweek (June 24, 2016), http://www.newsweek.com/craziest-moments-and-quotes-oj-made-america-474222. Watch O. J.: Made in America here: http://espn.go.com/30for30/ojsimpsonmadeinamerica/. As the documentary continues, past O. J.'s acquittal, it follows O. J.'s life where he was found civilly liable for Nicole Simpson's death and incarcerated for a different crime. As in client-centered lawyering in general, the documentary raises the question of whether the lawyering in the original criminal trial successfully accomplished O. J.'s legal and non-legal goals in the short and long-term. Similarly, one can ask the question of how one measures whether cross-culturally competent lawyering was effective in this instance.

cultures and of the cultures of others with whom they interact. It is also essential that lawyers become more culturally competent when doing cross-cultural relationship building.

Cross-cultural competency may seem obviously implicated in the practice of lawyers who represent culturally diverse clients. Public Defenders, Legal Services, and many law school clinics, for example, represent clients experiencing poverty and/or other marginalization by society that may or may not be shared by the law students or lawyers. The Legal Services Corporation has publicly recognized this part of their mission by stating, "Legal aid organizations should strive to offer services in a culturally competent manner to those who come from diverse cultures in the service area. This includes, to the extent possible, having staff who are bilingual in the most frequently spoken languages other than English."[9]

Cross-cultural competency may also be implicated in the corporate world, where a lawyer may represent a corporation whose board members have different identities, such as geographic and class histories, educational background, gender, race, ethnicity and language identities; or different values, knowledge and behaviors. Indeed, due to the increased diversity of the workforce and clientele, both domestically and internationally, law firms recognize the need to practice cross-cultural competency.[10]

Further, the self-governing rules of the lawyering profession instruct us in the importance of cross-cultural competency. For instance, in the Model Rules of Professional Responsibility, the rule on "Competence" requires that the attorney represent the client with the legal knowledge, skill, thoroughness and preparation necessary for the representation.[11] If the attorney does not under-

---

9. Legal Services Corporation, *Language Access and Cultural Sensitivity*, http://www.lsc.gov/grants-grantee-resources/resources-topic-type/language-access-cultural-sensitivity.

10. Blanco Banuelos et al., *Embracing Diversity and Being Culturally Competent is No Longer Optional* (2012), http://www.americanbar.org/content/dam/aba/events/labor_law/2012/03/ethics_professional_responsibility_committee_midwinter_meeting/mw2012_cultural_compentancy.authcheckdam.pdf; Michelle Ramos-Burkhart, *Do You See What I See? How A Lack of Cultural Competency May Be Affecting Your Bottom Line*, The Jury Expert (May 31, 2013), http://www.thejuryexpert.com/2013/05/do-you-see-what-i-see-how-a-lack-of-cultural-competency-may-be-affecting-your-bottom-line/ (identifying that cross-cultural competency is required for law firms to increase their financial opportunities); Richard Susskind, Tomorrow's Lawyers: An Introduction to Your Future 31 (2013) (identifying an example requiring cross-cultural competence: law firms' disaggregation of their lawyering across the globe, such as outsourcing document review to third parties in low-cost countries).

11. Model Code of Prof'l Conduct R. 1.1: Competence (2016) ("A lawyer shall provide competent representation to a client. Competent representation requires the legal knowledge, skill, thoroughness and preparation reasonably necessary for the representation"),

stand the client's actual issue and goals, the attorney may not be able to provide competent representation. As seen in the *The Spirit Catches You* example, the medical professionals were dedicated to providing competent treatment to the patient, but ended up taking severe and ultimately detrimental action without understanding the parents' concerns and desired outcome and treatment.

Similarly, the Model Rules implicate an attorney's cross-cultural competency in the rule on "Communications," which requires the lawyer to inform, consult with and explain issues to the client.[12] The lawyer needs to recognize any impediments to understanding she might create based on her own cultures, and she must identify ways to overcome these barriers to ensure successful communication with the client. In addition, the Model Rule on "Due Diligence" requires zealous advocacy,[13] which again demands an understanding of the client's actual goals and her evaluation of the options to address them without being colored unreflectively by the attorney's cultures. Indeed, at a meeting of the ABA Ethics and Professional Responsibility group, cross-cultural competency was described as "no longer optional."[14]

D. How to Practice Law with Cross-Cultural Competency

Given its importance, how does one practice law with cross-cultural competency? The answer is simple, but hardly easy: one practices cross-cultural competency through critical self-reflection about one's identities and cultures, the role of power in one's relationships and in society, and one's appropriate role in the relationship at issue, such as lawyer-client, lawyer-community, lawyer-client-decision maker, lawyer-client-legal, or other system.

Narrative theory plays an important role in practicing cross-cultural competency. Without critical self-reflection and correction, assumptions and associations about cultures and identities can inappropriately shape the

---

http://www.americanbar.org/groups/professional_responsibility/publications/model_rules_of_ professional_conduct/rule_1_1_competence.html.

12. MODEL CODE OF PROF'L CONDUCT R. 1.4: Communications (2016) (discussing the lawyer's responsibility to inform, consult and explain issues with the client), http://www.americanbar.org/groups/professional_responsibility/publications/model_rules_of _professional_conduct/rule_1_4_communications.html.

13. MODEL CODE OF PROF'L CONDUCT R. 1.3: Diligence (2016) ("A lawyer must also act with commitment and dedication to the interests of the client and with zeal in advocacy upon the client's behalf"), http://www.americanbar.org/groups/professional_responsibility/publications/model_rules_of_professional_conduct/rule_1_3_diligence/comment_on_rule_1_3.html.

14. Banuelos, *supra* note 10.

construction and deconstruction of the narrative elements of character, events, causation, normalization, masterplot and closure. As an Estates and Trusts lawyer wrote, "[t]he danger of implicit bias lies in the lack of self-awareness because [implicit bias] can present itself and allow discrimination not only in situations of conflict, such as in litigation, but also in situations without conflict, such as in interactions with clients from certain backgrounds."[15] It is essential, therefore, that you practice cultural awareness and cross-cultural competency as you and your client construct your legal narratives.

The starting point for building a practice of cross-cultural competency and self-reflection about identities is to identify and address your own implicit assumptions about cultural identities (or character traits, causation, and even masterplots). Identifying one's cultural assumptions may sound scary: no one wants to learn or reveal themselves to be biased. But as we all know, everyone—no matter how well-intentioned—has assumptions about cultural identities.[16] Understanding this leads us to also understand that we can increase our cross-cultural competency if we surface these assumptions. Only then can we identify ways to address them so they do not control our behavior or relationships.

Many of the cultural identity assumptions we make rest on implicit understandings that we create unconsciously to help us quickly navigate the world. For instance:

> [j]ust as we might have implicit cognitions that help us walk and drive, we have implicit social cognitions that guide our thinking about social categories. Where do these schemas come from? They come from experience with other people, some of them direct (that is, real-world encounters), but most of them vicarious (that is, relayed to us through stories, books, movies, media, and culture). Although shorthand schemas of people can be helpful in some situations, such schemas also can lead to discriminatory behaviors if we are not careful."[17]

---

15. Madaan, *supra* note 2 ("[g]iven the critical importance of exercising fairness and equality in the court system, lawyers, judges, jurors, and staff should be particularly concerned about identifying such possibilities.").

16. Madaan, *supra* note 2.

17. ABA Section of Litigation Implicit Bias Initiative, *What Is Implicit or Unconscious Bias*, www.americanbar.org/groups/litigation/initiatives/task-force-implicit-bias/what-is-implicit-bias.html, quoting Jerry Kang, *Implicit Bias: A Primer for Courts*, prepared for the National Campaign to Ensure Racial and Ethnic Fairness of America's State Courts (Aug. 2009), www.americanbar.org/content/dam/aba/migrated/sections/criminal justice/Public-Documents/unit_3_kang.authcheckdam.pdf.

Harvard University runs a project on implicit associations that hosts numerous implicit association tests (IAT), including ones that focus on such identity characteristics as race, ethnicity, gender, sexual orientation, religion and disability.[18] As noted by Project Implicit, the IAT "measures attitudes and beliefs that people may be unwilling or unable to report.... For example, you may believe that women and men should be equally associated with science, but your automatic associations could show that you (like many others) associate men with science more than you associate women with science."[19] To learn more about implicit associations, the Project created the IAT that "measures the strength of associations between concepts (e.g., black people, gay people) and evaluations (e.g., good, bad) or stereotypes (e.g., athletic, clumsy)."[20] As the Project explains, it is measuring for implicit stereotypes, "beliefs that most members of a group have some characteristic" that are "outside of conscious awareness and control."[21] Showing an implicit bias towards a group does not necessarily mean one is prejudiced, because such biases often are contrary to one's conscious thoughts and beliefs. But research shows that the bias does predict one's behavior.[22] As the Project states: "[w]hen we relax our active efforts to be egalitarian, our implicit biases can lead to discriminatory behavior, so it is critical to be mindful of this possibility if we want to avoid prejudice and discrimination."[23] Accordingly, identifying one's implicit associations can help improve one's cross-cultural competency.

In addition, engaging in a series of cross-cultural competency practices can be helpful. Professors Sue Bryant and Jean Koh Peters have developed a set of exercises that foster both self-reflection regarding the role of cultures in lawyer-client relationships, as well as strategies for practicing cross-cultural competency. Their "Five Habits of Cross-Cultural Competency" are summarized below with additional guidance towards their practice by using narrative theory:

1. Habit One involves the lawyer identifying any and all similarities and differences between herself and her client.[24] If one list—of similarities or of differences—is shorter than the other, the lawyer should go back and see if she can amplify that list. In this habit the lawyer and client are the *char-*

---

18. Project Implicit, https://implicit.harvard.edu/implicit/takeatest.html.
19. Project Implicit, https://implicit.harvard.edu/implicit/education.html.
20. Project Implicit, https://implicit.harvard.edu/implicit/iatdetails.html.
21. Project Implicit, https://implicit.harvard.edu/implicit/faqs.html.
22. Project Implicit, *supra* note 21.
23. Project Implicit, *supra* note 21.
24. Susan Bryant, *The Five Habits: Building Cross-Cultural Competence in Lawyers*, 8 Clinical L. Rev. 33, 65–67 (2001).

acters in the constructed narrative and the lawyer is asked to generate their *traits* and then characterize them as similar or different. One insight gained from the initial listing is that trait identification and characterization is relational not intrinsic. Moreover, what is listed in the first go round versus the second may be the result of cultural assumptions.[25] The habit then asks the lawyer to reflect on the meaning of those similarities and differences to explore how they "might affect issues of trust, role of the lawyer and the content ... of interviews."[26] In narrative terms, the lawyer explores whether there is *normalization* at play in the constructed narrative of who she perceives herself to be and who the client is, based on assumptions of cultural similarities or differences. The goal is to construct a narrative that is true to the lawyer and the actual client.

2. Habit Two asks the lawyer to map in a three-circle Venn diagram overlapping areas of cultural *traits* between lawyer and client and decision maker or other system actor. This habit asks the lawyer to reflect on how the shared and unshared traits may affect the perception of each individual (lawyer, client and decision maker or other system actor) towards another. In addition, Habit Two asks how this mapping may affect collaborative case theory construction. The goal here is to ensure that the lawyer and client construct a case theory that meets the client's actual goals and is likely to be effective with the actual decision maker.[27] This is akin to our earlier discussions regarding constructing stories that will be compelling, persuasive and comprehensive to our audience.

3. Habit Three questions any initial ascribed meaning by the lawyer to client conduct, and prompts the lawyer to slow down and, instead, consider "parallel universes" or any and all other possible explanations for the client's conduct.[28] In narrative terms, this requires the lawyer to consider what other *causation* might be at play in the constructed narrative being told by the client, and to identify alternative plot lines that could be more effective. This "parallel universe" thinking intends to surface any unconscious

---

25. Mark Aaronson, *We Ask You to Consider: Learning about Practical Judgment in Lawyering*, 4 Clinical L. Rev. 247, 313 (1998) (citing Martha Minow, *The Supreme Court 1986 Term Forward: Justice Engendered*, 101 Harv. L. Rev. 10, 13 (1987)).

26. Susan Bryant & Jean Koh Peters, *Six Practices for Connecting with Clients Across Culture: Habit Four, Working with Interpreters and Other Mindful Approaches*, in Affective Assistance of Counsel: Practicing Law as a Healing Profession (Marjorie Silver ed., 2006). *See also* Bryant, *supra* note 24, at 33.

27. Bryant & Peters, *supra* note 26.

28. Bryant & Peters, *supra* note 26.

cultural interpretations the lawyer might be making based on her own culture, and any assumption that the lawyer's interpretations are universal. It might surface that the lawyer ascribed inaccurate meaning to the client conduct because the lawyer unilaterally had tried to fit the client into an inaccurate *masterplot*. One goal of this habit is to focus on the client's narrative as told through the client's perspective, not the lawyer's.[29]

4. Habit Four focuses on how to improve struggling communication between lawyer and client that is due to cultural assumptions or interpretations.[30] Such miscommunications often occur as the result of the lawyer's unconscious construction or reconstruction of the client's narrative through the lawyer's own cultural context. This can also be called "gap-filling." This habit identifies strategies to minimize such unconscious gap-filling, such as permitting the client to *construct his own narrative* by encouraging the lawyer initially to engage in listening rather than questioning, probing, or redirecting.[31] When the client is given the space to construct his own narrative in his own cultural context, he will fill in the gaps himself.[32]

5. Habit Five has the lawyer exploring her own implicit associations, without judgment, and working towards eliminating or minimizing the harm from them by employing critical self-reflection to address any bias or discrimination.[33] Again, *narrative theory* can be important as one engages in this habit by using the strategies already discussed above and in Chapter Three discussing critical self-reflection.

---

29. Bryant & Peters, *supra* note 26.

30. *See* Chapter Five discussing interviewing, client construction of narratives, and narrative listening.

31. Bryant & Peters, *supra* note 26 (strategies suggested are as follows: using narrative to permit client to convey herself in her own context; listening to understand the client's narrative; parallel universe thinking; communicating in light of client's cultural context especially concerning lawyers and legal systems; using interpreters to promote understanding and communication; actively analyzing any communication struggles to employ strategies to improve communication). We discuss listening, including narrative listening and active listening, in Chapter Five.

32. Bryant & Peters, *supra* note 26 (another benefit of the client constructing his own narrative is that the power and authority of constructing the narrative is confirmed in the client).

33. Bryant & Peters, *supra* note 26. Paul R. Tremblay and Carwina Weng explore the effects that bias and stereotypes can have on lawyers' work and suggest approaches that lawyers can take to minimize these effects. Paul R. Tremblay and Carwina Weng, *Multicultural Lawyering: Heuristics and Biases*, in Affective Assistance of Counsel: Practicing Law as a Healing Profession (Marjorie Silver ed., 2006).

E. Exercise: Taking Steps Toward Cross-Cultural Competence

Now it is your turn to start practicing some of these habits and exercises. Pick one of your own clients and try your hand at this two-part exercise.

Part One: Exploring Differences and Similarities

In a quick write,[34] create a two column document. Label the column on the left "similar traits" and the column on the right "different traits." Take two minutes to write down all similar and different traits between you and your client. At the end of the quick write, review your lists; if one is longer than the other, take one more minute and try to write down more in the shorter list.[35]

Now ask yourself:

1. What do you think are some difficulties you might encounter from the different traits between you and your client? What about from the similar traits?
2. What might be some of the strengths resulting from the different traits? What about from the similar traits?
3. If one list of traits was longer than the other at the beginning, what insight do you have about why that was? What did you do to add to the shorter list? How might that strategy be helpful as you continue your lawyering?
4. Follow the process of self-reflection discussed below:
   a. Considering the list of similar and different traits, take a fresh look at your client's situation and reconsider the question of what it is your client actually wants and cares about.
   b. Consider how the similar and different traits you identified might have affected your ability to attend to your client? How can you address that now?
   c. Consider how the similar and different traits you identified have affected your belief and/or doubt in your client's narrative? Do you have any new thoughts now?

---

34. A quick write requires a writer to listen to a prompt, think about it for a minute, and then put pen to paper and not lift it up for at least two minutes. During the two minutes, the writer should write whatever comes to her head, understanding it is not going to be reviewed or evaluated by others for grammar or coherency. The quick write technique is used to help brainstorm ideas without self-judgment getting in the way, as well as incorporating the benefits of writing for the development of critical thinking. Harvard University, *Quick Write*, ABL CONNECT http://ablconnect.harvard.edu/quick-write.

35. This part of the exercise is based on "Habit One" of the Five Habits of Cross-Cultural Competency created by Sue Bryant and Jean Koh Peters. Bryant, *supra* note 26, at 33.

    d. Is there anything on your list that may be affecting your rapport and relationship with your client? How can you address that now?

    e. Considering the similar and different traits, identify any ethical or strategic issues you may be confronting and how the list might help you address them.

Part Two: Cross-Cultural Competence and Critical Reflection

Now, using the narrative elements (characters, events, causation, normalization, masterplot and closure) construct a brief narrative about a trouble your client has faced that has disrupted his steady state and for which he is seeking a resolution. Write it down. Go back and examine your list of similar and different traits between you and your client. How is your cultural context or your client's cultural context affecting the narrative you have drafted? Is it improving your understanding of the client's narrative and his goals, or impeding it? Revise your narrative if appropriate.

Using narrative elements (characters, events, causation, normalization, masterplot and closure) construct a brief narrative about any trouble you have faced in the representation of your client that has disrupted the steady state of your representation of your client and for which you are seeking a resolution. Write it down. Go back and examine your list of similar and different traits between you and your client. How is your cultural context or your client's cultural context affecting the narrative you have drafted? Is it improving your lawyering on behalf of your client or impeding it? Revise your narrative if appropriate. Consider how you can use these narratives to help guide your lawyering for your client.

III. Collaboration

As discussed above, a goal of cross-culturally competent lawyering is to build better rapport, understanding, and communication between lawyer, client and decision maker or other system actor. We now turn to the lawyering skill of collaboration, which relies on cross-cultural competence, and shares its goals of building rapport, understanding, and communication when engaging in work together or creating a joint work product.

A. Collaboration and Lawyering

The dictionary defines collaboration simply as "to work with another person or group in order to achieve or do something."[36] Again, a seemingly simple skill, but not an easy one to execute. In breaking down the definition, we see there are choices to be made. For instance, how will we work with another person or group? And how will we define success for achieving or doing something? These are issues we explore in this section of this chapter.

For lawyers, collaboration has always been a critical skill. Lawyers collaborate with their clients and others within their own law practice, such as other lawyers, paralegals, administrative assistants and librarians. Lawyers also collaborate with other professionals, stakeholders and workers outside the legal practice on the same matter for the same client. And lawyers collaborate with opposing parties, decision makers, government officials and others while working on various matters.

Highlighting the importance of collaboration, Richard Susskind argues that big firm lawyering now urgently requires restructured work by assigning tasks to workers in different countries to achieve greater efficiency, and a streamlining of tasks best suited to each individual's strengths.[37] To successfully disaggregate lawyering across people not only outside of one's firm, but across the globe, as Susskind suggests, requires collaboration.

Professor Sameer Ashar also identifies effective collaboration as critical for lawyers' work with clients who partner with the community to "mediate complex decision making within organizations and communities, frame social problems, and think carefully about power—how it is created, distributed,

---

36. Merriam Webster, *Collaborate*, http://www.merriam-webster.com/dictionary/collaborate; see also Virginia Rowthorn and Jody Olson, *All Together Now: Developing a Team Skills Competency Domain for Global Health Education*, 42 J.L. MED. & ETHICS 550 (Winter 2014) (defining collaboration as "a way to ... allow partners to reach an aspiration that would be impossible to achieve without each member of the team working toward the same end. It requires the partnership and the commitment of all members working toward a common goal to succeed") (internal citation omitted).

37. RICHARD SUSSKIND, TOMORROW'S LAWYERS: AN INTRODUCTION TO YOUR FUTURE 29–31 (2013). For instance, Richard Susskind deconstructs litigation into the following tasks—"document review, legal research, project management, litigation support, electronic disclosure, strategy, tactics, negotiation, and advocacy"—and recommends these tasks be allocated to workers across the globe based on cost and effectiveness. *Id.* Susskind similarly disaggregates transactional work into the following components: "due diligence, legal research, transaction management, template selection, negotiation, bespoke drafting, document management, legal advice risk assessment." *Id.* at 33.

used, and lost."[38] So you see that understanding and making intentional choices about how to collaborate and why continues to be an essential part of effective lawyering, implicating as it does global working relationships with multiple parties across many kinds of cultures.

And collaboration is important in law school and other learning settings. Professor Sophie Sparrow articulates that cooperative learning improves student learning, develops "problem solving, reasoning, and critical thinking skills," and increases cross-cultural competency.[39] Professor Susan Bryant has articulated that for lawyers, collaboration: (1) increases "professional satisfaction;"[40] (2) improves work product;[41] and (3) creates a process for work in diverse workplaces.[42]

Collaboration to achieve these professional, service, and learning goals happens in many different ways. Bryant identifies the following three models for working together:

- The Collaboration Model—where workers share decision-making;
- The Input Model—where the decision maker seeks contributions from others; and
- The Parallel Work Model—where workers work toward a common goal but on separate, related projects.[43]

So lawyers can collaborate by working together on a project, by working separately but sharing strategic decision-making, and/or by dividing up the tasks to achieve the overall outcome.[44] Each type of collaboration offers different benefits and disadvantages.

In the Collaboration Model, workers decide how best to allocate work based on each worker's goals and strengths, as well as to promote the overall goal of shared decision-making.[45] Because everyone is involved in the decision-making, the collaboration model requires a good process for synthesizing multiple ideas, as well as mechanisms for identifying and resolving conflict among the workers.[46]

---

38. Sameer M. Ashar, *Deep Critique and Democratic Lawyering in Clinical Practice*, 104 Cal. L. Rev. 201, 223–24 (2016).

39. Sophie Sparrow et al., Teaching Law for Design By Adjuncts 11 (2010).

40. Susan Bryant, *Collaboration in Law Practice: A Satisfying and Productive Process for A Diverse Profession*, 17 Vermont L. Rev. 459, 468–472 (1993).

41. Bryant, *supra* note 40, at 472–476.

42. Bryant, *supra* note 40, at 476–477.

43. Bryant, *supra* note 40, at 491.

44. Bryant, *supra* note 40.

45. Bryant, *supra* note 40, at 494.

46. Bryant, *supra* note 40.

The Input Model has one worker as the ultimate decision maker. So while input and discussion is invited from other workers, the final decision-making power and responsibility rests with one person. This model avoids some of the conflict resolution issues that may arise when using the collaboration model, but using this model means that not everyone has equal responsibility for the work and outcomes.[47]

Finally, the Parallel Work Model works well when tasks are to be done in a sequence and no synthesis of ideas is required.[48] A downside of working this way is that the final work product may lack synthesis.

All three of these collaboration models may be part of your lawyering practice. The following discussion focuses on collaborations with other lawyers, but it could easily be applied to work with your client or others. If you are working in a pair or on a team of other lawyers, your work may be organized in the collaboration model to share jointly in the professional responsibility of your work product, including decision-making and synthesis of ideas. If you are working alone on a client's matter, but are assigned to a team for case rounds or supervision, or if you raise a lawyering issue during a firm meeting, then you may be engaging in an input model where your lawyer colleagues are providing ideas and feedback but you, under your supervisor's supervision, are the ultimate decision maker. While working with a team on legislative advocacy, you and your colleagues may collaborate using a parallel work model and decide to conduct legal research separately. In this situation, there will probably be shared decision-making around what issues are important to research and how best to record that information, but the actual research and work is conducted individually, with each person making decisions about her own tasks. The important thing to remember, though, is that no matter which type of collaboration you engage in, it should be an intentional choice. Therefore, it will be helpful to have a conversation with your collaborators about which type of collaboration will best fit the work you are undertaking. Without such intentionality, you might end up falling into a work pattern or relationship that is not best for you, your partner(s), and ultimately your client and the project.

B. Collaboration, Self-Reflection and Narrative

So how do you make these intentional choices? Just as in practicing cross-cultural competency, critical reflection and narrative theory will help you iden-

---

47. Bryant, *supra* note 40, at 495–496.
48. Bryant, *supra* note 40, at 497–498.

tify strengths and obstacles to collaboration, as well as strategies to help improve collaborations.

The exercise you tried in the first part of this chapter—mapping *character traits* that are similar and different between you and your client—can also work in determining a good collaboration model for you and your work-partner. As you and your work-partner individually generate the list of traits, include not only categories of cultural traits you might have focused on earlier, but also ones that involve your collaborative style, such as how you learn from others, how you like to teach others, and how you handle feedback and conflict. Then you and your work-partner should compare your lists and consider which similar and different traits could help or hinder the collaboration and why. From there, consider guidelines for your collaboration that will address the challenges you anticipate. Finally, consider any processes you want to put in place to address any situation where one of you does not meet the guidelines.[49]

In addition, you and your work-partner could employ critical self-reflection as you encounter difficulties in your collaboration to explore the *causation* for the difficulties and how in the future you can address those difficulties. The Five Habits discussed above to address cross-cultural competency can be used to improve communication and address pitfalls in collaboration as well.

In addition, a tried and true approach to any problem in a collaboration is to assume good intent by your collaborator. Assuming good intent means you will adopt a listening posture as you try to understand what happened and why. It will enhance communication by decreasing the likelihood that your work-partner will feel defensive or judged. It will permit better critical reflection by your team to understand what the pitfalls are and how they can be addressed and prevented in the future.

C. Examples of Collaboration

One example of the importance of listening and being present in a collaboration is shown in a playful retort by Sarah Koenig in *Serial*. In Episode Five of *Serial*, Sarah Koenig and Dana Chivvis reconstructed the events of the afternoon when Hae Min Lee was murdered by driving and timing the same route Adnan supposedly took that afternoon. During the drive, Sarah is discussing and

---

49. See Deborah Epstein et al., The Clinic Seminar Ch. 9 (2014) and Deborah Epstein et al., Teaching the Clinic Seminar 9 (2014); Sophie Sparrow et al., Teaching Law for Design By Adjuncts 11 (2010); Rachel Camp, *Creating Space for Silence in Law School Collaborations*, 65 J. Legal Educ. 897 (2016).

seeking Dana's assistance in analyzing whether Adnan had enough time to have committed the murder. Rather than engaging in that dialogue, Dana states: "There's a shrimp sale at the Crab Crib." Sarah Koenig responds in an aside to the audience, "Sometimes I think Dana isn't listening to me."[50] Koenig and Chivvis' exchange might have been playful, but it also makes an important point that collaborative partners do need to listen to each other for an effective collaboration.

Another more serious example of collaboration is later in *Serial* when there is a collaborative strategic discussion of case theory. In Episode Seven of *Serial*, two student attorneys and the director of the University of Virginia Innocence Project Clinic examine the evidence against Adnan and discuss back and forth the strengths and weaknesses of the case to determine if there is enough for them to take on the case and investigate further.[51] This is an example of the collaborative input model where the student attorneys were providing ideas to the clinic director who seemed to be the decision maker as she was talking with Koenig about lawyering strategies.

D. Exercise—What Kind of Collaborative Model Works for You?

Now it's your turn. If you are working with another lawyer in practice or a student attorney in clinic, conduct the collaboration exercise described above of mapping similar and different traits between you and your work-partner. When you and your work-partner compare your lists and consider whether any of the similar or different traits could help or hinder the collaboration, identify strategies that could assist overcoming any hindrances. Would utilizing a particular collaborative model help? Would utilizing any of the Five Habits discussed in the cross-cultural competency section of this chapter help? Would establishing any communication or other work guidelines help? Finally, would establishing any processes to address any collaboration pitfalls help? If the answer is yes to any of these questions, create a shared document identifying your answers to guide your collaboration into the future.

IV. Conclusion

In this chapter, we have shown how cross-cultural competency and collaboration are important skills and values that apply to all facets of lawyering. We

---

50. *Serial*, Episode 5: Route Talk (20:32).
51. *Serial*, Episode 7: The Opposite of the Prosecution (22:40–end).

have explained these skills and values and shown ways to practice them. We have shown how critical self-reflection and narrative theory can be used to enhance these skills and values. We have learned the importance of being aware of our cultural similarities and differences when representing clients. We also learned how cultural competency influences narratives, particularly how we represent the characters, their relevant traits, and normalization. We introduced tools to practice cross-cultural competency, such as Project Implicit tests and the Five Habits of cross-cultural competency, and how narrative can enhance the use of them. Learning the importance of collaboration and finding a collaborative model that works is also important, especially for clinic students and new lawyers, and we showed how narrative can help lawyers establish and maintain effective collaborations.

Chapter 5

Interviewing and Listening

I. Introduction

Client interviewing is where the lawyer-client relationship begins. It is also a great place to start applying narrative theory and storytelling practice. These tools make lawyers more effective interviewers and ultimately counselors. In this chapter, we will examine the basics of client interviewing, and how narrative theory and storytelling practice help master those basics. As with the chapters that follow, we will provide a general theoretical overview about the lawyering activity at issue; we will offer some practical guidance on how to conduct the lawyering activity, using accessible popular media examples; and we will show concrete examples of the lawyering activity in a lawyering context. This chapter begins with a general theoretical overview about interviewing, divided into narrative probing and narrative listening, and then provides practical guidance on how to conduct interviews with examples and exercises to help you learn this essential component of lawyering.

When interviewing a client, a lawyer must listen to the client's narrative, paying attention to how the client describes the closure he seeks, as well as the trouble he wants resolved, and the characters he includes. By attending to these narrative elements as she listens to the client's description of his issues, the lawyer learns about the client's actual goals and values. Such careful listening can override a lawyer's assumption about what the client's problem is, and how that problem should be resolved. Lawyers need to inquire and listen as well as understand and empathize with the client. Attending to the client's narrative helps lawyers do all of these things.

II. Narrative Probing and Narrative Listening

The lawyer's goals for a first interview may be manifold, but certainly include: to begin to develop an effective professional lawyer-client relationship, and to gather enough information about the client's situation to make the relationship a fruitful one.

A. Narrative Probing

The relationship between lawyer and client connects deeply with the lawyer's goal of gathering information about the client. The more comfortable the client feels, the more likely he is to give the lawyer information, and vice-versa. So in thinking about that first interview, the lawyer must put front and center this idea of connection—between the client and others in his life, AND between the client and the lawyer. Only once the lawyer understands that in order to do her job of counseling and shaping the LAW she has to engage with and be curious about the client's FACTS will she be able to enter into a fruitful lawyer-client relationship.

For many, the initial interview cements the foundation for the attorney/client relationship by beginning to establish personal regard and trust. Acknowledging your client's feelings is key to client-centered lawyering. While effective lawyers might have sympathy for their clients, truly effective lawyers have empathy. Here's a quick differentiation between the two: sympathy means feeling sad about the hardships that another person encounters, while empathy means understanding that person's values/feelings, often by putting yourself in their shoes.

How do you show empathy to a client? Here is a great (short) animated video by Brene Brown on the difference between sympathy and empathy, and how to be empathic. https://www.youtube.com/watch?v=1Evwgu369Jw. Try to simply listen to your client and say something like "wow, that sounds really hard." Or, "I can't imagine how that must have felt. Thank you for sharing that with me." Those kinds of exchanges will go a long way toward making your client feel safe and comfortable with you.

Which, of course, will make it a lot easier to do the work of the initial interview: figuring out the client's situation so you and the client together can determine how to proceed. There are great learning moments as students and new lawyers realize that by not doing enough inquiring into the facts of the client's life, they missed the essence of his concern, and were unable to do effective legal counseling.

Information gathering about the client breaks down into three distinct sub-areas:

- What is the client's situation, or, to use narrative terminology, his *steady state*?
  - Think about the narrative elements of *character, events,* and *normalization.*
- What is his legal issue/concern, or, to use the narrative term, the *trouble*?
  - Think about the narrative elements of *character, events,* and *causation.*
- What are his goals or desired outcomes, what *closure* does he seek?
  - Think about the narrative elements of *causation, normalization,* and *masterplot.*

So when a client walks into your office for the first time, you want to learn as much about him as you can. You want to identify both the content and feelings in the client's narrative. And you want to be sure that you are gathering and listening for the client's actual FACTS (as he describes them), rather than filling in gaps on your own, based on what you assume his story is. Remember the discussion in Chapter Two about the absence of something called "absolute truth." While facts appear to be fixed, we know that stories and narratives can change from telling to telling. So you want to be careful not to make assumptions and/or rely on stereotypes as you interview your client. Ask yourself, who did you expect to see? Was the client what you expected? Was the narrative what you expected? Be a person, not a "lawyer."

The goal of all this information gathering is, of course, to determine what brought this client to you. That is obviously the main information you are trying to gather during your interview. You need to get a sense of the legal claims the client might have or need to defend against. You also want to get a sense of any "non-legal" concerns the client might have, issues that might rub up against his legal claims, but don't appear — at least to him — to be legally relevant. You can decide what is legally relevant only after you have heard all the possible sources of tension in the client's life. You want to know everything that is causing a disruption to the client's steady state.

Having learned as much as you can about the problem, you also have to learn about the client's desired outcome. Most clients have a general goal of achieving satisfactory, effective solutions, but what are this client's particular goals? And if he has more than one goal — which people generally do — what are his priorities among those goals? You need to elicit information that will allow you and the client to move forward toward that outcome. Clients are autonomous owners of their problems, and are in the best position to make important decisions about their lives.[1] Legal problems raise both legal and non-legal concerns; the client is best placed to assess non-legal consequences, and clients are happier with solutions that consider such consequences. Clients are also better placed to assess their own willingness to take risks. So you and the client need to learn from each other what means there might be to achieve the desired outcome(s).

How does narrative theory and storytelling practice help lawyers prepare for and conduct an interview in such a way as to achieve these goals? Amsterdam and Bruner describe how "as clients and lawyers talk, the client's story gets recast into plights and prospects, plots and pilgrimages into possible worlds."[2] Narrative theory reminds us that clients exist within contexts, and those contexts include relationships—with family, with culture, with institutions, with neighborhoods, communities, and state. Seek information about the *characters* in your client's life, about the *events* that have taken place, or that the client anticipates will take place, about the *causal connection/causation* between the various characters and events, and how that connection might contribute to or detract from the client's desire for *closure*.

Lawyers too exist within contexts—professional, personal, cultural, and familial. For our purposes in this chapter, the lawyer's context is the legal system, beginning a relationship with a client. Just as the client's context is comprised of multiple relationships and dynamics, so too is the lawyer's. What relationships might be important to consider as the lawyer prepares to interview her client for the first time? Are there power dynamics that might need to be explored? Does the lawyer have support and resources to help represent this client? Is this a client the lawyer has identified herself, or has the lawyer been given the client by the court, or a senior partner, or some other referral mechanism?

How do the answers to these questions affect the lawyer's ability to be empathic with her client, to build rapport, and to gather information? We explored in Chapter Three how the practice of critical reflection helps lawyers be more effective client representatives. Answering these questions about the lawyer's context is part of that critical reflection. By placing herself squarely within a context she identifies and understands, the lawyer learns to recognize her own power to ameliorate tension, to elicit information, to counsel, and to manipulate/elicit the client's narrative.

Narrative theory can also help you as students and new lawyers come to see yourselves as professionals who hear, construct, and retell narratives, and, in

---

1. David A. Binder, et. al., Lawyers as Counselors: A Client-Centered Approach 318–321 (3d ed. 2012).

2. Anthony G. Amsterdam & Jerome S. Bruner, Minding the Law 110 (2000).

so doing, make choices about how to do so and to do so in a client-centered, professional, and justice-driven way. You will begin to see that when made with intention, those choices can result in narratives that are persuasive, compelling, and respectful of your clients; and when made without intention, those choices can result in narratives that fail to achieve your client's goals or fail to reflect their lives in a way that feels familiar and comfortable to the client.

Attention to the process of recasting a client's facts into "pilgrimages into possible worlds" helps us slow down and explore our client's context more fully. By attending to narrative, we recast the client's recitation of her situation into its narrative elements of character, events, causation, normalization, masterplot, and closure. Curiosity about all the elements of a client's story— also described as narrative probing—guides lawyers to pursue all of these paths to exhaustion. They are then much more likely to get a fleshed out contextual story before moving on to the more comfortable realm of the story's "legal elements" and the legal counseling that comes next. As such, narrative theory helps students become more effective lawyers.

B. Narrative Listening

Now what about the other part of the conversation—the listening? Wisconsin Supreme Court Justice Geske has observed "lawyers who were good empathetic listeners and creative problem solvers best represented their clients' interests by guiding them to peaceful resolutions of their disputes."[3] This section explores the importance of listening in interviewing, and how narrative and story can help improve your listening.[4]

Let's start at the basics, namely what is *listening?*[5] At its most basic, listening is "making meaning from sound."[6] By listening, we distinguish noises from

---

3. Janine Geske, *Why Do I Teach Restorative Justice to Law Students?*, 89 MARQ. L. Rev. 327 (2005).

4. Linda F. Smith, *Was It Good for You Too? Conversation Analysis of Two Interviews*, 96 KY. L.J. 579 (2008). In her article, Smith demonstrates that interviewing that permits the client to construct her narrative is more effective than legal element driven interviewing for obtaining information but is equal in its ability of building rapport. Similarly, Linda Smith writes that most lawyering scholars and teachers agree that good interviewing requires lawyers listening, using empathy and active listening, to clients so the clients can "describe the situation in their own words and ... give a narrative or time line." *Id* at 579.

5. Of course, listening is important in lots of other contexts as well and we hope you will apply it beyond interviewing.

6. Julian Treasure, *5 Ways to Listen Better* (2011), https://www.ted.com/talks/julian_treasure_5_ways_to_listen_better?language=en.

signal and differentiate different sounds to make the meaning.[7] By listening, we are engaging in a process to understand what the speaker is trying to communicate both verbally and nonverbally.

As lawyers, we engage in *active* listening, which is not only a process of attending to and understanding what is being communicated but also of conveying to the speaker that you respect him and value what he is communicating. The fact is that clients value lawyers who listen to them. And, as the literature shows us, active listening does in fact grow the trust between lawyer and client, which increases the access to information and ideas, and results in better counseling, problem-solving, drafting and advocacy—in short, better lawyering.[8]

Below we explore some suggested behaviors and identified choices you can make to enhance your active listening and explain how they tie to the goals of interviewing.[9] The first set of behaviors help to communicate that you are listening to the speaker and to build rapport. The building of rapport is important for communication and the sharing of information, both important goals of interviewing.

- **Face the person who is speaking and maintain eye contact.** If the listening person is looking down all the time taking notes or staring out the window, the speaker may feel unattended to, may start to feel self-conscious about his story or judged, and may trim or stop his story accordingly. Maintaining eye contact and facing the speaker communicates to the speaker that you want to listen to what he is saying.
- **Reflect back the speaker's feelings and contents.** Being able to show the speaker you are listening by stating back to him the feelings he has expressed or summarizing the content of what he has said helps to build rapport. Through these actions the listener shows she is listening and the speaker can settle in to share more comfortably his story. For example, you can provide responses like "I understand," or "I see," or even just "mm-hm." You can also reflect back the client's content by saying something like, "Let me make sure I have this right, are you saying that your husband came home at 9:00 p.m.?" And you can reflect back any emotions he displayed in the telling of his story by stating something

---

7. *Id.*

8. Binder, et al., *supra* note 1, at 40–62.

9. Dianne Schilling, *10 Steps to Effective Listening* (2012), http://www.forbes.com/sites/womensmedia/2012/11/09/10-steps-to-effective-listening/#52d8554526fb.

like, "When your husband came home at 9:00 p.m. and slammed the door you were concerned."[10]

- **Relax.** Communicating that the speaker's story is important to you will convey respect. Listening takes focus and a lot of energy but don't let it make you tense as that may dampen rapport. Try to be yourself and relaxed as you listen to make your speaker feel comfortable in telling his story.

This second set of behaviors and identified choices focus on enhancing your active listening for the meaning of your client's story.

- **Listen nonjudgmentally and permit the speaker to tell his story at his pace.** If the speaker feels that the listener is judging him then the speaker will start to make strategic choices about what he shares in his story to avoid being judged. Accordingly, try not to interrupt unless you and the speaker have agreed that interrupting is fine. Also, try not to suggest solutions while the speaker is still getting his story out. Wait until the conversation shifts to problem-solving or counseling for discussing potential solutions to problems.
- **Listen to the words and try to visualize what your speaker says.** Sometimes it is hard to attend for long periods of time. If you focus on the words or draw a picture in your head about the story being told this will be helpful.
- **Be intentional about your questions to the speaker.** There will be times when you have clarifying questions. You have a choice to interrupt to ask them or wait for pauses in the conversation. Consider what will be the best approach for this particular speaker and context. If you decide to wait for a pause, you could consider jotting down an idea for a clarifying question to ask later. In addition, understand that different questions have different effects on your speaker and choose which to ask during the interview. For example, clarifying questions continue the speaker on course with his story while other questions may lead the speaker to a different topic or story.
- **Pay attention to what is not said.** We communicate a lot nonverbally. If we only attend to the verbal content of the speaker, we may be missing a lot about what he is trying to convey. Therefore, as a listener, pay at-

---

10. As discussed in client-centered lawyering and transformative mediation literature, reflecting back what was said "provides a natural platform for elaboration, deliberation, and clarification [by the client] — it allows the client to hear what s/he is saying, think about it, and thus refine and confirm what s/he wants to say." Robert A. Baruch Bush, *Mediation Skills and Client-Centered Lawyering: A New View of the Partnership*, 19 CLINICAL L. REV. 429, 458–9 (2013).

tention to facial expressions, body expressions, and pauses to gain even more understanding of the speaker and what he is saying.

- **Be conscious of filters that can assist or block your understanding.** The meaning from listening is created through filters that assist us with understanding.[11] These filters include "culture, language, values, beliefs, attitudes, expectations, [and] intentions"[12] and determine what we will attend to while listening. We can enhance our listening by being aware of these filters and checking ourselves as we listen to see if the filters are helping us to focus and understand or distracting us and causing misinterpretation.

- **Consider changing your listening position from time to time.** Consider changing your listening position along the critical/empathic filter spectrum, sometimes referred to as the methodological doubt or belief spectrum.[13] Methodological belief is listening and trying to believe the speaker's idea or hypothesis and not trying to construct a counter-argument. The result of this kind of listening is that we expand our knowledge as we open ourselves to really listening to other ideas and experiences.[14] On the other hand, methodological doubt involves criticizing arguments and engaging in critical thinking.[15] This is a common listening position in law school courses focused on Socratic teaching that engages the listener to attune to the speaker with an analytical approach.

Now let's tie in narrative theory to active listening. As we learned in Chapter One, we are hardwired to look for a story in what people say. Therefore, active listening helps us to listen for the constructed story (narrative) of the speaker

---

11. Treasure, *supra* note 6.

12. Treasure, *supra* note 6.

13. Mark Weisberg and Jean Koh Peters, *Experiments in Listening*, 57 J. LEGAL ED. 427, 432 (2007) (citing PETER ELBOW, EMBRACING CONTRARIES: EXPLORATIONS IN LEARNING AND TEACHING 253, 258 (1986)).

14. PETER ELBOW, EMBRACING CONTRARIES: EXPLORATIONS IN LEARNING AND TEACHING 253, 258 (1986) (as cited in Weisberg and Peters, *supra* note 13, at notes 8 and 9). As Weisberg and Peters state, "Methodological belief 'forc(es) us genuinely to enter into unfamiliar or threatening ideas instead of just arguing against them without experiencing them or feeling their force. It thus carries us further in our developmental journey away from mere credulity.' Rather than encourage us to accept unquestioningly, to embrace false beliefs, believing helps us examine our beliefs and consequently, become better able to assess what knowledge is trustworthy." Weisberg and Peters, *supra* note 13, at 427 (citing Peter Elbow though internal citations were omitted).

15. Weisberg and Peters, *supra* note 13, at 432 (citing ELBOW, *supra* note 14, at 258).

without inserting our own constructed story. And listening for the speaker's story will help to improve rapport because the speaker wants to tell his story and does not want to be directed to tell a different story.[16]

When we listen through the lens of story, we can start to categorize the information: who are the *characters*, what are the *events*, what *causation* exists between events; what is the listener's experience in trying to *normalize* the story; what *masterplot*(s) are presented in the story; and what *closure* is being sought, including what is the steady state and problem as described by the storyteller. Listening for a story lets the listener learn more about what happened.

On another level, the listener can reflect upon what is not in the story. For instance, the listener can learn about the unspoken motivations and feelings of the speaker by analyzing how the speaker constructed the narrative. The listener can learn what is important to the speaker by what is included and what is not included in the story from characters to events to causation to masterplots. It is listening to both of these levels of story—what's included and omitted from the story—that will help the listener as lawyer become in tune with what is being told.

And, as with active listening, listening to the story means permitting the client to control the narrative, at least initially. Accordingly, lawyers listening should consider which questions to ask and when with the understanding that all questions disrupt the flow of the story, some questions will fill out the story, and other questions may end the current story and start another.[17]

Exercise:

Here is an exercise to build your active listening skills. For a day, try to practice the above behaviors during the various conversations you have with different people. Pay special attention to reflecting back the speaker's emotional and substantive content, being intentional about what questions to ask and when to ask them, and listening nonjudgmentally and at the speaker's pace. See if at the end of the conversation you can summarize the speaker's story— who are the characters, what are the events, what closure is being sought. And see if you notice gaps the speakers placed in the story. Share your summary with any speakers you know well and get their feedback on how well you listened. Based on the feedback from the speaker, consider whether any of your filters enhanced or diminished your understanding.[18]

---

16. Smith, *supra* note 4.

17. Baruch Bush, *supra* note 10, at 454, 456–57.

18. Another listening exercise is from Julian Treasure and goes by the acronym RASA. The first step when you are engaging in listening is to receive (R), in other words, pay attention to the person talking. The second step is to appreciate (A) the person who is talking

III. Planning for the Interview

How do narrative probing and narrative listening help you plan for and conduct a client interview? There are three phases of the client interview experience: preparation, performance and reflection. Let's go through each one.

A. Preparation

Well before the interview takes place, here are some things to think about:

Prepare for the facts. Identify the factual elements you want to explore in your potential client's situation. Develop an outline of topic areas to ask about. Use the narrative elements of character, events, causation, normalization, masterplot and closure to guide you in identifying topics and questions to ask.

Prepare for attorney and client (or potential client) relationship. Spend some time anticipating potential questions the client might have about the process, fees, confidentiality, any retainer agreement, other forms, etc. You will want to remember your goal of establishing rapport with the potential client and think about ways to start building the relationship. Watch the Brene Brown video again to remind yourself about empathy, and the importance of connection. And gather together any forms or pamphlets or other informational resources you might want to share with the client during or after the meeting.

Prepare for the law and the process of the matter. Research what you can about the area of law you imagine the client's situation might involve (if you have received any information from an intake form, or the client himself when he made the appointment). You also want to consider any procedural rules that might be implicated by the client's problem or issue, and/or what process might be followed to address the client's problem or issue. As we will explore in Chapter Seven on Fact Investigation, focusing too much on what you think legal elements might be as you prepare for an interview risks closing your mind to potential "non-legal" elements. So you want to prepare for the law only to the extent that it is relevant to your firm's practice and offers some ground over which to connect with your client. Your legal research should never override your factual research and/or your openness to alternative legal narratives.

---

and what they are saying, such as by making noises like "ok" or "uhuh." Active listening's concept of reflecting back the content, including the emotional content of what is said, is part of the appreciating step. The third step is to summarize (S) what you just heard to ensure you have heard the person talking correctly. For instance, you might say, "To make sure I understand you, you just stated...." And the final step is to ask questions (A). Treasure, *supra* note 6.

Think about the setting. Where will this interview take place? Do you have control over that? If you can choose where to meet, think about the pros and cons of meeting in your office, in the client's home, or at a coffee shop. Wherever you end up meeting, what might you want to do to create a comfortable atmosphere for the client? Where, for example, will you plan to sit, and where will the client sit? Are there ways to make the setting feel safe and private for the client, even if you are meeting in a public place? These may sound like relatively minor issues, but things like lighting, sound, relative placement of chairs can make a huge difference. Think back to the last time you went to a doctor. Where did you meet with the doctor—in her office? In an exam room? What were the rooms like? Were there things about the setting that made you feel more or less at ease? What were they, and why?

Think about your personal appearance. Again, this might seem like a minor issue, but remember, you are preparing to meet with someone for the first time (probably) about a problem or concern he has. You want to signal at every opportunity that you are trustworthy and professional, and that you respect the potential client. Dressing respectfully is one way to do that. This doesn't mean necessarily that you should put on the crispest business suit and shiniest shoes for every interview. Indeed, for some interviews, such attire would have the opposite effect than the one you are hoping for. You don't want to intimidate your potential client or make him feel less powerful than you. You just need to be intentional about your appearance—think about the goals you have for this meeting, and dress in a way that seems likely to facilitate your achieving those goals.

B. Agenda and Outline

How do you anticipate the interview will proceed and what are your goals? It is helpful to break an interview down into several stages, each of which warrants its own mini-outline. As you think about how you hope the interview will unfold, consider how much of this agenda/outline you want to share with your client during the opening stage. It is generally a good idea to give your client a sense of how the interview will proceed, so he feels part of the process.

1. Opening Stage

What icebreaking will you do? Do you have a patter you use with all your clients—about the weather, parking, current events? Has that been effective at putting your client, and yourself, at ease? If so, great. Keep using it. If not, why do you think that might be the case? What other techniques can you use? Think about your last visit to the doctor again: what kind of opening conversation did you have with each professional you interacted with. Did any of those work to relax you and make you comfortable? Why or why not?

It is important to remember why you engage in ice-breaking: to ease your client into the interview, to ease yourself into the interview, to get you both to relax and settle into the conversation; and to set the tone for rapport-building and information gathering. So ask yourself these questions as you prepare for your interview's opening stage:

What information does the client need to know from you for you to meet your professional obligations and for your client to be comfortable in providing his narrative? How best can you explain client confidentiality and your position as a student attorney to meet these goals?

How will you set the tone for the client to be able to construct his narrative from the beginning? How will you be prepared to listen actively?

2. Information Gathering and Rapport Building

Remember the goals of narrative probing are to explore the following areas: the client's situation (his character and traits), his steady state; his legal issue/concern, the trouble or problem; and his goals or desired outcomes, or closure. How are you going to do this exploration?

Ask open-ended questions. They reflect your openness to multiple narratives, and increase the likelihood that your client will feel empowered to present his narrative on his terms. Classic reporter questions of "who, what, where, when, why and how" or "can you explain, can you describe" permit the client to talk more and thereby construct his narrative.

Ask narrower, follow-up questions. These show your attention to detail, and your interest in the client's narrative. It is important that these narrower questions be used only after an open-ended question that has allowed the client to present his narrative first. Otherwise, you risk conducting what might feel to the client like a cross-examination, rather than an information-gathering interview. Remember your goals and strike a balance between open and closed questions. Some lawyers call this the "T-Funnel" approach: you start broad, at the wide top of the funnel, and then get progressively narrower, getting deeper into the client's narrative, eliciting more details about your client and his situation.[19]

---

19. Jeffrey L. Kestler, Questioning Techniques and Tactics § 4.11 (3d ed. 2016).

Engage in active listening. We explored earlier in the chapter the importance of listening to a lawyer's goal of gathering information, building rapport, and constructing effective narratives. Use some of the techniques described above in the active listening section of this chapter to effectuate these goals.

Loop back. This means that you use the client's own words when you ask a follow up question. For example, if the client has described coming home late one night, you might follow up with a question like, "you say you came home late that night; can you remember what time it was?" Again, this shows the client you are paying attention to him, and that his actual words matter to you. It also gives him the opportunity to correct his earlier statement—"well, it wasn't really late, I guess. Probably like 8 or 9pm."

Let the client know why you're asking hard questions. No one comes to a lawyer if everything is perfect. People come to lawyers because they have or anticipate having a problem. In order to help clients, lawyers have to ask questions that some clients might not want to answer: questions about money, sex, death, relationships, guilt, wrongdoing, crimes, arrests, and embarrassing moments. This is very hard for students and new lawyers to do, especially if you have been raised in a culture that has unspoken rules about privacy and discretion and respect for others' business. It is also very hard for the clients to be asked—let alone answer—these kinds of questions. But they must be asked and they must be answered for you, the lawyer, to gather the information you need to help the client. This is very tricky because while you are trying hard to develop trust between yourself and the client, such trust does not exist at the outset of the relationship—which is, unfortunately, when you are having to ask these hard questions. Try explaining all this to your client: you know it's awkward and uncomfortable—for you too!—but you have to ask these questions, and here's why. When you do this, you signal that you recognize your client's possible discomfort, and that you are sorry to put him in that position. That might further your goal of developing trust and building rapport. Second, by letting your client in to your thinking about why you need to ask these questions, you are signaling that he is a partner in this relationship, not a subordinate. You need him, and here's why. And third, you might end up getting the answers you need!

3. Answering Client Questions and Initial Counseling

At a certain point in the interview, you will feel a lull in the information gathering conversation. You might have gone through and developed a narrative timeline with the client, and followed up with questions to fill in any gaps and missing details. And now you have a basic idea of the situation. This is a good moment to shift gears and give the client a chance to ask any questions he might have. The client might have questions about the law, about the process, about his chances of success. Think about how you will respond to these questions.

At this stage of the representation, though, you are probably not prepared to engage in full-blown legal counseling (which we explore in Chapter Eight). It is perfectly appropriate to respond to a client question by saying something like, "that's a great question. Based on what I know about your situation right now, and the little research I have done, here are my initial thoughts." If you are not confident that you know the answer, don't try to fudge that. Simply acknowledge the question and then admit that you don't know the answer at this point, but here is how you would work to find the answer. For instance, you could say, "I don't know the answer, but I will research it and get back to you at the beginning of next week." That shows the client that you are taking his concerns seriously, and that you have a plan to address those concerns.

4. Ending the Interview

This stage of the interview has two purposes: identify next steps in the representation, and formalize the attorney-client relationship. Let's look at each.

Identify next steps. In the final moments of the interview, you will want to outline a series of next steps. First, what will you, as the lawyer, do next—today, tomorrow, next week? Second, what will the client do next—today, tomorrow, next week? And finally, what is likely to happen next in the legal matter you and the client are discussing. Some lawyers find it useful to write up a "to do list" for the client and either email it to him, or hand him a hard copy at the end of the meeting. You could do the same thing for your own "to do list" and give it to the client as well, so he can track your progress as well as his own. This act of identifying the tasks you are committing to, and asking him to commit to, furthers the development of your relationship as well as moves the case or project along efficiently.

Formalize relationship. Depending on the kind of client and kind of legal services being sought and provided, this will look different. You and your client might need to review and sign a retainer; you might need to ask your client for a payment; you might need to schedule another meeting to get or give more information; and/or you might just need to shake hands and agree that you are moving forward. Whatever the formalities, you and the client need to reach agreement on what is happening next in the relationship. This will not be hard to do once you have developed the "to do lists" described above.

C. Post-Interview Reflection and Analysis

Congratulations! You have completed your initial interview. Whether or not you now have a new client—not all potential clients turn into actual clients—there is one more step to the interview process. You've done your preparation and performance. Now it's time for reflection, as we discussed in Chapter Three. This is an important step because it gives you a chance to review the substance of the interview—which will be helpful if you move forward with the case or project—and your interviewing techniques and strategies. This is helpful to your professional development as an attorney.

Here are some reflection questions to get you started.

- What was the story you expected to hear today?
  - Why did you expect to hear that story? Were you relying on master-plots?
- What is the story you did hear today?
  - Was it different from what you expected? How? How do you explain the differences?
- What narrative do you think you might construct with your client based on what you heard today?
  - Think about the narrative elements: who are the characters, what are the important events, what is the causal connection, what about normalization and masterplots? What closure is the client seeking?
- What parts of the story seem odd, don't make sense? Why don't they make sense?
  - Again, are you relying on masterplots or your own assumptions?
  - Are you missing information about narrative elements?
- What do you think might happen in the future?
  - What closure is the client seeking?
  - Is the client's goal/desired outcome realistic? Why or why not?

Use these questions to guide you in drafting a post-interview memo about the client and potential case or project. Your answers will give you information about how to pursue your next steps in the representation, and will also identify anything you failed to address with your client that might require follow-up communication. You will also learn a bit about your own performance as you reflect on these questions and answers. And hopefully, that will help you prepare for, perform and reflect on your next interview!

IV. Exercise and Example

A. Serial

A compelling story, the producers of *Serial* state, requires three critical components: (1) Action (motion where one thing happens and then another and then another); (2) Reflection (where audience gets inside the head of the human experiencing the action and the human says something we can connect to, making the experience relatable); and (3) Stakes (a question or problem that keeps the audience listening to figure out if it will be answered or resolved). After listening to Episode One of *Serial*, answer the following questions about interviewing:

a. **Questioning:** How does the form of the question that Ms. Koenig uses in her interviewing differ from the form of the questions the police use in interviewing Jay? Which is more effective in getting information?
b. **Rapport Building:** Identify one thing that Ms. Koenig does to build rapport or that hurts rapport with the people she interviews.
c. **Time Line:** How did Ms. Koenig construct a time line? Why was a timeline important to construct? (For more information on constructing the timeline, visit https://serialpodcast.org/maps/timelines-january-13-1999.)

B. Clinton Derrico[20]

Two students receive a letter from an inmate at a Supermax prison (the letter appears below).

In preparing to go meet him for the first time, the students identify their goals as: (1) to determine whether they will take this prisoner's Eighth Amendment case; (2) find out enough facts to state a cause of action (or not); and (3) provide some initial information to the potential client about his likelihood of success.

---

20. This is based on a hypothetical developed by Laura Rovner, Marty Guggenheim, Jean Koh Peters, and Margaret Johnson for the 2011 AALS Conference on Clinical Education, Plenary 1, https://memberaccess.aals.org/eweb//DynamicPage.aspx?Site=AALS&WebKey=ec949d5c-f291-497a-b244-9aca5f8e7e67&RegPath=EventRegFees&REg_evt_key=dad1e1f2-9807-46f5-9f92-5cd25784e7bb.

CLINTON DERRICO
24691-076
U.S. PEN- ADMAX
P.O. BOX 8600
FLORENCE, CO 81127

April 23, 2011

Dear Law Students,

I'm writing to you from the federal supermax prison in Florence, Colorado. I've been in solitary confinement for **26** years. I am in dire need of legal assistance and advice. I read in the paper that law students at the University of Denver won a case against the federal Bureau of Prisms last year. I *really* need lawyers who aren't afraid of the feds so I hope you'll be able to help me too.

I know you are very busy so I'll try to keep this letter short. These people have been torturing me for 26 years by keeping me in TOTAL and EXTREME isolation. I killed a guard in 1983 and I've been locked down ever since. I was at the federal prison in Leavenworth, KS for most of that time in a cell that gaurds call the "Derrico Suite" cuz they built it specially for me so that I would have "no human contact." It was in a separate building, and I got was so far away from

OVER ↷

everyone else that sometimes they even forgot to feed me.

They brought me here to the supermax 4 years ago. I didn't think anything could be worse than Leavenworth but THIS PLACE IS. When I left Leavenworth, I had more than 20 years of clean time and I thought they were finally gonna put me in gen pop. They brought me here instead and I've been in the hole ever since. It seems like ~~the reason~~ the only reason they're keeping me in isolation is to make me suffer. This endless solitary confinement is like a slow constant peeling of the skin, the nerve-wracking sound of water dripping from a leaky faucet in the still of the night while you're trying to sleep. Drip, DRIP, DRIP — the minutes, hours, days, WEEKS, MONTHS, YEARS constantly drip away with no end or relief in sight.

NEXT PAGE →

I really truly need your help in ending this TORTURE. I don't know much about "the law" but I do know that this is CRUEL and UNUSUAL. Thank you for taking the time to read my letter.

I hope to hear from you soon.

※ RESPECTFULLY YOURS ※

(signature)

(CLINTON DERRICO)

* THANK YOU *

Based on the information contained in the letter, the students learn as much as they can about the law. This is what they found:

The Eighth Amendment, which forbids "cruel and unusual punishments," governs the treatment of convicted prisoners. To establish an Eighth Amendment claim for conditions of confinement, a prisoner-plaintiff must satisfy a two-prong test, which has both an objective and subjective component.[21] The objective component asks whether the deprivation is sufficiently serious. With respect to living conditions, prisoners must demonstrate "unquestioned and serious deprivations of basic human needs" or of the "minimal civilized measure of life's necessities." *Rhodes v. Chapman*, 452 U.S. 337, 347 (1981).

The Supreme Court has listed as basic human needs food, clothing, shelter, medical care and reasonable safety as well as warmth and exercise. *Helling v. McKinney*, 509 U.S. 25 (1993); *Wilson v. Seiter*, 501 U.S. 294, 304 (1991). The list does not purport to be exhaustive, however, and the lower courts are beginning to grapple with the idea of human contact and environmental stimulation as human needs as well.

Based on the letter and this Eighth Amendment research, the students begin to think about topic areas they want to discuss with Mr. Clinton. They have identified the fact that sometimes guards forget to feed him as a potential claim, but they worry that they won't have enough questions about this topic to fill the 30 minutes they will be allowed. In a pre-interview supervision, the students try to imagine what a 24-hour day is like for Mr. Clinton. Using narrative elements, they brainstorm topic areas and questions to ask:

- Get full description of his last meal—use of five senses in describing meal.
- What is his least favorite meal/his favorite meal?
- Describe the entire process in the minutest detail.
- What role in his day do meals play?
- Describe all props involved—is there a tray, trapdoor, cutlery, etc.?
- Who are the cast of characters—does he ever see any of those involved in preparing, delivering, or retrieving the tray?

Now watch three clips—first of the supervision meeting, and then two of the interview itself.

https://vimeo.com/channels/1258334

---

21. For purposes of the hypothetical, only the objective prong of the Eighth Amendment inquiry is relevant. Consequently, this description of the law omits discussion of the subjective prong.

As you watch, pay attention to the interviewing goals/techniques we discussed earlier in the chapter, and make notes for yourself of what the students did well, and where they might have done better regarding:

- Question formation
- Rapport building techniques
- Attention to narrative details
- Openness to other narratives

What do you notice about the narrative the students end up exploring? How do the students move into that exploration? Is this the narrative they expected to hear and/or construct?

V. Conclusion

In this chapter, we learned the difference between sympathy and empathy, and the importance of empathy when interviewing a client. We also learned how to gather information. In an initial client interview, it is important for lawyers to get information relating to the narrative elements—characters, events, causation, and closure. We also learned the purpose for behaviors that will enhance active listening the first set of behaviors is to communicate that you are listening to the speaker and build rapport and the second set of behaviors is to enhance active listening for the meaning of the client's narratives. This chapter also includes an agenda and outline that students can refer to when drafting initial client interview plans.

Chapter 6

Case and Project Theory

I. Introduction

Have you ever submitted a paper only to have it returned with the comment that you don't have a thesis? The professor asks you to go back and clearly articulate your main idea and purpose at the beginning of the paper. And then, the professor asks you to make sure that each section of the paper, each paragraph of the paper, each idea in the paper relates back to that thesis, and furthers the idea and purpose set forth in the thesis. Because without a thesis, a paper does not effectively guide the reader about how to interpret the information. The reader doesn't know what he should be learning or understanding from the paper. The reader doesn't have a road map for synthesizing the various ideas presented.

A case or project theory is like a paper's thesis—it is the main idea and purpose of your lawyering. The case or project theory is necessary to guide the representation to ensure that your lawyering is in line with your client's goals. A case theory must synthesize the facts, law and client goals in order to create a comprehensive narrative that will persuade your audience to do what your client wants the audience to do for him.[1] In transactions, there is no dispute requiring the proof of facts, so the project theory focuses primarily on your client's goals and how specifically you and the client will achieve them.[2] In addition, the project theory helps to evaluate the quality of the work product created to achieve the client's goals.[3]

---

1. David F. Chavkin, Clinical Legal Education: A Textbook for Law School Clinical Programs 40 (2002) (client theory urges audience to "do something for our client").
2. Alicia Alvarez and Paul R. Tremblay, Introduction to Transactional Lawyering Practice 85 (2013).
3. *Id.*

This chapter explains how to use case or project theory, the components of a case or project theory, and how to construct a case or project theory. We use example of case theories from *Serial*, and then provide an exercise for you to develop a case or project theory for a particular client.

II. The Use of a Case or Project Theory

The two goals of a case or project theory are that it be persuasive and a guiding force for our lawyering. When will you use a case or project theory? Always. Once constructed, your case or project theory will serve as a flexible tool that guides all lawyering you do, including, but certainly not limited to:

- your first words in a negotiation session,
- your closing argument in a trial,
- your testimony to a legislative body,
- your counseling of a client,
- your engagement in a community organizing meeting.

When you are weighing options in strategic decision-making, you will check your case or project theory to evaluate which options make the most sense. The case or project theory can help you decide what discovery to serve, which exhibits to enter into evidence, how to structure the contract that you are drafting, or how to describe the nonprofit organization's mission in its 501(c)(3) application. The case or project theory can guide you in all these ways because you have constructed a theory that synthesizes the important and relevant facts with the relevant law, and with your client's short- and long-term goals. Moreover, if you have constructed your theory using narrative theory, it will be comprehensive, compelling, and persuasive as well.

One more important point to note: as you continue representing a client, new events will occur in his life and in the world, and his goals for the representation may change. Your case or project theory needs to keep up with those changes. You will need to revisit and revise your theory to ensure that it is still an effective and compelling thesis for your client's case or project.

III. Components of a Case or Project Theory

Knowing the goals of a case theory (that it should be persuasive and a guiding force for your lawyering) and the goals of the project theory (that it should identify your goals in representation and guide your evaluation of your work product), we need to figure out how to construct a case or project theory. As we have explored in earlier chapters, narrative is a compelling way to persuade audiences, and an excellent communication tool. Accordingly, we will construct a case or project theory as a narrative. But to be able to use your case or project theory as a flexible tool to guide each and every lawyering decision, we need to ensure that your theory is nimble. It really needs to be the gist of your narrative, also known as the storyline. So to construct a case or project theory, we need to construct a storyline.

What goes into the case or project theory storyline? For case theory, the storyline should include the client's story, the relevant law, and the client's view of *closure*.[4] And for project theory, it should also include a focus on what will be accomplished in the representation and how.

When constructing your theory, you need to keep the various audiences in mind. These are your client, you the attorney, the other attorneys and parties involved, the decision makers and any other relevant stakeholders. Let's explore each of these audiences.

First, the case or project theory has to make sense to the client as a persuasive story designed to obtain his desired outcome. The theory also has to make sense for the client's life—not just his case.[5] Usually, a client has come to you because he faces a legal issue and, therefore, may have a particular case or project in mind in his crafting of the theory with you. But this case or project is a narrow moment—involving maybe one issue and a few other stakeholders in the client's life—that sits within the broader context of his current life—involving all of the myriad issues the client faces in his personal and professional life, as well as the many people and organizations with whom he interfaces.

For Example: a man comes to a lawyer wanting to bring an adoption action to adopt his step-child. In addition to the activity of this case, the client has lost his job and is looking for new work, his house has been foreclosed upon and he is seeking new housing for his family, his step-child is acting out as a teenager, the

---

4. *See* CHAVKIN, *supra* note 1, at 40 (2002) ("an integration of the *facts* surrounding the client (the client's 'story') and the *law* relevant to the client's concerns"); Binny Miller, *Give Them Back Their Lives: Recognizing Client Narrative in Case Theory*, 93 MICH. L. REV. 485, 487 (1994) (case theory is "an explanatory statement linking the 'case' to the client's experience of world" that acts as "a lens for shaping reality in light of the law, to explain the facts, relationships and circumstances of the client and other parties in the way that can best achieve the client's goals.").

5. This is why David Chavkin urges attorneys to create a client theory with their clients. CHAVKIN, *supra* note 1, at 39 ("'Theory of the client' is the sum of the legal and non-legal strategies that can be created to achieve the goals of the unique individual you represent.").

client's other two children (the step-child's half siblings) do not know the step-child is not their father's child; and the biological father whose rights the lawyer seeks to terminate in the adoption was physically abusive to the children's mother, and threatens to be so again if the adoption goes through. In other words, the step-parent has a lot going on in addition to the adoption case itself. There are a lot of other issues that might be affected by or could affect the adoption case, which may involve a lot of other people than simply the step-parent, his wife and the step-child. And whether or not the step-parent succeeds in adopting his step-child, he is committed to raising the child as his own and as a full member of his family. This case is a short-term moment—it may last a few weeks, months or years— while the client's life will hopefully continue for decades after the case is over.

Second, you and your client must construct a case or project theory that meets your professional responsibility of having a legal claim that is either viable with existing precedent, or reasonably extends that precedent. In addition, the case or project theory must be based on facts that exist or will be found, and that are in your possession or discoverable. Ideally those facts would be difficult for the other side or a reviewing entity to disprove.

Third, the case or project theory needs to communicate an understanding or persuade the audience. The theory must be comprehensive of the case or project, and be consistent with the facts, law and reasonable inferences you will be asking the audience to make in understanding the storyline. The storyline's moral or values should either comport with those of the decision maker or other relevant stakeholders, or be explained in a way that makes the decision maker or other relevant stakeholders change their value or morals to be in line with the storyline's.

What to avoid: Before he became the famous "People's Court" judge, Judge Wapner was a trial judge in California. Overseeing a wrongful death trial between an airline and the parents of a deceased passenger, the judge was not persuaded by the airline's argument that the damage award should be little or nothing because the deceased passenger was merely the son of a tailor, and therefore not worth that much in damages. Why did the Judge find that argument unpersuasive? Because, as he said from the bench, "my father was a tailor."[6]

Finally, the decision maker needs to understand the story you are communicating. The case or project theory should convey a simple storyline but one that will be expanded upon throughout the course of a negotiation, community meeting or trial. So while the theory needs to be comprehensive, it should be concise.[7]

---

6. The People's Court (Warner Brothers 1981–1983; 1997–present).

7. As our colleague Peter Knapp states, "Elegance is a virtue."

IV. Constructing a Case or Project Theory

So we need to create a storyline, guided by the storytelling elements of characters, events, causation, normalization, masterplots and closure, while also considering the legal context of the story.

A. Step One: Narrative Facts[8]

Because our case or project theory is a storyline, we want to focus on the facts in the theory. Your case or project theory should be developed with your client, as it is the story you and the client will be telling about him. Therefore it needs to be comfortable to the client, and comprehensive, accurate and persuasive.

1. Character

Think about who your client is as a character. What are your client's traits, motivations, intentions, emotions and beliefs as well as his will to self-determine and self-direct his life (a.k.a. agency)?

Example of Character in Case Theory

In a racial employment discrimination case, let's say your client, Bea Taylor, sought a promotion to team leader because she has a vision for how her group can perform its work more efficiently. She was passed over for the promotion, which was awarded to her white female counterpart.

What are Ms. Taylor's character traits?

- African American,
- female,
- intelligent,
- hard-working,
- received a less than favorable performance review,
- leader,
- proactive,

---

8. To create what they call a theme, but is akin to a case theory, Krieger and Neumann offer the following steps:"(1) what is the injustice that has been done to you client?; (2) How do you define the "trouble" in your case?; (3) what are the three 'best' facts in your case?; (4) Are there any refrains that recur in the sequence of events in your case?; (5). what stock stories favorable to you client are similar to your case?; (6). will your theme still have meaning at the end of the trial?" STEFAN H. KRIEGER & RICHARD K. NEUMANN, JR., ESSENTIAL LAWYERING SKILLS: INTERVIEWING, COUNSELING, NEGOTIATION, AND PERSUASIVE FACT ANALYSIS 165 (4th ed. 2011).

- strong collaborator
- feels like an outsider because her colleagues are white, there are few African Americans in the group, and none are leaders.

What other characters are there in this story? There is the white female employee who received the promotion, and the Vice President of the company who selected the white female for the promotion over the client. What are their traits?

Example of Character in Project Theory
YouthSpace, a drop-in center for homeless youth, seeks your counsel to become a separate organization from its parent entity. As a character, the drop-in center has the following traits:

- caring,
- understanding of the impact of poverty on youth,
- comprehensive in the services it provides,
- creative in its approach to addressing issues for youth,
- accessible to the youth
- struggling with organization structure and managerial responsiveness to administrative issues because it is not autonomous.

YouthSpace wants to become a stand-alone entity to be able to better serve in a professional and moral way the City's homeless youth. Other characters in the project are YouthSpace's clients, who receive little to no services from the City. In addition, YouthSpace relies on young people in the community to run programs for other youth, and to bring energy and commitment to the youth drop-in center. What are these characters' traits?

2. Setting

What is the setting? In the case theory example, the setting is a private company with a very non-diverse workforce and no African Americans in leadership positions. In the project theory example, the setting is the "City" and also the drop-in center itself.

3. Events

Next, let's turn to events. What has your client Ms. Taylor or YouthSpace experienced that has developed into the **problem** they are facing and for which they are seeking your assistance in achieving a **resolution**. What is the timeline of those events?

4. Causation

In describing the events, be sure to explain why the events happened the way they did. In other words, what is the causation or the cause and effect of the events? For instance, in describing the Company's Vice President's selection of the white female over the client, you might explain that Ms. Taylor's being passed over for the promotion resulted from the VP's racial bias, which in turn resulted in heightened scrutiny of Ms. Taylor and lesser scrutiny of the white employee. In the project theory example, YouthSpace has been unable to handle some unforeseen events, such as when its parent organization failed to be fiscally responsible and was almost unable to pay the rent for the drop-in center. YouthSpace wants to become its own entity one day soon in order to control its own finances.

5. Normalization

Make sure to include facts that promote the audience's normalization of the story. Ensure that the story is internally consistent, that there are no discrepancies within the story. For instance, in the race discrimination matter, if your fact investigation reveals that your client had received excellent performance reviews except for one, don't overstate the reality by saying that Ms. Taylor received only excellent performance reviews. Instead, the story can state that except for one review, Ms. Taylor received excellent reviews.

Also, ensure that your story is externally consistent, meaning that it comports with your audience's understanding of how the world works. For instance, the audience to the employment discrimination case probably believes that employees have their performance reviewed every year, and that people from time to time can get less than excellent reviews even if they are excellent employees. Therefore, providing the fact of the less than excellent review could fit within the audience's understanding of varying reviews.

In the project theory example, the story is internally consistent that the YouthSpace organization wants to be a separate 501(c) (3) in order to control its own finances and avoid challenging unforeseen events. It is also externally consistent because it is understandable that an organization may not be able to control its finances without organizational control as well.

6. Masterplots

Check your facts for masterplots and use them to tell your persuasive story. As we learned in Chapter One, masterplots can be compelling narratives because they appeal to our values and morals so we root for the character in line with the masterplots. In addition, masterplots are familiar stories that are told over and over in differing forms. In the case theory example of the employment discrimination case, one masterplot is that good workers should be rewarded for their merit and discrimination is antithetical to that meritocracy. Another masterplot is that racism exists in workplaces where white people are promoted or retained at a larger percentage than blacks. The types in these masterplots are the hardworking but overlooked minority employee and the insensitive, biased boss.

The masterplot in the project theory example is that homeless youth deserve a well-funded, well-run, professional and moral drop-in center and organization that provides necessary services. YouthSpace is seeking organizational change in order to do so.

7. Closure

Last, but certainly not least, ensure that you have identified the problem that has disrupted the steady state, and what needs to happen to reach closure. Can your facts offer a resolution where questions will be answered, enlightenment gained, and expectations fulfilled? Identify those facts that need to occur to achieve a resolution. Identify why your client should be provided with or obtain the resolution she desires. Then identify each and every fact that supports why your client should receive the outcome.

In the race discrimination example, the Vice President's racial discrimination disrupted Ms. Taylor's excellent work history and performance, denied her a promotion, and created isolation in the job. The discrimination must be stopped, she should be promoted retroactively, compensated for her harm, and the company should diversify its workforce. In the project theory example, the problem that disrupted the steady state was that the parent entity's own management, or mismanagement, was detrimental to YouthSpace and the youth they serve. For closure, this problem needs to be solved by separating from the parent entity.

B. Step Two: Storyline

Now that you have the facts that go with components of the story, construct with your client the *brief* storyline, using the narrative theory devices we discussed earlier.

Visually compelling. To make your storyline visually compelling, try to *show* not *tell* your storyline. This is advice we have all heard since elementary school, and it remains true for your case or project theory. To show not tell, try using language that is compelling to all of your senses. Your audience should feel a part of your story, not detached from it; they should be able to use their imagination. Make your story immediate and sensory. When you consider your details, ask yourself, can you see them, touch them, smell them, hear them or taste them? If not, try to revise your storyline so the details come alive to the senses.[9] Can you edit out conclusions and insert facts instead?

Emotionally compelling. We know the storyline will be emotionally compelling if you ensure that it contains the various narrative theory and story components we discussed above. Be sure to provide likeable traits for your main character that make the audience root for her as she addresses the problem that disrupts the steady state. Also, as discussed in Chapter One, providing some flaws for your main character that are forgivable makes your character seem relatable. And for any so-called bad actor characters, ensure they have some positive traits to avoid the audience refusing to believe your version of the character as all bad. You need to ensure that your traits are such that you provide your audience with insight into how your client aims to overcome the trouble, and what sort of reflection and change of character he experiences as a result.

Once you have described your character and the problem, or conflict, then you want to consider the "spark," which is the "wisdom or the process that the character in your story receives in order to overcome the conflict."[10]

Use this simple graphic to guide the construction of your storyline:

Character → Conflict → Spark → Change in Character → Takeaway Message[11]

In the racial discrimination case, Ms. Taylor's spark is that she learned that her evaluations were far and away better than the white employee who was selected. As a result, she decided she deserved the promotion, as she believed she was better qualified. This change in her character led her to bring a lawsuit claiming a violation of her civil rights. The takeaway message in your case theory for Ms. Taylor might be that people are not permitted to unfairly treat employees due to bias on the basis of race.

In the project theory example, YouthSpace's spark was almost being evicted due to the parent company's mismanagement of the finances. As a result, YouthSpace wants to ensure that it can control its own finances and be an internally strong, professional and moral organization. The takeaway message in your project theory for YouthSpace might be that organizational autonomy will give YouthSpace the ability to control its fiscal management and be the organization it wants to be for its clients.

---

9. Akash Karia, TED Talks Storytelling: 23 Storytelling Techniques from the Best TED Talks 21–25 (2014).

10. *Id.* at 40.

11. TED Talks Storytelling, *supra* note 9.

C. Step Three: Legal Theory and Law

Only after you and your client have constructed your storyline do you consider what law might apply to the client's situation. It is important to construct the factual storyline first because if you begin with the law, you risk defining—and offering solutions for—only legal problems. As we have seen, those may be much narrower than what your client is actually facing in his life, and you do not want to be unnecessarily restrained in identifying potential options for resolution and closure.

We are lawyers, though, so we tell stories that are bounded at least partially by law. Taking the problem as constructed in your and your client's story, consider whether there is a legal theory that would address the problem and provide a resolution. For instance, in Ms. Taylor's case, the law might be either Title VII under federal law or the state or local human rights law. For YouthSpace the law would be that governing the creation of 501(c)(3) nonprofit organizations. Once you identify the legal claims or governing law, you would develop a legal theory that furthers your client's goal given the context of their storyline. Once you have identified a theory, go back to your facts and incorporate them into your legal theory. You might find that you need to include additional facts, and/or that you need to edit out others. Again, check the facts as you have written them against story: **character, events, causation, normalization, masterplots, and closure.** While your storyline will necessarily be partially bounded by law, the law should not be explicit in the case or project theory because it may detract from what is compelling about the narrative.

D. Step Four: Normative Theory

Narrative theory shows us as lawyers what the choices are, but it is the client's goals that tell us how to make the narrative choices. The storyline in your case or project theory is the narrative you will present about your client in public fora. Your client must agree that that is the story to be told about him. He must be comfortable with it. When defining the trouble and closure, you want to make sure they are consistent with your client's view of his issues as well as his goals, including his goals from the representation. You want to ensure that the closure sought is in line with those goals.

As we explored in Chapter One, all narrative is normative: when the character addresses the problem and seeks closure, he reflects upon his morals, or norms, and thus gains insight. Thus as client-centered lawyers, you should draft your case or project theory in such a way that your client sees himself—and his transformation—reflected accurately. Although you have many audiences for the constructed narrative—the court, regulators, stakeholders, policy makers, witnesses, the opposing party, yourself, your client—it is the client's goals that must drive your narrative.

Further, we as lawyers can ensure that the moral of the story comports with the client's and justice goals by filtering the narrative through normative theory, such as client-centered theory. In addition, we as lawyers may find it useful to filter the narrative through other normative theories such as feminist theory, critical race theory, class and Latino critical theory, which provide structured critiques of society and the operation of power as it relates to different identity groups.[12] Accordingly, for Ms. Taylor's case theory, you will have a specific focus on race and the discrimination against African Americans, and African American women in general, in the workplace and may highlight the way race is utilized as a sorting function for promotions in the workplace. In YouthSpace's project theory, you may focus on agency theory from feminist legal theory, which uses the law to support the ability of people to self-direct and self-define despite normal societal operation that might undermine their autonomy. YouthSpace's mission is to support a youth-centered and youth-run drop-in space and unless it becomes independent, it will be unable to do so due to its parent organization's financial mismanagement.

E. Step Five: Put It All Together

Now you are very close to having constructed your case or project theory. But you need to do one more check.

As you construct your case or project theory, consider that you are building a house. The foundation of the house—the unseen but critical portion of the construction—is the legal and normative theory. The frame of the house—the part of the construction visible to everyone—is the factual storyline and the client's goals. Your case or project theory is the frame of the house: where the facts and the goals are visible, but the law and normative theory are not. As the foundation of the house, the law and normative theory will be apparent in the case or project theory through the facts and goals you have chosen to emphasize.

Why do we suggest that you construct your case or project theory this way, with the law and normative theory invisible? Because from narrative theory we have learned that story is the powerful tool to communicate and to persuade. Therefore, we suggest you use the components of story to make your case or

---

12. For more on this, see Margaret E. Johnson, *An Experiment in Integrating Critical Theory and Clinical Education*, 13 Am. U.J. Gender Soc. Pol'y & L. 161 (2005).

project theory as effective as possible. And the law, legal elements and normative theory rarely break down into characters, events, causation, normalization, masterplots, and closure, all of which help to make the theory persuasive.

Having constructed the first draft of your case or project theory, edit to ensure that the theory is:

- Consistent with the facts—your understanding of them, the client's understanding of them, and any witness's understanding of them.
- Using strong evidence and explaining away bad or inconsistent evidence that undercuts your client's case or project theory.
- Consistent with the law—are you seeking to expand or narrow the accepted legal framework?
- Consistent with your client's goals—for the short-term and the long-term. If the client has competing goals or they appear inconsistent, it is important to try to reconcile them through legal counseling of the client.[13]
- Normatively consistent with your client by using critical theories to challenge any assumptions embedded in the theory. Does it address masterplots by employing them or diffusing them with counterstories?[14]
- Provides insight into why things have happened in a particular way, and not merely what has happened.
- Emotionally compelling, making the audience want to root for your client.
- Comprehensive in such a way that it explains the circumstances in anticipation of the audience wanting to normalize the story to make the circumstances and relationships of the party "fit together."
- Helpful in strategic planning, investigation, and moving to resolution.

F. Step Six: Edit Again!

Having edited as instructed above, you no doubt have a very capable case or project theory. Now it is time to conduct one final edit! To help with keeping the theory nimble and elegant, we recommend that you construct it using approximately 40 words. Such a short storyline makes you consider each and every word that you use, and also ensures that you can easily memorize it to use in any situation. We like to say that the case theory should fit in your back pocket so you can pull it out whenever and wherever you might need it: a negotiation, a deposition, a client counseling session, a contract drafting session,

---

13. See Chapter Eight.

14. Richard Delgado, *Storytelling for Oppositionists and Others: A Plea for Narrative*, 87 MICH. L. REV. 2411 (1988).

a community meeting, an opening statement or closing argument. This final stage is your chance to examine every word, to consider every inference, and to trim your theory down into a lean, mean lawyering tool!

Below are examples of a case theory and a project theory for our clients Ms. Taylor and YouthSpace.

Bea Taylor

Bea Taylor, a well-qualified, generally well-reviewed, African American woman was denied a promotion unjustly because of her race when her employer promoted a less-qualified white woman. Ms. Taylor seeks what is rightly hers: a retroactive promotion and no more race discrimination in her workplace.

YouthSpace

YouthSpace, a drop-in center for homeless youth, seeks to become a 501(c)(3) organization separate from its parent organization. To fulfill its charitable work and mission of supporting underserved youth's agency and empowerment, YouthSpace needs financial and moral independence.

V. *Serial* Example

In the *Serial* Podcast, dueling case theories are presented by the State and by Adnan Syed in order to persuade the jury. The parties created these case theories from the same broad set of characters and events and applied them to the same criminal law. Yet they are different case theories, and whichever one is believed by the jury will lead to the outcome of the trial.

In *Serial* Episode Ten (12:00–14:00), the prosecutor described Adnan Syed's motive to kill Hae Min Lee: he was a Pakistani male enraged over the loss of control over Hae Min Lee because they had broken up. The prosecution's case theory played into a masterplot that has been used as recently as Donald Trump's 2016 presidential campaign: immigrants such as Adnan (despite the fact that Adnan was not an immigrant at all) from a non-western country (Pakistan) are untrustworthy and dangerous. This masterplot played into anti-immigrant fears, including those regarding Pakistanis because of the so-called "War on Terror." And finally, the prosecution's story played into the masterplot of domestic violence, as relied upon by the prosecution in the O. J. Simpson case: a male partner is shunned by his female partner, and he uses physical violence to harm or control her.

On the other hand, in Episode Ten (19:00–20:30), we hear the defense case theory, which is that the prosecution (and the police) bungled the investigation and arrested and prosecuted the wrong guy.[15] This story played into the masterplot of a corrupt or inept police department and prosecutor's office that overlooked clues that could exonerate Adnan. *Serial* leaves the impression that the prosecution successfully convicted Adnan in part because of the persuasiveness of their case theory, and in part because the defense failed to construct the best case theory it could have. *Serial* thus offers an example of how constructing case theories is important to achieving desired outcomes.

VI. Exercise: Drafting a Case or Project Theory

Prepare to and then draft a case or project theory.

Ask questions to gather content for case or project theory. Before drafting your case or project theory, work through the following questions with your client and use the other factual information you have:

1. Who is your client? What are your client's likeable and less likeable traits?
2. What does he describe as the trouble he is facing? What is the causation of the trouble?
3. What other characters are involved in the trouble (or its closure)? What are their likeable and less likeable traits?
4. How can you normalize your client in this trouble? What makes normalizing your client difficult?
5. What is the steady state your client experienced before the trouble?
6. What closure does he seek? Why should he get it? What stands in his way?
7. What facts are favorable to your client?
8. What facts are not favorable to your client?
9. What legal claims are available to your client to address the trouble he is facing and attain closure? What legal claims or defenses make your client's claim difficult?
10. What is the legal authority for all of those claims?
11. What are the legal elements for those claims? And which facts will you use to analyze and argue the legal elements?
12. Go back and check your facts. Have you included all good and bad facts that meet the legal elements for your claims? If not, do so now.

---

15. The defense did not identify who the murderer was. Of course, legally the defense does not have the burden of proof in a criminal trial and only needs to show there is reasonable doubt that the prosecution's case is correct.

Draft case or project theory using the six steps described earlier:

1. Gather your narrative facts.
2. Create your visually and emotionally compelling storyline.
3. Develop your legal theory.
4. Develop your narrative theory.
5. Put it all together into one case or project theory.
6. Edit!

VII. Conclusion

In this chapter, we have identified how to use narrative and story through six steps to create a case or project theory for your clients. We also learned that as we continue to work with our clients, we will revisit the case or project theory as new facts, law or client's goals shift. Therefore, as the story changes, our constructed narrative may change. We also learned about the importance of incorporating normative theory in a case or project theory. This requires the lawyer to make sure that the case or project theory is consistent with the way the client (and any decision maker) views the trouble and the client's closure.

Chapter 7

Fact Investigation, Development and Case Planning

I. Introduction

A whole chapter on facts? Aren't we supposed to work with *the law*? Turns out that while the law is obviously integral to what lawyers do, cases are much more likely to involve factual disputes than they are to involve true legal disputes. In this chapter, we consider the lawyering that must take place in order to find and develop the factual parts of the narratives lawyers and their clients construct.

Throughout the litigation process, from motions practice to settlement and to trial, most case outcomes are driven by the facts. It is rare that a case resolves based on a new interpretation of a legal standard. However, many cases are decided in settlement or at trial by a party or decision maker deciding which facts led to the dispute at issue and analyzing them and applying them to the law. This large population of cases are decided because one side provides the most persuasive or comprehensible narrative. For instance, in the famous Property case, *Pierson v. Post*, the following is the entire recitation of the facts:

> ... *Post*, being in possession of certain dogs and hounds under his command, did, "upon a certain wild and uninhabited, unpossessed and waste land, called the beach, find and start one of those noxious beasts called a fox," and whilst there hunting, chasing and pursuing the same with his dogs and hounds, and when in view thereof, *Pierson*, well knowing the fox was so hunted and pursued, did, in the sight of *Post*, to prevent his catching the same, kill and carry it off.[1]

---

1. *Pierson v. Post*, 3 Cai. R. 175 (Supreme Court of New York, 1805).

These limited facts name the two parties, Post and Pierson, and relate that Post was pursuing a fox with his dogs on a beach, and Pierson killed and took away the fox. And these facts lead to the legal question, framed by the court, of who occupied, and thereby owned the fox.[2] We have some understanding of traits—the fox is a "noxious beast" and Pierson "well-knew" that Post was in pursuit. But how were those determined to be the facts upon which the decision of the court would be based? Those facts were extracted by judges from the narratives constructed by the lawyers and clients during the course of the litigation, including the trial testimony and exhibits.

Further, in *Pierson v. Post*, there was a larger story at play than two men battling over who gets the dead fox. Post was considered nouveau riche, as evidenced by the many hounds and dogs he had during the fox hunt, and discussed in the case opinion. Pierson, on the other hand, was an old-line town citizen among other educated, gentleman farmers and civic officials. As a result, the controversy was about more than who had rights to the dead fox but also about the "growing conflict over who could regulate and use the common resources of the town, and over whether agricultural traditions or commerce and wealth would define its social organization."[3] This larger context plays a role in the decision-making in favor of Pierson in this case, as it does in many other legal matters. For this reason, the role of relevant and contextual facts is important throughout the litigation process, from settlement to trial, in persuading the other side or court that you should prevail.

In other litigation matters, a party may win a case because he is able to show there is no dispute of facts and the law favors the party. As you learned in civil procedure, if there is no dispute of material fact, then cases can be determined on a motion for summary judgment.[4] Therefore, even in the situation of undisputed facts, we see that knowing all of the legally relevant and narrative facts is critical to determining whether the case can be disposed of pre-trial.

In transactional law, case outcome again is determined by the facts, more often than not. For instance, in a community development clinic, a team of students represented a client to explore gaining 501(c) (3) status as a nonprofit organization, and legal rights to its slogan and logo. To do so, the students had to research the law relevant to nonprofit creation as well as copyright and trademark law. But the students spent as much time conducting the fact investigation regarding the client's current 501(c) (3) status, the facts necessary to complete

---

2. *Id.* at 177.

3. Bethany R. Berger, *It's Not About the Fox: The Untold History of Pierson v. Post*, 55 DUKE L.J. 1089, 1089 (2006).

4. Celotex Corp. v. Catrett, 477 U.S. 317, 322–323 (1986).

the relevant application, and the legally relevant facts to copyright and trademark as they might relate to the client's slogan and logo.[5]

In traditional law school courses, most of the reading and work you do emanates from appellate opinions. In those opinions—and in the analysis around those opinions—there is rarely much discussion about the lawyering that took place before the litigation commenced; and the events that gave rise to the controversy itself become the small recitation of facts at the beginning of opinion.

For every one of those cases, the lawyering tasks of fact investigation and development is what lead to the "findings of fact" or factual summaries that appear as a static part of the appellate opinion. But remember, facts are never set or determined. And of course, with the passage of time, more facts are created. The shades of facts change based on emphasis, context, and meaning. And we have already seen how we can explain facts persuasively and communicate them better with story and narrative. Because so much lawyering does not involve novel issues of law, the advocacy and other work we often do for clients is around developing the factual narrative that fits the law to meet our clients' goals.

In this chapter we will discuss the importance of facts, how narrative theory helps lawyers to investigate and develop facts, the process of fact investigation and development, and how to plan the development of a case.

II. Facts and Narrative

Why are facts critical? Facts help you (and your audience) know both what happened and why it happened. These are the essential pieces of a coherent and compelling story. It is because of the critical nature of facts that fact investigation, development and case planning are highly sought after skills by legal employers. The ABA report on legal education fundamentals, known as the "MacCrate Report," stated that fact investigation is a "fundamental lawyering skill essential for competent legal representation."[6] Effective fact in-

---

5. Other examples of transactional lawyering activities that focus heavily on fact investigation, gathering, and assessment include contract and other document drafting, with its focus on facts and emphasis on plain English, and negotiations with their focus on future facts. *See e.g.,* OFFICE OF INVESTOR EDUCATION AND ASSISTANCE, UNITED STATES SECURITIES AND EXCHANGE COMMISSION, A PLAIN ENGLISH HANDBOOK: HOW TO CREATE CLEAR SEC DISCLOSURE DOCUMENTS (1998).

6. ABA SECTION ON LEGAL EDUCATION AND ADMISSION TO THE BAR, LEGAL EDUCATION AND PROFESSIONAL DEVELOPMENT—AN EDUCATIONAL CONTINUUM: REPORT OF THE TASK FORCE ON LAW SCHOOLS AND THE PROFESSION: NARROWING THE GAP, July 1992, at 135.

vestigation involves "determining whether factual investigation is needed, planning an investigation, implementing an investigative strategy, organizing information in an accessible form, deciding whether to conclude the investigation, and evaluating the information that has been gathered...."[7]

In our study of narrative and story, facts are critical. The narrative facts are intentionally selected to create informative, compelling and persuasive narratives. And as we have shown, facts are critical to the lawyering we do for our clients. Legally relevant facts construct legal narratives that incorporate the relevant law, facts and client goals.

Because facts are critical to legal narratives, we need to do everything we can to learn, identify and support the facts used in the construction of legal narratives. If you are engaged in transactional lawyering, you and your client will not be able to construct the legal narrative for your negotiations, contracts, or other drafting; and if you are engaged in the litigation process of a case, you and your client will not be able to construct a legal narrative for opposing parties or the decision maker, until you know the facts critical to narrative construction:

- Characters (including their likeable, unlikeable and neutral traits, agency, goals, motivations, emotions and beliefs);
- Events (including setting);
- Causation;
- Normalization;
- Masterplot; and
- Closure.

And you need to construct not only your and your client's legal narrative, but the alternate narratives that might be constructed by other stakeholders relevant to your matter, such as a present or future opposing party, regulator, or decision maker. To do so, you need to find favorable and unfavorable facts to ensure that you and your client can construct the strongest narrative, and anticipate narratives constructed by the other potential stakeholders.

III. Fact Investigation — Process

Because facts are so critical to a case or project, before you can tell a decision maker what happened and why, you have to work with your client to figure it out and understand it yourself. You need to learn, develop, and understand the facts.

---

7. *Id.* at 163.

Fact investigation is as important to transactional lawyering as for litigation. As discussed in Chapter Four, project theories differ from case theories in that they are not always as concerned with persuasion.[8] Project theories are similar to case theories in that they provide the strategic summary of what you hope to accomplish in your representation. Unlike litigation, transactional work does not involve a present adversarial process with disputed facts where each party is trying to persuade the decision maker as to the party's version of facts. Of course, transactional work may anticipate potential future disputes. Nonetheless, fact investigation is still an important part of transactional work. For example, fact investigation can be necessary to transactional lawyering to learn more about the context of the client and client's work, any other party with whom the lawyer is negotiating and their work, any inconsistencies in documents or records, and any divergent views among stakeholders.[9]

How do we conduct fact investigation and development? We want to start broadly and work toward the specific. Below we suggest a process that, although apparently linear and clearly articulated, might, in fact, end up being quite recursive. The steps may not always go in the sequence provided, or even be discrete steps. So at each step along the way, consider what new information you have learned, and whether you might need to revisit earlier steps before moving on to your next. We suggest that, after reading this section, you follow this process with a case or project on which you are working, in clinic or in your practice, to plan a fact investigation for your client.

A. Step One: Case or Project Theory

Let's work through this process using the following car accident tort litigation. We represent the plaintiff, who is the City; the defendant is Mr. Mitt. As we discussed in the previous chapter, your case theory must be consistent with what you know about the facts, the law, and your client's goals. You will, of course, go back and revise your case theory frequently, as you learn more about all three categories. But at the outset, here is what we know about the facts, law and client goals:

---

8. ALICIA ALVAREZ & PAUL R. TREMBLAY, INTRODUCTION TO TRANSACTIONAL LAWYERING PRACTICE 84, 84 n.11 (2013) (discussing case theories) and GARY BELLOW & BEA MOULTON, LAWYERING PROCESS: NEGOTIATION (2007) and John B. Mitchell, *Narrative and Client-Centered Representation: What Is a True Believer to Do When His Two Favorite Theories Collide?*, 6 CLINICAL L. REV. 85, 99 (1999)("[t]heories of the case are stories").

9. Because transactional work involves less informal fact finding and no formal fact finding, we do not discuss it in the rest of the chapter, though the principles laid out here could be used for fact investigation in transactional work.

The basic facts are that a city bus (driven by Ms. Angoulo) and a car (driven by Mr. Mitt) crashed in the middle of an intersection. The plaintiff claims that Mr. Mitt caused the accident by speeding through the intersection; the defendant claims that Ms. Angoulo (and, through her, the City) caused the accident by failing to stop at a red light.

The basic law is negligence, whose elements are: legal duty, breach of duty, causal nexus and damages. In addition, in the relevant jurisdiction, there are statutes against speeding, using a cell phone while driving and failing to stop at a red light. Also, since there will probably be competing claims of fault, we need to know the law around comparative fault. In the relevant jurisdiction, the rule is that if plaintiff's negligence/fault is greater than 50%, then plaintiff will receive no damages; if plaintiff's negligence/fault is 50% or less, then plaintiff's damages will be reduced by that percent.

Now for our client's goals: Our client's main goal is not to have to pay for any of the damages suffered by the City bus, Ms. Angoulo, or Mr. Mitt and his vehicle. Another goal is public safety—the City wants riders, drivers and pedestrians to feel safe when on the road with, or when riding, a City bus. Another goal of the City is that people, no matter their access to wealth or resources, be able to transport themselves around the City for work and pleasure at a reasonable price.

Based on all this, here is our initial working case theory:

> Plaintiff (City): Mr. Mitt's excessive speed and inattention caused him to hit the City bus at the intersection. Despite Ms. Angoulo's extensive bus driver training and the proper functioning of the bus, she could not prevent the accident and did not cause it. Mr. Mitt should pay.

B. Step Two: Identify Important Narrative Facts

Highlight, or circle, every fact in the case theory.

> *Plaintiff (City): Mr. Mitt's excessive speed and inattention caused him to hit the City bus at the intersection. Despite Ms. Angoulo's extensive bus driver training and the proper functioning of the bus, she could not prevent the accident and did not cause it. Mr. Mitt should pay.*

We talk about sources of "facts" as people, places or things. As plaintiff's lawyer, how did we find the facts included in our preliminary case theory? In creating an initial case theory, we often rely on the initial interview with our client, and any documents we might have obtained, either during that interview and/or in a preliminary search of publicly available information. But we also use our imagination, our curiosity, and our knowledge of how things work in the real world. We then continue to investigate and develop more facts, and revise our case theory with our client, as appropriate.

So other than interviewing our client's employee, Ms. Angoulo, the bus driver, do we have other sources for the provided "facts"? Are there any documents or photos available? Are we building our theory on facts we assume to be accurate, but for which we do not have a source for proving them? Are there other facts we would love to include in the story, but we do not know what they are?

Those are general brainstorming questions. Now, to get more specific, go through the narrative elements.

What *characters* exist in this story? So far we know about the City (the plaintiff), Ms. Angoulo (an employee of the City), Mr. Mitt (the defendant), and even the two vehicles: Ms. Angoulo's City bus and Mr. Mitt's car. Are there other characters we should consider? Think about what other characters are likely to have been involved—even if only tangentially—in this incident: people who were walking by that intersection at the time of the accident, other drivers near the intersection at the time of the accident, any police who responded to the accident, any passengers in the City bus or Mr. Mitt's car. We can imagine any or all of these potential characters as sources of information for us as we develop our factual narrative.

Are there more *traits* we would like to learn about for each of the characters? For instance, in the case theory, Mr. Mitt is described as driving at an excessive speed and distracted by his cell phone. In order to support the theory that Mr. Mitt has the trait of "excessive speeding," we would like to investigate Mr. Mitt's driving record. To buttress our claim that he was distracted, we need to investigate whether he owns a cell phone, and we would love to look at his cell phone records to see whether he made phone calls or wrote texts during the relevant time. We might also want to explore Mr. Mitt's physical and mental health to see if there were any other barriers to his driving safely.

And what about Ms. Angoulo? What was she doing at the time of the accident, and right before? Don't we want to learn something about her driving record? About her attentiveness and care for detail? What about her record as an employee? Has she ever had an accident before? And might there be something in her physical and mental health history that could have contributed toward the accident, or that could undermine the claim that she herself was at fault?

And the bus and car? What *traits* might be important for our narrative that the accident was Mr. Mitt's fault? We want to find facts about the bus's history of repairs and maintenance. We would like to know how old the bus is, and whether it has ever been in any accidents. We would like to be able to argue that the bus was running impeccably and had the highest safety rating possible. Are we likely to find evidence like that? From where? What facts might help us make that claim—or one like it? We also want that same information about Mr. Mitt's car. Wouldn't it be great if his car had a history of brake malfunction, or needed a tune up? Where can we find those facts?

In terms of *events*, the major event is the accident, but widening our lens and using our imagination and what we know of the world, we know that other events took place as well. What was Mr. Mitt doing right before the accident—making a telephone call? Rushing to get to an appointment? What was Ms. Angoulo doing before the accident—helping folks get on the bus? Rushing away from the bus stop to keep to her schedule?

In addition, the *setting* here is critical to the event. So we want to know more about the intersection where the accident occurred: what does the intersection look like? What is the speed limit at the intersection? How much traffic—auto and pedestrian—does there tend to be at that intersection at the time of day the accident occurred? Are there particular people or vehicles regularly at that intersection at the time of day when the accident occurred? Are there any traffic cameras at or near the intersection that might provide additional information? What kind of buildings line the streets at the intersection—houses, apartments, store fronts, stoops, bus stops, etc.?

Turning to *causation*, we want to identify, find and develop other facts that will help explain the timeline of events and what caused the accident. The case theory as written suggests that Mr. Mitt's distracted driving at excessive speed caused the accident. So we have identified facts about Mr. Mitt, Ms. Angoulo and the two vehicles that might support that claim.

But are there other explanations for the accident? We've identified potential mechanical failure of either or both vehicles. We might want to rule out weather issues or road conditions as causes of the accident. So we would want to look at those facts for the day and time in question. What was the weather like that day? How do these vehicles perform in weather like that? Same with the road condition—were there potholes or puddles or loose gravel that might have affected the driving at or near the intersection?

We might want to consult with a reliable expert who can determine causes of accidents. We may also need an expert who can decipher and convey the meaning of the cellphone records we discussed above. We may also want an expert who will identify the speed at which Mr. Mitt was driving and how, given that speed, he could have caused the accident.

Next we want to investigate ways in which plaintiff's story will be subject to *normalization*. Can we investigate or develop facts that show that the City's explanation of the accident is internally and externally consistent? For instance, if we are able to gather facts showing that Mr. Mitt was on his cellphone or texting at the time of the accident, this would support an internally consistent story that he was distracted while driving. We may want to investigate his car and cellphone as well to see if he has Bluetooth on his cellphone, how it is operated, and how much attention it takes to place a call or answer a call. As for externally consistent, we may want to consult an expert who does research on distracted drivers to understand what usually happens when people do the things Mr. Mitt was doing while driving. Also, we would want to make sure to know the information we identified under *events* and *causation* that identify the speed limit at the intersection, the speed at which Mr. Mitt was driving, and how that speed caused the accident.

For *masterplots*, we want to identify any and all masterplots that could be at play here. Could we develop a masterplot around Ms. Angoulo, a dedicated public servant who takes pride in safely shepherding her riders from stop to stop? What facts would we need to find and develop to make this masterplot persuasive?

Or could we develop a masterplot around Mr. Mitt, a selfish man who always put his needs ahead of the public good? If so, we might decide to investigate whether he was racing to a meeting for which he was late, and what the meeting was, and how important or trivial the meeting was. And we might want to investigate what phone call or text he was making and how important or trivial it was.

What other masterplots might there be, and what facts might we need in order to develop them?

Finally, in order to complete our narrative, we need to find and develop facts that provide closure for the characters and for the audience. As attorney for the City, we want to identify and develop facts that will lead to a resolution of the problem caused by the accident. Of course, we need to work with the client to determine what closure it wants. What is the client's goal here—to resume the steady state that existed immediately before the accident, or to create a new steady state? Depending on the client's goal, we could investigate whether speeding and distracted driving are generalized problems, and whether such things as a safe driving campaign, speed bumps or increased signage around the intersection would be useful. We could investigate the City's protocols around drivers sticking (or not sticking) to schedules, and determine whether steps could be taken to ensure that such protocols do not undermine public safety.

Once you have gone through all of these narrative elements—some of which lead to overlapping fact investigation and development—you should have a pretty thorough sense of what facts you are looking for and how you would like to develop them. Time to move on to the next step, for now.

C. Step Three: Alternative Narratives

Now open up your fact investigation to *alternative narratives*. This means you need to identify alternative explanations for why your client should win, and alternative explanations for why the opposing party should win!

D. Step Four: Identify Legally Relevant Facts

Other than using narrative elements to guide you in fact investigation, you also need to consider the legal elements that you need to prove or satisfy through your case or project theory. Identifying those elements guides you to do further investigation and development. Let's go back to Mr. Mitt and Ms. Angoulo and the City Bus. This is a tort case, based in negligence. The City alleges that Mr. Mitt breached his legal duty of safe driving because he violated both the statutes against speeding and using a cell phone; and because he failed to use reasonable care as a driver. The City also alleges that this breach of Mr. Mitt's duty to drive safely caused the accident, which severely damaged the bus. And finally, we know the rule about comparative fault. We must show that Ms. Angoulo was less than 50% at fault for the City to recover.

What further fact investigation and development should you do given these three sets of legal rules? And what further legal research is necessary based on the further fact investigation and development?

E. Step Five: Identify Normatively Relevant Facts

Planning for fact investigation regarding narrative and legal elements alone is not enough. We also need to consider the justice goals of your client and this representation. Such justice goals may be surfaced by scrutinizing your lawyering through the lens of normative theories, such as client-centered lawyering[10] or critical legal theories, such as race or feminist theories.[11] Depending on which lens you use, you might be guided to develop different investigation and development plans.

---

10. *See* Chapter Two for our earlier discussion of Client-Centered Lawyering.

11. Alina S. Ball, *Disruptive Pedagogy: Incorporating Critical Theory in Business Law Clinics*, 22 Clinical L. Rev. 1, 24 (2015) ("critical legal theory explains and theorizes how subordination of classes of people is perpetuated even absent formal systems of intentional discrimination"). For further discussion of critical legal theories, *see* Chapter Six discussing normative theories.

For example, in *Serial*, Koenig initially describes Adnan as a "typical American teen" rather than a teen who is a Muslim and Pakistani American. As a result, Koenig's investigation never fully explores the way in which Adnan's "arrest, his indictment and his conviction were all influenced by his faith and the color of his skin."[12] If you were to use the lens of critical race theory, after conducting a narrative and legal elements approach to fact brainstorming, a race-conscious approach would explore whether race played a factor in the prosecution of Adnan due to explicit or implicit bias. If Koenig had conducted this inquiry, her investigation could have led to other important facts such as those developed by Rabia Chaudhry, who did pursue these facts and reported on them in her own podcast.[13]

So how might these normative lenses affect our fact investigation and development in the *City v. Mitt* case? As lawyers who practice client-centered lawyering, we want to ensure our representation is in furtherance of our client's goals and case theory. Here, one of our client's justice goals in the representation is public safety. What fact investigation might you want to undertake to flesh out a claim that action is needed to ensure or enhance public safety? What sources of information might you gain access to in this area? And what if you were to apply another critical normative lens, like class or poverty law theory? Another goal of the City is that persons no matter their access to wealth or resources be able to transport themselves around the City for work and pleasure at a reasonable price. Using a class or poverty theory lens, a new "masterplot" might come into focus: Mr. Mitt used his class privilege as a private driver to put his needs over those who take public transportation by negligently texting and speeding, thereby risking their safety.

F. Step Six: Make a Fact Investigation/Discovery Plan

The steps we have discussed so far help identify the *categories* of facts to investigate, find, and develop. These categories include the *narrative elements* (characters, events, causation, normalization, masterplot, and closure), the *legal elements*, and the *normative theory* elements of a case or project. Now, we need a plan for how to find and develop these various categories of facts.

As lawyers, we have two modes available to us for investigating facts, *informal* and *formal* mechanisms. Whether you are undergoing informal or

---

12. Jay Caspian Kang, *White Reporter Privilege*, THE AWL (Nov. 13, 2014) https://theawl.com/white-reporter-privilege-541a743ad90d#.cfuy3obw0.

13. *Undisclosed, Episode 6—The Suspect* (June 22, 2015) http://undisclosedpodcast.com/episodes/season-1/episode-6-the-suspect.html

formal fact investigation, the Rules of Professional Conduct apply to your lawyering.[14] For *informal investigations*, we recommend that you put on your journalist or private investigator hat and think about good old-fashioned gum shoe detective work—talking to *people*, visiting *places*, and identifying, discovering and analyzing *things*. *Formal investigation* is what we call "Discovery"—the legal procedures available for gathering information and tangible items from the opposing party or third parties in a litigation. It is a good idea to have a fact investigation plan that incorporates both kinds of tools, even if you do not end up using all of them.

Informal fact investigation and development focuses on all of the ways you and your client can gather information and tangible items for all of the fact categories (narrative, legal, and normative theory) without relying on formal legal mechanisms. Common tools of informal investigation include: interviewing people, internet research, going to physical locations, accessing publicly available documents, accessing voluntarily disclosed private documents, and finding other media sources that might be helpful, e.g., security camera footage and news coverage.

How does formal investigation vary from informal investigation?[15] Unlike informal investigation, formal investigation, or discovery, can only be undertaken in accordance with legal authority or court approval. In addition, the opposing party is provided notice of the discovery.[16] The most common tools of formal discovery include: depositions, interrogatories, requests for admission, and requests for production of tangible items. All of these formal mechanisms help you gain information and tangible items necessary to develop your narrative, legal, and normative theory facts. The information you gain, as with your informal investigation facts, may require you to then alter your case or project theory and your case plan for further fact investigation and development.

As you consider informal and formal investigation methods, you should consider what pros and cons they present to your case planning. For instance,

---

14. Model Rules of Prof'l Conduct, Rules 3.3, 3.4 and 4.4 (2016), http://www.americanbar.org/groups/professional_responsibility/publications/model_rules_of_professional_conduct/model_rules_of_professional_conduct_table_of_contents.html.

15. For civil litigation, jurisdictions have developed rules of civil procedure for most courts and cases. This section focuses on the civil litigation process. For criminal litigation, formal discovery exists but is generally more limited than formal discovery in civil cases.

16. You have most likely studied the discovery rules in the Federal Rules of Civil Procedure that govern litigation in federal courts. Discovery rules in state civil matters are governed by state rules of civil procedure.

informal investigation, because it is not governed by court rules, can be begun at any time, including before filing a case. For formal investigation, most discovery must be begun after the filing of a complaint.[17] Benefits of formal investigation include that the other party must attest to its accuracy under oath, so you can use the facts to impeach a witness at trial. Another benefit of formal investigation is if the party upon whom you serve the discovery does not comply, you may be able to seek a court order compelling the discovery responses and/or obtain sanctions for the failure to provide discovery. Some disadvantages for formal discovery is it can be expensive and take a long time.

G. Examples

To help you learn how to conduct narrative fact investigation, we provide two examples by non-lawyers. The first example involves a non-lawyer group who investigated narrative facts about an event. The investigators were located in Dublin, Ireland, and used their journalistic skills to identify the exact location of a U.S.-based explosive thunderstorm they saw on a YouTube video. In other words, they saw the explosion on the video and wanted to identify the veracity and the *setting* for the *event.*

So how did they do it? They acted like detectives. They primarily used free internet resources (as they were in Ireland, not the U.S.) to identify the storm's location, and to verify and accurately source what they learned.

The explosive thunderstorm video at issue identified that "Rita Krills" posted it. The investigators were not sure if Rita Krills was a real person or a pseudonym, so they had to investigate this *character* in the story. They started by using Spokeo (http://www.spokeo.com/), a telephone-directory type search engine, to identify all Rita Krills in the U.S. Then they used WolframAlpha (https://www.wolframalpha.com/examples/WeatherAndMeteorology.html) to search the history of weather on the day of the video they saw. Next they used the white pages (http://www.whitepages.com/) to locate Rita Krills in Florida. Then they used Google maps to locate the homes of the various Rita Krills and match them with the home depicted on the video. Finally, they called Rita Krills to verify that she was indeed a person, who had shot the video, and that

---

17. And under the federal rules, generally there are required disclosures by the parties and actual discovery cannot be begun until after the parties have conferred. See FED. R. CIV. P. 26(a) and 26(d)(1). There are special rules for permitting a deposition before the complaint is filed. *See* FED. R. CIV. P. 27(a).

the posted video accurately portrayed the thunderstorm and the subsequent explosion, or, in narrative terms, the *causation*.[18]

In the second example, Sarah Koenig and her producer, Dana Chivvis, conducted narrative fact investigation in *Serial*. How do Koenig and Chivvis investigate the prosecution's and Adnan's competing stories of what transpired on the afternoon of January 13, 1999, when Hae Min Lee was murdered? Multiple ways:

1. They go out into the real world and recreate the afternoon of Hae's murder. Koenig and Chivvis drive from the high school to the Best Buy, reconstructing the driving route, and checking it against the time that would have been available to Adnan if he had committed the murder. (Episode Five at 3:36–8:04, 8:48–11:02).

2. They identify that Jay's story requires Adnan to have made a call from the Best Buy without a cellphone. This leads them to investigate whether there could have been a pay phone at the Best Buy in 1999, and to review old store blueprints and old telephone company records.

3. They test the driving route Jay states he and Adnan took on the afternoon of Hae's murder against Adnan's cell phone call records; and they determined where the cell phone must have been located based on cell tower locations. (Episode Five at 12:29–14:11, 14:33–21:03, 22:32–27:50).[19]

Similar to these non-lawyer fact investigations, you as a lawyer will engage in similar types of fact investigations to support your client's case or project theory, or to defend against your opposing party's case theory. To do so, you too will need to imagine what would or could have taken place, and then use whatever resources are available to you both technologically and out in the real world to gather and develop the relevant facts.

H. Exercise

So let's dive into a lawyering exercise of fact investigation. Can you brainstorm a list of ways in which you could informally investigate and develop the

---

18. In this TedTalk, Markham Nolan explains how the investigators were able to locate the site of the thunderstorm: https://www.ted.com/talks/markham_nolan_how_to_separate_fact_and_fiction_online?language=en (6:45–8:57).

19. And Episode Five continues with a discussion of the investigation of the cell phone tower records. Other examples of fact investigation in *Serial* include investigating Hae Min Lee's diary entries (Episode 2, 3:00) and researching the AT&T customer service agreement from 1999 regarding whether one would be billed for an unanswered call (Episode 12, 23:48).

facts we have identified for the *City v. Mitt* tort case? Can you brainstorm a list of ways in which you could informally investigate and develop facts in your own clients' cases or projects?

If you find visual tools to be helpful, Appendix A is a chart that shows how you can organize your fact investigation around narrative elements. There is no one way to organize your case plan for fact investigation and development, though it is important to find a system that works for you. While the charts offer visual organization, a downside is that it may become a checklist and discourage constant revision and expansive thinking. Accordingly, we offer the chart as a potential resource, but not as the only resource. The chart has four parts geared towards a litigation scenario—room not only to address plaintiff's affirmative claim and defendant's responsive claim, but also defendant's affirmative claim and plaintiff's responsive claim too, if applicable in your matter. This chart can be easily adapted to transactional lawyering scenarios. Also, Appendix B is a similar chart for organizing your fact investigation around legal elements.

IV. Conclusion

In this chapter, we have discussed how a lawyer can use narrative to conduct fact investigation and development as well as plan one's case or project. We learned that most case outcomes are driven by facts, so it is important to do a thorough fact investigation in the beginning, and stay aware of any changing facts and circumstances throughout the matter. Learning and understanding the facts is also important in constructing a narrative and case or project theory. We learned how to identify narrative facts in a case or project theory, as well as alternative or opposing case or project theories, and use the facts to determine what investigation needs to be done to support those facts.

This chapter also introduced how identified facts can be used to create a discovery plan. A discovery plan can then be divided into a formal discovery plan and an informal discovery plan. The case planning chart provided in the Appendix can be used to help with identifying facts to support the narrative elements, and the sources of information for the facts. In the next chapter, we discuss how narrative helps lawyers to conduct legal counseling of their clients.

Appendix A

Narrative Elements Case Planning Chart

Case Name:

Plaintiff's Affirmative Claims				
Narrative Elements	Information	Potential Sources of Information (People, Places & Things)	Informal Investigation & Timeline	Formal Investigation & Timeline
Characters (and traits)				
Events (and setting)				
Causation				
Normalization				
Masterplots				
Closure				

Defendant's Defensive Claims				
Narrative Elements	Information	Potential Sources of Information (People, Places & Things)	Informal Investigation & Timeline	Formal Investigation & Timeline
Characters (and traits)				
Events (and setting)				
Causation				
Normalization				
Masterplots				
Closure				

Narrative Elements Case Planning Chart (Cont.)

Defendant's Affirmative Claims				
Narrative Elements	Information	Potential Sources of Information (People, Places & Things)	Informal Investigation & Timeline	Formal Investigation & Timeline
Characters (and traits)				
Events (and setting)				
Causation				
Normalization				
Masterplots				
Closure				

Plaintiff's Defensive Claims				
Narrative Elements	Information	Potential Sources of Information (People, Places & Things)	Informal Investigation & Timeline	Formal Investigation & Timeline
Characters (and traits)				
Events (and setting)				
Causation				
Normalization				
Masterplots				
Closure				

Appendix B

Legal Elements Case Planning Chart

Case Name:

Defendant's Affirmative Claim					
Legal Claim	Elements of Claim	Information Related to Each Element	Potential Sources of Information (People, Places & Things)	Informal Investigation & Timeline	Formal Investigation & Timeline

Plaintiff's Defensive Claim					
Legal Claim	Elements of Claim	Information Related to Each Element	Potential Sources of Information (People, Places & Things)	Informal Investigation & Timeline	Formal Investigation & Timeline

Legal Elements Case Planning Chart (Cont.)

Plaintiff's Affirmative Claim					
Legal Claim	Elements of Claim	Information Related to Each Element	Potential Sources of Information (People, Places & Things)	Informal Investigation & Timeline	Formal Investigation & Timeline

Defendant's Defensive Claim					
Legal Claim	Elements of Claim	Information Related to Each Element	Potential Sources of Information (People, Places & Things)	Informal Investigation & Timeline	Formal Investigation & Timeline

Chapter 8

Counseling and Problem-Solving

I. Introduction

In this chapter, we examine two related lawyering activities, and explore the ways in which narrative theory and storytelling can guide students and practitioners to be more effective problem solvers and client counselors. We begin by deconstructing the skill of problem-solving, and then move on to applying that skill in the particular activity of counseling clients. As you read through the theory of these lawyering skills, put your narrative theorist hat on to identify and apply the tenets of narrative theory we are now familiar with: character, events, causation, normalization, masterplot, and closure.

II. Problem-Solving

Lawyers are problem solvers—you've heard it said, but what does it mean? In this section we will explore what a problem solver is and does, and how narrative theory helps lawyers be more effective. Take a moment to reflect back on a problem you have been involved in trying to solve. What was the problem and how did you try to solve it? Did you succeed? Why or why not? Write a brief description of what happened. You might want to refer back to this as we proceed through our analysis of problem-solving.

A. Definitions

Let us begin by defining three common terms, so we can all be on the same page. First, what do we mean by "problem," "problem-solving," and "decision-making"?

A **problem,** for our purposes, means that the *existing* set of circumstances is different from the *desired* set of circumstances, and there is no obvious way to reach that desired set of circumstances.

Problem-solving is the process of navigating through the problem space. Problem-solving concerns "understanding, specifying, or diagnosing the problem."[1] The Problem Solver recognizes that the current situation is different from the situation we would like, and tries to move the current situation toward the desired situation.[2] Problem-solving is a process of moving from a current state to a desired state.[3]

Decision-making is related to problem-solving, but it is narrower. If problem-solving is navigating across problem space, decision-making is selecting a particular pathway to take across that space. Problem-solving is a working methodology; it is more about the questions we ask ourselves, and our work and mental habits in getting information.[4] Decision-making involves "selecting among and implementing alternative courses of action."[5] Decision-making is best understood as the choices we make at certain decisive junctures.[6]

B. Problem-Solving by Lawyers

All legal problems can be seen as client goals that are impeded by obstacles; all legal work can be seen as efforts to avoid those potential obstacles (transactional work) and/or playing out the conflicts that result from those obstacles (advocacy).[7] Solving problems is what lawyers do in practice. But while a competent, experienced, practitioner may be able to solve problems, make decisions, and exercise practical judgment at the same time without much self-conscious reflection, an understanding of how to do each is not clear to the student or new lawyer.

---

1. Paul Brest and Linda Hamilton Krieger, *The Phyllis W. Beck Chair in Law Symposium: New Roles, No Rules? Redefining Lawyers' Work. New Role: Problem Solving*, 72 TEMP L. REV. 811 (1999).

2. See *e.g.,* Gerald P. Lopez, *Shaping Community Problem Solving Around Community Knowledge*, 79 N.Y.U. L. Rev. 59 (2004) and Gerald P. Lopez. *Working with Communities and Organizations,* in SOCIAL JUSTICE: PROFESSIONALS, COMMUNITIES, AND LAW 158–71 (Martha Mahoney et al. eds., 2003).

3. Linda Morton, *Teaching Creative Problem Solving: A Paradigmatic Approach*, 34 CAL. W. L. REV. 375 (1998).

4. James M. Cooper, *Towards a New Architecture: Creative Problem Solving and the Evolution of Law*, 34 CAL. W. L. REV. 297, 302 (1998).

5. Brest and Krieger, *supra* note 1.

6. Cooper, *supra* note 4.

7. Brest and Krieger, *supra* note 1.

Exploring the skill of problem-solving allows us to focus on the whole picture of what lawyers do, which includes legal skills and development of cognitive, experiential thought processes. Thus, in order to be an effective problem solver and thoughtful decision maker, an attorney must have the following:[8]

Skills: listening, collaborating, empathizing, holistic vision (seeing the big picture), consensus building, creative thinking, assessing needs, ability to work across disciplines if necessary.[9]

Attitudes: open-minded, persistent, humble, curious, trusting, aware of one's perspective and bias, able to challenge assumptions, accept criticism, and deal with ambiguity.

Values: respect, appreciation for decentralized decision-making, inclusiveness, creativity, and self-awareness.

And perhaps most important, such a practitioner must be intentional and conscientious in choosing and applying those skills, attitudes, and values to fit the needs, values, and culture of those involved.[10]

C. "Stages" of Problem-Solving

Problem-solving is not a linear process. Instead, multiple "decision nodes" present themselves as practitioners navigate through the problem space. Each of these decision nodes occurs at a fork in the road, offering a glimpse down at least two—often more—potential pathways. The problem solver must be willing to venture down these pathways, some of which might be dead ends, requiring a backwards or sideways step. Thus effective problem-solving **must be a flexible, multidisciplinary approach** to understanding and resolving problems.[11]

One way to understand this approach is to disaggregate the stages of the process to ensure that at each stage, the lawyer makes intentional and effective

---

8. See Linda Morton, *A New Approach to Health Care ADR: Training Law Students to be Problem Solvers in the Health Care Context*, 21 Ga. St. U. L. Rev. 965 (2005) (citing the rounds structure taught to Morton by Deborah Epstein). *See also* Janet Weinstein & Linda Morton, *Stuck in a Rut: The Role of Creative Thinking in Problem Solving and Legal Education*, 9 Clinical L. Rev. 835 (2003) (arguing that creative thinking is an essential component to problem solving and encouraging the incorporation of creative thinking into legal education); Janet Weinstein, *Coming of Age: Recognizing the Importance of Interdisciplinary Education in Law Practice*, 74 Wash. L. Rev. 319 (1999).

9. Cooper, *supra* note 4.

10. *See* Morton, *supra* note 8; *see also* Weinstein & Morton, *supra* note 8; Weinstein, *supra* note 8.

11. Morton, *supra* note 8.

choices about how to proceed through the problem space. When confronting an issue or problem, imagine four distinct phases: (1) fact gathering about the client's situation and goals, (2) brainstorming a definition or diagnosis of the problem, (3) generating options and strategies that might resolve the problem as defined in Stage 2, and (4) evaluating the options in order to make a decision.

1. Stage One: Fact Gathering

The goal of this stage is to gather as much information as possible about the relevant narrative elements. Therefore, throughout this stage the problem-solver seeks facts that address the narrative elements of character, events, causation, normalization, masterplot, and closure. Consider whether there are narrative elements of the story that are not clear.

For instance, with regard to characters, this stage could provide information about client context, background, goals, and desired results. It could also provide information about the characters' relationships.

This stage can also provide information regarding the **events** that have transpired and what **caused** them to occur. This stage can provide information about whether the problem as presented is the actual problem disrupting the steady state or whether there is a different problem or issue that needs to be addressed or a different steady state than the one previously understood. This stage can also provide information about **normalization** by explaining any previous apparent internal or external inconsistencies. This stage can also provide information about a **masterplot** that may be overly relied upon and is not credible or persuasive or a masterplot that has been rendered invisible and needs to be utilized. Finally, this stage can provide information about **closure**, how the problem that disrupts the steady state can be resolved.

Let's consider a problem lawyers frequently encounter: some version of "We can't reach our client. He isn't responding to our attempts to contact him." You might start your fact gathering with basic questions like "What have you done to try to contact the client?"; "How long has it been since you heard from him?"; "Are there other phone numbers or email/postal addresses you could try?" What other questions might you have for someone describing this problem to you, or if you yourself are having this problem?

You might move from these questions to wondering about why the attorney needs to contact the client, "What information are you looking for?" "Why do you need the information?" This leads to asking about other **characters** as sources for the information: you might start to wonder about the client's family and friends network, e.g., "Is there someone else we can contact to get information to/from the client?" Or even farther removed from the client: "Are there public agencies where you might be able to get reliable information that you need?"

These questions lead the problem solver to wonder about pursuing information from sources other than the client: "Is there any reason not to trust what the client's daughter might tell you?" "Is it worth it to the client to have you reach out to people he doesn't want you to, even if they have information that could help him?" and "Is it okay with the client for you to look elsewhere?"

The problem solver might wonder about her own feelings about the situation. Is she frustrated? Angry? Overwhelmed? Curious? The problem solver might drill a little deeper to wonder why she feels this way? And what is underneath those feelings?

For this stage, narrative theory provides a vehicle for both gathering facts and generating areas of inquiry. Narrative probing and narrative listening help the problem solver focus on and explore the problem through its narrative elements. The problem solver should allow herself to be curious about the network of **characters** in the narrative, the chain of **events** that might have transpired, how those events and characters might be **causally connected**, and whether and how the problem solver and/or other characters might be using **normalization** or **masterplots** to understand any aspects of the problem.

2. Stage Two: Problem Definition/Diagnosis

Problem definition is the most important tool of creative problem-solving. The main question for problem definition is: What is the nature of the problem to be solved? When a problem is properly recognized, it can be properly solved. An attorney must recognize that the client exists in a contextual web of relationships and dynamics, and that the problem, therefore, inhabits that contextual web. Defining or diagnosing the problem, therefore, requires attention to the narrative elements we have explored thus far: characters, events, causation, etc. Identifying all potential causes for the disruption of the client's steady state— those with legal elements and solutions and those with non-legal elements and solutions—allows attorneys to act as counselors and to yield sound advice. Interviewing, fact-finding, and active listening skills should be deployed.[12]

That is the second stage of problem-solving. You, as the problem solver, should brainstorm ideas about the contours of the problem itself and how it might differ from the problem as presented originally. To do this, you have to integrate the factual information you have gathered, and come up with a plausible explanation for the behavior presented.

---

12. Cooper, *supra* note 4.

In order to jump start the brainstorming of problem definition, try using Jean Koh Peters' and Sue Bryant's "Parallel Universe Thinking" exercise.[13]

Write a plausible explanation for the situation as you understand it. Then imagine a parallel universe, and come up with a second, equally plausible, explanation for the situation as you understand it.

In other words:

- What do you think is the explanation/theory that explains the situation; what more facts do you need to know to prove/disprove this theory?
- What ELSE do you think could be the explanation/theory that explains this situation; what more facts/information do you need to know to prove/disprove this theory?

Building on these written reflections, you work to differentiate symptoms—the factual information gathered in the first phase—from the problem itself. Your initial diagnosis of the problem might have been a fairly simplistic response to the facts you had learned. The parallel universe exercise pushes you to explore beyond that initial assessment to consider other possibilities, and develop a more complex understanding of the problem.

Let's go back to our hard-to-reach client. Your initial assessment of the problem (part one of the parallel universe exercise) might be "the client is not responsive because he doesn't care about the issue/doesn't understand how important it is." Pushed beyond that simplistic explanation by part two of the parallel universe exercise, you might suggest other possible explanations such as that the attorney (or you) might not have been using the right methods to try to get information; the attorney (or you) might not understand what information she needs; the client might not understand what the attorney is asking for and why; the client might not be clear about what his goals are; the attorney might not be clear about what the client's goals are; the attorney might not feel comfortable prying for information; the client might not feel safe with this particular attorney for some reason; the attorney might not feel safe/confident with this particular client for some reason, etc.

The brainstorming that follows this exercise is richer and more fruitful than it might have been without reflection. You force yourself to consider hypothetical explanations beyond the knee-jerk ones; you explore different avenues, and wonder about other possible unknown/unknowable facts. You come to understand, quite quickly, that this portion of problem-solving boils down

---

13. Susan Bryant, *The Five Habits: Building Cross-Cultural Competence in Lawyers*, 8 Clinical L. Rev. 33, 70–73 (2001). For more discussion of this and other habits, *see* Chapter Four.

to: "What problem could explain the symptoms presented? And, what OTHER problem could explain the symptoms presented?"

The problem solver gets to this point by starting in the fact-gathering process, which provided richer context and awakened empathy, and then by engaging in a rigorous exploration of symptoms and explanations, and counter-explanations, to come up with a diagnosis. The originally stated problem becomes more intimate, in that this particular version of this particular problem is very much about these particular characters and events and causal connections.

3. Stage Three: Problem-Solving

Having gathered information and determined both what you know and what you don't (but should?) know, and developed a working understanding of the "problem," you can now turn to the task of solving the problem.

This is the stage we are all most comfortable with because it is what we do all the time, as people, law students and lawyers: strategize actions based on information we have gathered. In fact, we tend, if left to our own devices, to START in this phase, and only work backwards to fact gathering and problem definition if forced to slow down and deconstruct the problem more fully.

In our example of the attorney who can't reach his client, if you, the problem solver, had started where we tend to be most comfortable—i.e., in the strategizing/problem-solving stage—you might have concluded that the attorney should simply try harder—call again, email, write a letter. Or, if things became desperate, you might have concluded that the attorney should send the client a warning shot that his case is about to be closed. These are what we call "connect-the-dot" solutions. They fail necessarily to identify, consider and solve any underlying or overlapping issues that might exist. They fail, in other words, to recognize that not being able to reach the client might be a symptom, not the problem itself.

Having gone through the lengthy process of gathering information and defining the contours of the underlying problem, however, the problem solver can generate solutions and actions that are quite different from theses connect-the-dot options.

The problem solver might have diagnosed the problem as that the client was not responding to the attorney's efforts to contact him because he did not feel safe or comfortable in the legal system. Accordingly, in this problem-solving stage, you might suggest that the attorney write a letter or email acknowledging that and offering to meet somewhere neutral or affirmatively safe for the client, to offer some reassurance.

The problem solver might have diagnosed the problem as that the client was not responding because the attorney hadn't made it clear why she needed the information. So you might suggest that the attorney write a letter or email laying out what she needed to know and why, and the consequences to the client if the attorney is unable to get the information.

You learn, as you proceed through Stages One and Two, that you have to take action on the fact that most problems are multidimensional and require multidimensional solutions. What started here as a problem with an "unresponsive client" might evolve into a situation with an unresponsive and frightened client, or maybe a client who didn't know he was expected to respond, or how to respond. With these thickening problem frames comes understanding that your problem-solving has to be nuanced and layered, not simply figuring out how to get your client to answer the phone.

4. Stage Four: Reflection

This final stage is easy to skip over, but very important—so don't be tempted. This is where you assess the process you have gone through to determine your next steps.

Here are two takeaways from this process, generally:

First, the personal feelings/positions of the relevant characters are really important. In the fact-gathering stage, you should explore those personal feelings and positions. In diagnosis, you realize that those personal feelings might play a big role in deciding what the problem might be. And in problem-solving, you need to take those concerns seriously and attempt to address them.

Second, lingering in the definition/diagnosis phase provides a deeper, richer, more holistic understanding of the problem and the solution. It is really important to go through each stage of the process in order to prepare for the next stage, and ultimately to come to a satisfying set of strategies. Problem description leads to problem definition leads to problem-solving: the more detailed you get at each phase, the more you discover, and the more satisfying and effective the solution.

Breaking down problems and the process of solving them into these distinct stages leads to complex, long-term solutions quickly and authentically. This practice of taking a problem and deconstructing it very deliberately before attempting to solve it is essentially a practice of critical reflection.[14] Moreover, the deconstruction of problems in this way is flexible and transferable, and

---

14. For more on critical self-reflection, *see* Chapter Three.

can thus increase your ability to critically reflect on your role and identity within a particular framework, or in general practice. The bottom line is that a good problem description leads to better problem definition, which generates more effective problem-solving. In other words, the more you flesh out your client's story, the better you are at working with him to develop long term and successful solutions.

III. Counseling

So we've established that problem-solving is a process of moving from a current state to a desired state. In a legal context, one way to think about a client's problems is that the client's *goals* are impeded by obstacles. In narrative theory terms, closure will be obtained by resolving the problem that is disrupting the steady state of the client's goal realization. Our role as lawyers, therefore, can be seen as anticipating and avoiding those obstacles if we are engaged in planning or transactional work, and engaging with those obstacles in the hopes of eliminating or reducing them if we are engaged in dispute resolution work.[15] In both kinds of cases, the lawyer's job is to help the client move from his current state to his desired state, so that he can achieve his goals. One of the main ways we engage in problem-solving with clients is through client counseling.

A. What Is Client Counseling?

Client counseling is sometimes conflated with or subsumed by discussions of client interviewing. And while the two are obviously related—counseling often takes place within the client interview—it is important to isolate the skills and values necessary for lawyers to engage in effective client counseling.

In Chapter Five, we described the goals of an interview as being primarily to gather information about the client and his situation, and to begin to develop the lawyer-client relationship. The goals of counseling are to build on the foundation laid in the initial interview: to provide information to the client about his various legal and non-legal options—in light of the facts and goals the lawyer has learned about—and to work with the client to develop a plan of action. In narrative theory terms, client counseling is where the lawyer and

---

15. Morton, *supra* note 3.

client collaborate in constructing a narrative designed to resolve the trouble the client has come to the lawyer about.

B. *Client Counseling in Stages*

Client counseling involves the lawyer and client together actively engaging each stage of the problem-solving process. In short, a counseling session involves the following tasks and steps, each of which falls within one of the problem-solving stages described above:

Stage One: Fact Investigation
- Preparation
- Ice-Breaking & Fact Updating

Stage Two: Problem Definition
- Clarifying Client Goals/Values
- Clarifying the problem

Stage Three: Problem-Solving/Strategizing
- Identifying Options
- Evaluating Choices
- Deciding

Stage Four: Reflection
- Checking in
- Answering questions
- Identifying next steps

In this part of the chapter, we will examine each stage of a client counseling session, and consider ways that narrative theory enhances a lawyer's ability to counsel effectively.

1. Stage One: Fact Investigation

As you prepare for your counseling session, remember, you have probably already had at least one interview with your client, and might have been able to do at least some fact investigation already. Part of your preparation, therefore, will be to develop a working case or project theory based on your understanding of the client's facts and goals, and the applicable law.[16]

---

16. For more on case and project theory, *see* Chapter Six.

Before you welcome your client in for your counseling meeting, you should have as complete a grasp as possible of the client's situation as it stood at the time of your last contact with him. You should be able to identify the major characters in his story, the major events that have taken place, and the causal connection among those events and characters. You should also understand how your client describes his steady state and the disruption that has occurred—or that he fears might occur—to that steady state. And finally, you should have some sense of how the client wants the situation resolved—what closure, in other words, the client might be seeking. That is your starting point. This is the first stage in constructing your client's legal narrative.

It is not, however, your ending point. In order to be an effective legal counselor, you must recognize that the client's situation is not static, and that therefore his facts and goals might have changed and the applicable law might be different. Indeed, there might be facts the client doesn't want you to explore, or you might discover facts that would change the client's mind about how to proceed. It is important, therefore, that your counseling session begin with updating your previous fact gathering—a second round of fact investigation.

As with the initial interview, you will want to use some kind of rapport-building small-talk or ice-breaking technique to put the client at ease, remind him of why you and he are meeting, and how the session might progress. Ideally, you would create a conversational rhythm that will carry over to the presentation and discussion of options and increase the role of the client. You would want to continue with your narrative and active listening.

And as with the first round of fact gathering—conducted during your initial interview—you will want to ask open-ended questions to get a wide draw of information. But this time around, you have a clearer sense of the basic topics to explore, so you can also use directed questions to get particular updates. And you will want to use your natural curiosity about your client's story—any particular events, the characters he has mentioned, the problem and steady state as explained—to guide your questioning. These techniques, as we saw in the first part of this chapter, will result in a full and rich picture of the client's factual situation.

Let's imagine the following client: Harlan is a 73-year-old white man who wants to get his affairs in order. You've learned from the intake form that he has 4 children ranging in age from 25 to 51, and two ex-wives, ranging in age from 51 to 73. His first ex-wife is the mother of the two oldest children; his second ex-wife is the mother of the two youngest. He is quite close to his oldest and youngest children, but estranged from the middle two. Other than some oral surgery 5 years ago, he has had no hospitalizations or serious illness. He is in good health. He wants his will to provide that an autopsy be performed immediately after his death, paid for out of the estate. And he wants to disown the two middle children and leave his estate to the oldest and youngest.

What more do you want to know about this client and his situation? Let the narrative elements guide you—who are the characters and what are their traits? What events have transpired and what causal connection might there be between those events and the client's goals? What is the client's steady state? And what disruption, if any, has there been to that steady state? What kind of closure is the client seeking and why?

2. Stage Two: Problem Definition

Just as the client's facts are not static, nor, necessarily, are his goals. So you need to make sure you are counseling the actual client before you today and not a constructed client or the client who appeared before you during the initial interview. In order to do this, you need to make sure you understand the client's values, and how they inform his objectives and decision-making.

In Stage Two of problem-solving, we work to define the problem that needs solving. That is what you are doing as you work with the client to identify his values and explore how those inform his goals. You might collaborate with the client in shaping those goals, using techniques like the ones suggested in the first part of the chapter, e.g., having a modified parallel universe discussion with the client. You might ask, for example, these questions:

- What would a satisfactory resolution of your situation look like and why?
- What would a different satisfactory resolution of your situation look like and why?

Based on the discussion that follows from these questions, you and your client can work backwards to identify his goals (ideal resolution) and define the problem that needs resolution.

Let's go back to Harlan. Your information gathering from the initial interview and subsequent fact investigation reveals that Harlan believes that during his oral surgery five years ago, something was implanted or otherwise entered his back molars, causing him to experience radio frequency sensations in his jaw and head. He insists that he is not crazy—he is not claiming to hear voices or to believe that aliens are controlling or communicating with him. He claims only that something in his teeth is causing him to feel like a staticky radio is constantly playing in his jaw and head. While at first sympathetic, his second wife ended up not being able to handle his anger and frustration with this condition, and Harlan says she stopped believing his claims, which Harlan says caused their divorce. His kids were also very sympathetic at first, but over the past year or so, the middle two children have grown more skeptical of his claims and he fears that they too don't believe him. That is why he wants to disown them. And he wants to have an autopsy performed after his death to prove that something is indeed in his teeth, causing him this discomfort.

What questions do you have for Harlan about his goals? Does the closure he suggests connect effectively with his goals? How would you diagnose or define the problem Harlan is presenting to the lawyer? Is it the same diagnosis or definition of the problem Harlan himself is presenting?

3. Stage Three: Problem-Solving

The third stage of the client counseling—and problem-solving—process is the actual decision-making. Simple as it sounds, we saw in the first part of the chapter that the process of deciding on strategy has multiple layers. Here is a way to break it down into sub-processes:

a. Generating options

As we saw earlier, this stage involves brainstorming various courses of action based on what the lawyer has learned during the first and second stages—fact gathering and problem definition. This part of counseling should be very much a collaborative endeavor—the client has a lot of information and insight into his own life and goals; and the lawyer has a lot of insight into how the law might intervene or intersect with the client's life in order to achieve or impede those goals. In this stage, the two should simply identify the choices the client might have.

Let's imagine that during the problem definition stage of your counseling, you and Harlan determine that he has two primary goals: first, to get the radio frequency feeling to stop; and second, to have his kids believe him about his condition. You and he have diagnosed his problem, therefore, as being that his family does not support him in getting to the bottom of his condition, and ultimately finding a way to treat it.

Based on that problem definition, what options can you brainstorm?

b. Analyzing choices

Having brainstormed a list of potential options, the lawyer and client now have to analyze those options to determine which best fits with the client's goals, what the lawyer knows about the client, and what the law might allow or not allow.

As you and the client work together to analyze the various choices, you most likely will need to consider both legal and non-legal consequences, as well as both positive and negative consequences of a particular course of action. You will also need to give some kind of prediction about the likelihood of success of each alternative. In giving a prediction, there are a lot of factors that are uncertain such as, in litigation, what the actual judge or jury might do. You can provide information based on past behaviors, but there will be uncertainty. Accordingly, it is good client-centered lawyering to provide information about the basis of your predictions.

When called upon to predict, new lawyers may feel pressure to over assure a nervous client so he feels comfortable with the lawyer or to understate the value of the client's case in order to protect the lawyer from a client's later disappointment. Such impulses are based on the lawyer's interests and not the client's. Again, as the lawyer, you are counseling the client based on his goals and circumstances, not yours.

Additional approaches that help new lawyers to stay client-centered in their counseling are to stay neutral in tone, organization, language, and framing of the options so as not to sway the client with your own opinion of what he should do. It is important to remember that even—or especially—during this phase, the lawyer is not the "knower and director." Rather, the client and lawyer must generate choices and alternatives together.

You also want to play a bit of a devil's advocate role when counseling, if only by holding up the client's goals and asking how a particular course of action might or might not meet those goals. It is important to understand the bases for the client's evaluation of the options because it may clarify the goals or generate other options to be considered. You may want to probe inconsistencies among a client's choices or between his choices and his goals. You don't want to undo all that good rapport you have built by appearing to second-guess or dismiss a client's choice, so you might want to ask the client himself to project the consequences of a particular alternative; or you might suggest that you are trying to anticipate what the other side might say about your client's position. You also may want to help the client address perceived inconsistencies, to give the client space to identify and cure informational gaps and ambiguities.

Harlan himself has identified a couple of options he thinks address his goals: writing a will that provides for an autopsy, and disowning the two kids who don't believe him. How would you evaluate those options in terms of their connection to his goals? Given what you know about what happens when people die and are buried or cremated, is the will the best vehicle for providing that an autopsy be performed? And even if you and Harlan identified another vehicle better suited for such a provision—a Funeral Directive, for example—does a post-mortem au-

topsy lead to the kind of resolution that Harlan wants? Does disowning his two middle kids do anything to normalize the situation between them?

What other options did you come up with in Step (a)? How would you evaluate those?

c. Cooperating with client to choose option

Be aware of the potential to spend time only identifying and discussing choices, without deciding. If there are certain options the client won't consider, that may affect the way you develop the client's story.

You and Harlan have decided that you will do some fact investigation into his medical records and the procedure he had five years ago. You will also draft a letter for him to send to all of his children—and possible both ex-wives—laying out his concerns and feelings. You will suggest in the letter that the whole family meet to discuss the situation. You have offered to mediate that discussion, but Harlan isn't sure that will be necessary. For now, he just wants you to draft the letter. He also wants to read it over and adapt it to his voice. And he wants to be the one to send it. You've agreed that you will have the letter drafted within a week; he understands that the fact investigation will take longer than that.

4. Stage Four: Reflection

Once you and the client have agreed on a course of action, you want to take a moment to reflect on the process that got you there. You'll want to check in with the client to gauge his level of enthusiasm about the choices you both have made. You'll want to give him an opportunity to ask any questions he may have—about anything! And you'll want to very clearly identify what next steps both you and he have agreed to take.

Finally, remember that client counseling is a process. It happens throughout client representation. It is not a moment or an event. Counseling is related to decision-making and as there are decisions to be made at every step of your representation of the client, counseling will be a pervasive process throughout the representation.

What kinds of things will you want to be sure to ask Harlan about your counseling process? What questions do you think he might have about what you have decided to do, and what happens next? Are you clear what you are supposed to do next? Is he? Are there things you need him to do? Releases to sign?

Once you have finished the meeting, what will you do to continue your counseling? What is the next point at which you might need to engage in another round of fact gathering, problem definition and strategizing? After you have drafted the letter? Once you have gathered information from the oral surgeon's office? When else?

C. Example

Take a look at the following clips from *The Good Wife*, **Season 4, Ep. 18, 5:00 — 7:23**,[17] and consider:

1. How does Alicia Florrick, the attorney, respond to this client at the initial meeting?
2. How does Alicia Florrick respond to this client at subsequent meetings?
3. What stages of problem-solving are most illustrated by these clips?
4. What techniques does Alicia Florrick use to counsel this client?

IV. Conclusion

This chapter has identified and described a method for deconstructing and solving problems — those of lawyers and those of clients. By breaking problem-solving down into discrete stages, lawyers can take their time gathering information about the client's narrative — guided by their curiosity about the various characters, events, causal connections, steady state and closure — before moving on to defining and ultimately solving or strategizing to solve the client's problem.

Lawyers engage with this kind of problem-solving frequently in the context of counseling their clients. These counselling moments occur throughout the representation and require the lawyer's ongoing attention to the three stages of problem-solving — gathering information, defining the problem, and identifying strategies for resolution. Problem-solving and counseling might be fluid and flexible, with some stages truncated and others elongated. The important thing for lawyers to remember, though, is to go through each stage before moving to the next. That way lawyers and clients can determine solutions and strategies based on the client's full contextual narrative rather than on whatever masterplots either the lawyer or client might rely on. Client counseling includes problem-solving by the lawyer, but ultimately requires that the client is aware of the legal and non-legal options to address the problem. The lawyer helps the client evaluate the options, and the client chooses the course of action to address the problem.

---

17. http://www.cbs.com/shows/the_good_wife/episodes/211943/.

Chapter 9

Negotiation

I. Introduction

In this chapter we explore four questions: first, what is negotiation—when does it happen and what skills and values does it call upon; second, what are the goals of a legal negotiation, in general; third, what choices does an attorney have to make about how and what to negotiate. The overarching question, threading among all of these, is how does narrative theory and storytelling help lawyers be better negotiators?

To aid in this analysis, we suggest that you consider the following clip from the NBC comedy, *30 Rock*,[1] of a negotiation between Jack Donaghy and his nanny, Sherry: https://www.youtube.com/watch?v=a7-eoiY4bOo. You can watch it now to have something in the back of your mind as you read on, or you can wait and watch it after reading Parts I through III, when you will be asked to answer some questions about it. Either way, enjoy.

II. What Is Negotiation?

How many of you have engaged in a negotiation?

For those of you who silently answered, "I have," how many negotiations have you engaged in? What did you negotiate about in your most recent negotiation? How did it end up? Take a moment to jot down your answers.

For those of you who silently answered, "not me": think again! Every one of us has engaged in a negotiation. Indeed, every one of us has engaged in

---

1. 30 ROCK, Season 5, Episode 15 (NBC Feb. 17, 2011).

hundreds, thousands, perhaps tens of thousands of negotiations. We negotiate every single day, often multiple times a day. With our kids, with our parents, with our partners, with our employers and employees, with our professors, with service providers, clients, fellow drivers, public transport riders, pedestrians. And that's not to mention the negotiations we actually call "negotiations"—leasing an apartment, buying a car, a house, accepting or refusing a job offer, or asking for or giving a raise.

As social animals, human beings are negotiators. (So are cats and dogs and other social animals too, by the way. Ever wonder how a cat and dog figure out how to co-exist in the same house with the same limited number of cozy places to curl up? That détente is achieved through a series of non-verbal communications between these two social animals that amounts to negotiations about shared space.) So the bottom line is that you already know a lot about negotiation, just as you already know a lot about how to construct and hear a narrative. Now we will use that knowledge to explore how to negotiate in a legal context.

We have mentioned elsewhere that nearly all civil cases end in a negotiated settlement, usually after discovery and motions but before trial.[2] Likewise, the majority of all criminal cases end in a plea deal, also after discovery and initial motions, but before trial.[3] And almost by definition, transactional lawyering involves multiple negotiations throughout the representation, often with multiple different parties, over a variety of different issues.[4] So lawyers negotiate. A lot. It is a fundamental and essential set of lawyering skills.

What are those skills? Effective negotiation calls upon lawyers to be excellent interviewers, listeners, problem solvers, counselors, case and project theory developers, fact investigators, and persuaders, to name a few. The chapters preceding this one have explored and demonstrated ways that understanding narrative construction and storytelling helps lawyers practice all of these skills. It stands to reason, therefore, that understanding narrative construction and being able to present a compelling narrative are essential to the art of effective legal negotiation.

In their primer on lawyering skills, Professors Haydock, Juergens and Knapp suggest that good negotiators ask three sets of questions:

Goals: "What does my client want? What does the other side want?"

---

2. David F. Chavkin, Clinical Legal Education: A Textbook for law School Clinical Programs 130 (2001).

3. *Id.*

4. *Id.*

Information: "What do I know? What do I need to find out? What will the other side try to find out?

Choices: "What should I do during the negotiation? What will the other side do during the negotiation?"[5]

The first two sets of questions deal with negotiation goals; the third deals with negotiation techniques. We will explore these topics in this chapter.

III. Negotiation Goals

Just as with interviewing and counseling, a big part of successful negotiations includes preparation and research. And the first step in that process is to identify both the specific and the general goals of any potential negotiation. The answer breaks down into two parts: Substantive Outcome Goal and Information Bargaining Goal.

A. *Substantive Outcome Goal*

To determine this part of your negotiation goals, ask yourself, "what does my client want? What does the other side want?"[6] To determine the answer to these questions, you must first identify the relative *positions* and *interests* of the parties involved, and then you must analyze your goals in light of those *positions* and *interests*.

1. Positions and Interests

Let's imagine that you represent a nonprofit organization ("the NPO") that is seeking space for a retail shop. Your client has identified a potential unit to rent and would like you to enter into discussions with the building's owner ("the Landlord").[7] How do you go about figuring out what your goals are for this negotiation?

The immediate answer to this question is: to achieve an arrangement between my client and the potential landlord whereby my client is able to rent

---

5. Roger Haydock & Peter Knapp, Lawyering: Practice and Planning 180–181 (2011).

6. *Id.*

7. This hypothetical comes from Mitchell Hamline School of Law's first year Lawyering course. Thanks to Dean Raths and, before him, Mehmet Konar-Steenberg and Deborah Schmedemann for the excellent material.

the unit they want. That is a good initial answer, but in a negotiation, it's important to find out not only *what* your client and you want from the negotiation, but also *why* your client and you want it. You can distinguish between these two things by identifying your client's *position* and your client's *interests*.

Your client's *position* is what you have come to understand as the thing he wants or cares about.[8] You arrive at this understanding by interviewing and counseling your client, using narrative probing and narrative listening to flesh out the context of his legal problem, and to identify and evaluate potential resolutions. You can think of your client's *position* as the **closure** he seeks to resolve the disruption in his **steady state.**

In our example, your client's *position* is that they want a place to rent at a reasonable cost and with reasonable lease terms. You dig a bit deeper into what your client means by "reasonable cost," and "reasonable lease terms" and learn that they would like to pay no more than $100 per square foot, have a lease of no longer than 2 years, and be able to sublease or assign the unit. So your client's *positions* are:

- Up to 2-year lease
- Up to $100 per square foot
- Right to sublease/assign

In order to achieve these identified goals, however, you need to go deeper than the positions identified. You need to uncover your client's *interests*—the rationale that underlie their positions.[9] *Interests* are "needs, desires, concerns, fears—the things one cares about or wants."[10] Such interests could be financial, logistical, psychological, reputational, or relational.[11] How do you determine what feelings underlie your client's positions? Same way you determine their positions: through narrative listening, probing and constructing.

Going back to the NPO and the Landlord, what *interests* underlie the *positions* you have identified? Further narrative probing reveals the following:

- Up to 2-year lease so if the location or unit does not work out, NPO is not tied down for too long

---

8. William Ury, Getting Disputes Resolved: Designing Systems to Cut the Costs of Conflict 5 (1988).

9. Stefan H. Krieger & Richard K. Neumann, Jr., Essential Lawyering Skills: Interviewing, Counseling, Negotiation, and Persuasive Fact Analysis 310 (4th ed. 2011).

10. *Id.* at 310–311.

11. *Id.*

- Up to $100 per square foot because while the going rate in the neighborhood is a bit higher, NPO as a nonprofit does not have board approval to pay more
- Right to sublease or assign is for a similar reason as the two-year lease in that NPO wants to be able to cut their losses if the space doesn't work out

Knowing both your client's positions and interests allows you to craft and execute a nimble and context-rich negotiation strategy that is far more likely to be successful than if you understood only what your client wanted, and not why.

2. Goal Analysis

Part of your negotiation preparation, therefore, needs to include a refined understanding of goals through the identification and characterization of the positions and interests of each party: your client and the opposing party.[12] You also need to consider, analyze, and prioritize the relative importance of each position and interest. Is it essential, important, or desirable? Are the positions and interests among/between the parties shared, independent, inconsistent?

Use the narrative components to explore these questions. How do you know if a particular need (position and interest) is essential, important or desirable to your client? Narrative probing and narrative listening will lead you to a fuller understanding of why your client might feel the way he does about a particular position. By exploring your client's positions and interests using the narrative components of character, traits, events, causation, normalization, masterplot, and closure, you should get a clear sense of your **bargaining authority**: i.e., how your client prioritizes his needs as essential, important or desirable.

So in the NPO and Landlord example — how would the NPO prioritize its needs for a particular price per square foot, versus the length of the lease, versus the assignment/sublease clause? Which of those needs is essential — meaning that the NPO would want you to walk away from the bargaining table if that need were not met? And which is merely desirable — meaning that if you have to negotiate it away, the NPO could live with that?

---

12. Perhaps the lawyers on each side have positions and interests as well that need to be considered — one lawyer might have a large trial docket and would rather not have another case go to court; or the lawyer might be eager to argue the case, and will try to avoid settlement for that reasons. Are there ethical implications to these kinds of questions? Think back to our discussion in Chapter Two of narrative context when considering ethical questions.

You can use the same techniques—plus a little curiosity and creativity (which are also part of any good narrative!)—to determine the other side's positions and interests, and to guess at how those interests are prioritized. Once you've done that, you will need to compare your client's needs (positions plus interests) with the opposing party's needs (positions plus interests) and their respective prioritizations. You might discover that there are overlapping positions, and/or that what you know is essential to your client is not inconsistent with what is essential to the other party. You will also discover areas of potential conflict. Either way, this exercise of identifying and prioritizing both your client's needs and the other side's needs is an essential part of preparing for a negotiation.

So in our NPO and Landlord hypothetical, you know what your client's positions and interests are. What do you think the Landlord's positions and interests might be? How do you think the Landlord prioritizes those needs? What areas of overlap do you anticipate? What areas of conflict?

B. Information Gathering

It would be a mistake to think the only goal of a legal negotiation is to find the overlap and resolve the conflict between the two parties' positions and interests, however. Remember the second set of questions you should ask in every negotiation: "What do I know? What do I need to find out? What will the other side try to find out?"[13]

A negotiation provides an opportunity broader than simply to reach a settlement. Another very important goal is to gain information about the other side's "preparation, theory of the case, evidence, witnesses and competence."[14] Failure to come to agreement on all—or even any—issues does not necessarily mean the negotiation was a failure, if you engage in successful information gathering and bargaining.

Here, of course, is where narrative again really helps lawyers. You have already done excellent information gathering about your client and his interests, positions and needs. You have, using your curiosity and creativity, as well as the narrative elements, anticipated the other side's interests, positions and needs. Now you need to identify what more information you need to learn, and what information you need to confirm: what will bring resolution, what does each character think is the make-up of causation of trouble or causation

---

13. HAYDOCK & KNAPP, *supra* note 5.
14. CHAVKIN, *supra* note 2, at 131.

of closure? Is either side putting forward any masterplots to support or debunk? Do efforts at normalization get in the way or assist with finding common ground among the parties' positions and interests.

So in our NPO and Landlord hypothetical, you know what your client's positions and interests are. You have conducted research to try to figure out the potential positions and interests of your opposing party. From your research into the commercial real estate trends and practices, as well as the information you have analyzed from the Landlord's website and other marketing materials, you have a hypothesis about the Landlord's position. Specifically, you anticipate that the Landlord would like a lease longer than two years, a rental rate of something closer to the market rate (i.e., higher than $100), and a restrictive assignment/sublease clause. You have some idea of what interests underlie these positions, but your guesses are fairly generic: you imagine that a Landlord wants to make as much as he can in rent, and that he would like as low turnover as possible, to save on transactional and administrative costs of finding and signing new tenants. Those same interests would support the Landlord's position against assignment or sub-lease clauses.

So what information do you need to *confirm* during your negotiation, and what information do you want to *obtain*? This is called information bargaining. Again, let the narrative elements guide you in your planning. You can use something like the chart in Chapter Seven (Fact Investigation) to identify the facts you need and the facts you need to confirm. If you get stuck, go back to the narrative elements—character and traits, events, causation, etc.

Another aspect of this information bargaining has to do with your own information. Through interviewing and counseling of your client, you know the information you have about your client and its situation. Part of your negotiation planning, therefore, has to include identifying information you imagine the other side will want to obtain. What facts about your client, strategy, resources, and case theory do you want to hold close to your chest to prevent the other side from accessing, and what facts are you willing or strategically want to give up?

There are no hard and fast rules about the kind of information you should withhold and the kind of information you should reveal. It all depends on your client's goals for the negotiation, and your case/project theory for achieving those goals. The important thing to remember, though, is that a successful legal negotiation depends on having a strategy not only for finding the overlap between the parties' positions, but also for gathering, withholding and revealing information. Use the narrative elements to guide you in developing such a strategy.

C. Persuasion

A third important goal of a legal negotiation is to persuade the other party that your positions are compelling and likely to prevail. This should sound familiar, as it is what lawyers do in almost every major task they undertake. It should also sound familiar because it is directly connected to case or project theory, which, as we have explored, is directly connected to narrative construction.

As a negotiator, part of your job is to give the other side a reason to concede ground and meet you somewhere mutually agreeable to all parties. In order to do that, you need to figure out the other side's *interests* (not only *positions*), so you know what buttons to try to push or release. We saw in the previous section how considering the narrative elements can help lawyers gather and confirm such information.

But knowing the relevant *facts* about both parties is only part of what it takes to persuade the other side to act in a certain way. Remember that case and project theories are your most powerful tool of persuasion, and they consist of facts, and are defined by law. In a negotiation context, that might mean something a lot broader than just legal precedent and statute. Instead, you want to think about the various *rights* at play among the parties—that is "independent standards that demonstrate the legitimacy or fairness of a party's position."[15] These rights could be formal legal rules or contracts—negotiations are said to exist in the shadow of the law or against the background of common business practice or form provisions. But negotiations also exist in a context or framework of socially accepted standards of behavior such as reciprocity, equality, or seniority.[16]

What *rights* underlie the negotiation between NPO and the Landlord? Your legal research will provide you with the relevant legal standards in a commercial real estate transaction. But what about the other sources of rights? Narrative probing will help you uncover the relevant social context for this transaction, which will allow you to construct a project theory that rests on more compelling grounds than simply supportive case law.

Whether your negotiation ends with a settlement or a breakdown in talks, it is an opportunity to do three important things:

- Solidify your understanding of the relative parties' positions and interests, and the interrelationship among them;

---

15. Stefan H. Krieger & Richard K. Neumann, Jr., Essential Lawyering Skills: Interviewing, Counseling, Negotiation, and Persuasive Fact Analysis (4th ed. 2011).
    16. *Id.*

- Confirm, obtain, withhold and reveal information about the parties and the process; and
- Develop and present a persuasive case/project theory that incorporates the respective rights of all parties, and that is designed to achieve your client's goals for the negotiation.

IV. Context, Strategy and Style: Choices

These are the theoretical underpinnings of an effective, client-centered negotiation. But what does such a negotiation look like, and how do negotiators act? This brings us to Professors Knapp, Juergens and Haydock's third set of questions: "What should I do during the negotiation? What will the other side do during the negotiation?"[17]

There are no set answers to these questions: the bottom line is that you, as the lawyer who is negotiating, have to make intentional choices about how to conduct your negotiation substantively and stylistically, keeping in mind the ideas and principles set out above.

In particular, you will need to decide on the follow things: what approach do you want to take, what strategy will you follow, and what style do you want to use? Here are some things to consider when making these choices.

A. Approach

Your negotiation *approach* is the operational theory, as opposed to the substantive case/project theory, for your negotiation. There are two basic approaches you could take:

1. Distributive

This is the classic "zero sum game" approach to resolving issues. There is a set amount of money or resources to be divided and your goal is to get the most for your client. Each party's "gain must occur at the expense of the other party ... a pure conflict of interest exists between the parties."[18]

If we go back to the NPO/Landlord negotiation, a distributive approach might result in head-to-head conflict over the rent, length of lease, and lease-terms. If the Landlord insists on a higher rent, the NPO literally loses money,

---

17. HAYDOCK & KNAPP, *supra* note 5.
18. CHAVKIN, *supra* note 2, at 136.

and vice-versa. Likewise, a longer lease term might satisfy the Landlord at the expense of the NPO. And finally, a distributive approach would create a binary Yes/No question about the lease term about subletting/assigning: either the NPO can do it (and therefore win), or the NPO cannot do it (and therefore lose).

2. Integrative

The integrative approach widens the lens of the negotiation to consider money, resources, etc. as only part of the context. This approach considers the respective *interests* of the party and looks for ways to satisfy all of them. In other words, this approach shifts perspective on what the problem is that needs to be solved for closure. When parties' "interests are not directly in conflict— a 'win-win' outcome is possible. Agreements are possible in which the level of satisfaction of one party is not necessarily inversely related to that of the other party."[19]

There is no rule about when to use which approach, but you do need to decide which one to use as you are planning for your negotiation. You will want to make that decision—ideally in conjunction with your client—in light of considerations such as your client's goals, the issues in the negotiation, and available resources. We will explore these more below. It is also possible to use different approaches for different issues, or to start off using one approach and then shift to another depending on how the negotiation proceeds. You should note though that certain shifts in approaches may result in differing levels of success: it can be very difficult to move from a distributive, "zero sum game" approach to an integrative approach while it can be easier to start off integrative and convert to distributive.

Finally, choosing your approach must be based on a thorough understanding of the context of the negotiation—particularly all parties' goals and the important facts underlying those goals. Lawyers who fail to have such an understanding risk mischaracterizing the appropriate bargaining context. Consider the following illustration:[20]

Imagine that two children would like some cake. It is vanilla cake with chocolate icing, and there is only one small piece left (too small to divide in half!). Classic distributive negotiation, right? There is only once piece of cake, so one child is going to win (get the piece) and one child is going to lose (not get the piece.)

---

19. *Id.*
20. *Id.* at 137.

But what if you do further fact investigation to determine more accurately each child's *interests* in the cake. You could use narrative probing to understand the character of the cake. What traits does this piece of cake have? Among others, it has *icing* and it has *cake*. You ask each child what his/her *interest* in the cake is. What if it turns out that one child loves icing and one child loves cake? The problem that needs to be solved for closure has now shifted. All of a sudden, we have the makings of an integrative negotiation. By gathering this additional information about the goals of the parties, you are able to "fully satisfy needs of both parties by giving one child the cake and the other the icing."[21]

B. Strategy

Having decided what approach you want to take—based on the considerations we mentioned, and the information-gathering you have done—you need to decide which *Strategy* you want to use during the negotiation. *Strategy* is what is going on in your head—"the conceptual approach ... from planning through implementation, to achieve the underlying goals of the client."[22] Here are two common, opposing, strategies:

1. Adversarial

This is just what it sounds like. If you choose to adopt an *adversarial strategy*, you seek to undermine the other lawyer's confidence in his/her bargaining position by advancing positions to which you appear firmly committed, and restricting information flow between the parties. Further, you bargain along a linear continuum, from your opening offer through your bottom line, which is the point below which you walk away from the table. By the same token, you summarily reject your opponent's offers, and make concessions along the same continuum from your opening offer to your bottom line.

An adversarial negotiator constructs a narrative that seeks to persuade her opponent that the issues at stake should be viewed and analyzed consistent with the legal or other rights framework most favorable to the adversarial negotiator. In the NPO/Landlord negotiation, for example, an adversarial negotiator for the Landlord might frame the rental rate issue as purely a market value question. She might construct a narrative based on prevailing rates in the commercial rental market, under which the Landlord would succeed in

---

21. *Id.* at 137.
22. *Id.*

charging a higher rent per square foot than the NPO wants to have to pay. The adversarial negotiator would resist any attempt to broaden that context to include other considerations, such as the NPO's nonprofit status, or the Landlord's reputation as a charitable business.

2. Problem-Solving

This strategy too is just what it sounds like. Unlike an adversarial negotiator, a problem-solving negotiator tries to persuade the other side to "appreciate their world and to understand how that world relates to that of their opponent."[23]

A problem-solving strategy directs a negotiator to identify the parties' needs and brainstorm with the other side to develop solutions for mutual gains. In a problem-solving negotiation, both sides suggest positions to be discussed, accepted, rejected; neither side appears rigidly attached to any particular position. A problem-solving negotiator facilitates the exchange of data, and rejects or accepts solutions based in whole or in part on a needs analysis of both parties.

Whereas an adversarial negotiator focuses on the bottom line, the problem-solving negotiator focuses on the respective *needs* of the parties. Such a negotiator asks, "what will the client do, or be able to do, if the negotiation fails?"[24] The answer to this question leads to identification of the client's Best Alternative to Negotiated Agreement (BATNA). Rather than a rigid bottom line position, BATNA considers the broader context in which the negotiation—and respective parties' positions—exist.

Depending on that context, a party's BATNA could be taking the matter to court, for determination by a judge or jury. But the BATNA could also be more fact-based alternatives. In our NPO/Landlord situation, what is the NPO's BATNA? Finding another unit to rent, right? And the Landlord's BATNA might be to find another tenant. Consideration of these BATNAs—both your own client's and that of the other side—is essential to the success of the negotiation because now the parties will consider any offer on the table through the lens of whether it is better or worse than their BATNA, as opposed to considering whether the offer is better or worse than their position.

C. Style

Finally, what *style* are you going to adopt in your negotiation? Whereas *strategy* is what is going on in your head, *style* is how you present yourself to the

---

23. *Id.* at 144.
24. HAYDOCK & KNAPP, *supra* note 5, at 186.

other parties to the negotiation: "Style considers the interpersonal behavior of the negotiation and how that behavior affects the negotiation process."[25] Just like with *Approach* and *Strategy*, there are two apparently opposite kinds of *style*: Competitive and Cooperative, and both are what they sound like.

A competitive style of negotiation consists of making high demands, threats, and arguments. A competitive negotiator appears dominating, forceful, attacking, aggressive, and ambitious. A cooperative style of negotiation consists of making reasonable opening and follow-up offers. A cooperative negotiator seeks to find a fair and just solution; she appears trustworthy, honest, courteous, personable, tactful, sincere, perceptive, reasonable, convincing, and self-controlled.

D. How to Decide

How you decide on each of these issues—approach, strategy, style—depends on several factors. First, you must consider the **goals** of your client and those of the opposing party. If getting as much as possible of a limited commodity is the goal, you should consider an adversarial-competitive strategy-style. If a continuing a relationship between the parties is an important goal, you should consider a problem-solving-cooperative strategy-style.[26]

Next, you need to consider the **interests** of your client and the other party. Are the interests shared by the parties or are they independent of each other or are they in conflict? If the parties' interests do not conflict, you might consider using a problem-solving-cooperative strategy-style. If interests do conflict, consider using an adversarial-competitive strategy-style.

You will also need to consider the **resources** available to each side. If client resources are limited, consider a problem-solving-cooperative strategy-style as these negotiations may be less drawn out; if client resources are unlimited, you are better positioned to use an adversarial-competitive strategy-style as this approach may take more time.

V. Exercise

Okay, we have considered the theoretical underpinnings and the various choices that go into planning for and conducting a negotiation. Let's see one in action,

---

25. CHAVKIN, *supra* note 2, at 137.
26. *Id.* at 139.

and try to deconstruct it based on what we have discussed so far. Consider the following clip from the NBC comedy, *30 Rock*, of a negotiation between Jack Donaghy and his nanny, Sherry. https://www.youtube.com/watch?v=a7-eoiY4bOo

As you watch, consider the following:

- What's Jack's position? What's Sherry's position?
- What are Jack's interests? Sherry's interests?
- What approach, strategy and style did Jack use?
- What approach, strategy and style did Sherry use?
- What was Sherry's BATNA?
- What was Jack's BATNA?

Which strategy and style was more successful? Why?

VI. Conclusion

In this chapter, we explored the relationship between narrative and negotiation. To that end, we identified the various goals of a negotiation, and showed how attention to narrative elements and alternative case theories can help the process of identifying and analyzing the positions and interests of all involved in the negotiation. We also examined the steps of informational bargaining, and suggested ways that narrative theory supports the lawyer's goal to make intentional choices about gaining and revealing (or not revealing) important information. Finally, we learned different approaches and strategies to a negotiation and what each approach and strategy entails. In deciding which approach or strategy to use, lawyers should think about their narrative strategy and case or project theory—looking always to client goals to guide the process.

Chapter 10

Oral Advocacy

I. Introduction

By this point in the book, you might have started to think of lawyering as involving three basic tasks: "hearing stories, constructing stories, and telling stories." We have begun the process of identifying and exploring the substantive and technical elements of a story, introducing the ideas of the "what" and the "how" of stories. And we have seen how this theory and practice guide effective lawyers in the planning for and execution of many lawyering skills. In this chapter and the next two we are focusing on advocacy, narrative and storytelling. This chapter focuses on oral advocacy; the next chapter focuses on written advocacy; and the chapter after that focuses on two contexts—appellate advocacy and legislative advocacy—that involve both oral and written advocacy.

Now, let's turn to oral advocacy.[1] In many ways, this is the easiest and most obvious context in which to use storytelling. In this chapter, we will explore courtroom oral advocacy and the general idea of the lawyer as storyteller, and also the specific ways that storytelling and narrative can guide lawyers to be more effective advocates. There are many excellent trial advocacy resources;[2]

---

1. In addition to this chapter, please refer to Chapter Twelve, which focuses on oral advocacy in appellate and legislative advocacy.

2. This chapter is an introduction to oral advocacy. For a deeper dive, refer to the literature by STEVEN LUBET, MODERN TRIAL ADVOCACY: ANALYSIS AND PRACTICE (2009); DAVID FREDERICK, THE ART OF ORAL ADVOCACY (2010); MICHAEL R. FONTHAM & MICHAEL VITIELLO, PERSUASIVE WRITTEN AND ORAL ADVOCACY IN TRIAL AND APPELLATE COURTS (2013); Timothy Baughman, *Effective Appellate Oral Advocacy: "Beauty is Truth, Truth Beauty,"* 77 MICH. B.J. 38 (1998); and Jennifer Kruse Hanrahan, *Truth in Action: Revitalizing Classical Rhetoric as a Tool for Teaching Oral Advocacy in American Law Schools,* 2003 B.Y.U. EDUC. & L.J. 299 (2003).

our goal in this chapter is not to duplicate those—indeed, we commend them to you as guides for how to prepare for and conduct the skills of trial advocacy. Instead, our goal is to extract the principles of narrative theory and storytelling practice from the basic skills of trial advocacy.

II. Audience and Context

While in the chapters on Case Theory and Fact Investigation we focused on the role of lawyers as constructors of narrative, in this chapter, we focus primarily on the "telling" part of a lawyer's role, although the lawyer in consultation with her client remains a constructor of the narrative prior to its telling. As such, we need to explore questions of audience and context. So let's start there with the simple question: who is our audience?

Lawyers often have the opportunity to present their narratives to clients, opposing attorneys, and colleagues. But probably the most common audience for a legal storyteller is decision makers. What do we mean by decision makers? Judge and jury are the most obvious ones, but lawyers also try to persuade hearing officers and boards of directors, legislative bodies and administrative agencies, probation officers and social workers, public opinion and the media.

Each one of these potential decision makers has its own framework for making decisions. Elements of that framework of course include the relevant law, but also involve the decision maker's own values, personal experience, cultural and social influences. The decision maker might also be guided by expectations for them like a desire for efficiency or profit or public support.

In addition to what might influence the decision maker, beyond relevant facts and law, the lawyer has to recognize that each one of these potential or actual decision makers exists within its own particular context. While context is a complex idea, and can include all kinds of intangible layers, context can also be very concrete. As a storyteller in a particular legal context, you need to anticipate very basic things like: where will I be telling this story; who will be there with me; what kind of room will we be in; where will everyone be sitting; will there be a microphone; will there be visual aids; and what kind of timeframe will I have.

But fundamentally, the narrative itself must be a good story! That means it should be:

- Compelling
- Believable
- Comprehensible

- Comprehensive
- Memorable
- Emotionally appealing
- Persuasive

And you—the advocate, the storyteller—need to know who your audience is, what that means about the context, and therefore how to craft and present a compelling and persuasive narrative. So when you prepare to engage in oral advocacy of any kind, you need to consider these four questions:

- Who is our audience—whom are we trying to persuade, of what?
- What is the context—where are we presenting our narrative and why?
- What narrative should we tell in light of these things—what is the substance of our story? and
- How are we going to tell it—what organization, tempo, style, technique will we use?

We explore these questions in the remainder of this chapter.

III. Fundamentals of Oral Advocacy

The context most often imagined for lawyers preparing to engage in oral advocacy is a courtroom or hearing office. Because these are also the more formal contexts in which lawyers engage in oral advocacy, they provide a good framework to explore the skills of questioning witnesses, using exhibits and talking directly to decision makers. Of course, lawyers orally advocate in many less formal contexts, but the principles we develop in this chapter are in fact quite portable and can be used across many kinds of fora and with many kinds of decision makers.

As you may already know, a trial or hearing is an opportunity for a plaintiff or moving party to be heard by a decision maker—a judge or jury, arbitrator or hearing officer—on factual issues arising out of a dispute.[3] Different procedural rules apply depending on the context and decision maker, but basic principles of narrative theory and persuasion practice apply across these contexts. So in this section, we will explore some of these traditional oral advocacy tasks.

---

3. LUBET, *supra* note 2; FREDERICK, *supra* note 2; FONTHAM & VITIELLO, *supra* note 2; Baughman, *supra* note 2; Hanrahan, *supra* note 2.

A. *Talking to Decision Makers*

Whether in a trial's opening statement or a closing argument, opportunities to speak directly to your decision maker are the quintessential moments for an advocate to tell her story and persuade her audience. While the rules and specific goals of each of these activities might be different depending on whether you are arguing to a judge or jury, in an administrative proceeding or federal trial, all oral advocacy requires some basic practices and considerations.

Bottom line: the lawyer must tell a good story—a story that is consistent with her case theory, and that will persuade her decision maker to take action that benefits her client. Remember, the art of persuasion requires the story-teller—the lawyer—to make choices about both the substance and the technical aspects of the narrative and its presentation. Here is a good outline of choices the lawyer must make about both the "what" and the "how" of the narrative:

- What is the basic story and its elements? This includes decisions about:
  □ Characters and traits
  □ Events
  □ Causation
  □ Normalization
  □ Masterplot
  □ Closure

- How is the narrative structured? This might include decisions about:
  □ How to **begin and end** the narrative;
  □ How best to **order** the events within the narrative; and
  □ How best to **arrange the information** around each event.

Now let's look at some specific considerations for each of the opportunities a lawyer might have to present directly to a decision maker:

1. Opening Statement

In an opening statement, your audience expects some kind of introduction of the case, and a roadmap. You might want to focus the decision maker on the key issues of your case. You certainly want to leave the decision maker persuaded that your case theory makes sense. Given those goals, your opening statement should

- Contain a case theory. That is a brief explanation synthesizing the facts, law, and client goals, along with normative theory, for why your audience should take action that benefits your client.

- Highlight your strongest arguments, without making them. You want to choose and order facts to lead your audience to a certain conclusion, rather than state that conclusion.
- Summarize your story.

Take a look at this clip of an opening statement and consider how the attorney describes the evidence she will present to support her case theory. What is her case theory? How did she use her factual narrative to persuade without using argument? Did she veer into actual argument at any point? Notice also how the opening statement highlights and summarizes the prosecution's theory and asks the jury to find that the prosecution's theory is less credible that the defense's theory. What is the prosecution's theory? How did the defense attorney use a factual narrative to undermine the prosecution's theory without using argument? What choices did she make regarding when to begin and end her narrative and how to order the important events? https://www.youtube.com/watch?v=IzU2Zo37tpg/.

2. Closing Argument

Drafting your closing argument is an excellent way to *start* preparing for your trial or administrative hearing. Why? Preparing your closing requires you to put the whole case together—facts, legal theory, case theory. It is your end point so you can work forward in constructing your case. In a closing argument, you build on the opening statement—which introduced the court to your case theory and told the court what the evidence will show—and on all the evidence that comes into the record after. This is the moment of advocacy where you, as the lawyer, get to talk about the law; talk about how the facts fit in with the law; and talk about truth, justice, fairness, and any other big ideas that support your argument.

In your closing, you present your case theory in its complete form. Your closing is your chance to tell your story from beginning to end, with all the facts you have managed to get into evidence. You get to weave together all the strands of fact and argument-driven narratives, the characters, the events, the causation, the normalization, the masterplots, and the closure, that you introduced in your opening, and fleshed out in your direct and cross-examinations and exhibits. And your closing argument, unlike your opening statement, can now contain your explicit legal arguments based on your case theory; it also asks the decision maker to draw inferences from the evidence you've presented (inferential arguments), and to make judgments about witness testimony, or exhibit credibility or lack thereof (credibility arguments). The essence of your closing argument must be a compelling and emotional narrative that seeks to persuade the decision maker to find for your client.

Take a look at the following clips from the TV show, *Picket Fences*.[4] The plot of this particular episode involves a murder trial. The defendant is a doctor who is accused of murdering her patient. The undisputed facts are that after consultation with the patient and his family, the doctor administered a lethal dose of morphine to the patient, who was dying of cancer. Following the patient's death, the doctor told investigators (one of whom is the doctor's husband—because this is television!) that the patient had died of cancer.

You will see first a direct examination, then a cross-examination, and then the two closing arguments. As you watch, think about the different stories being told—one by the prosecution and one by the defense.

- What is each attorney's case theory?
- What facts does each attorney rely on as part of that case theory?
- What choices has each attorney made about characters, events, causation, masterplot, normalization and closure (the "what" of his narrative)?
- What choices has each attorney made about pace, tempo, beginning and ending, ordering of events, and arrangement of information within the events (the "how" of his narrative)?
- What kinds of arguments does each attorney make—factual, legal, inferential, credibility, emotional, political, moral?

B. Questioning Witnesses

Speaking directly to decision makers—whether in opening and closing arguments, or as an appellate advocate—frames the work of an oral advocate. Opening statements and closing arguments, for example, are the bookends of a trial. Between those bookends are the substance of the trial itself—the evidence, usually in the form of witness testimony and exhibits.

There are rules to storytelling through witness examination that makes it harder technically than simply making choices and constructing and telling a persuasive story. You cannot present the narrative yourself, you have to rely on your witness(es). That means there is not one narrator, and the story is not told in one piece. Rather, each direct examination represents one piece of the puzzle, not the whole puzzle. A big part of the lawyer's job, then, in addition to conducting the actual examinations, is to make choices about those "how"

---

4. Picket Fences, Season 3, Ep. 18 (28:36–35:42) (CBS 1992–1996), https://www.youtube.com/watch?v=46dnTxwu1f0.

questions of the overall trial narrative. Which witness should present his piece of the puzzle first? Which witness should have the last word? How should the presentation of evidence be ordered? Sometimes, these decisions are out of the lawyer's complete control—witness availability, decision maker preference, etc. But to the extent that you do have a choice about how to order your examinations and presentation of evidence, it is important to make that choice with an eye toward your overall narrative.

On top of that, every individual narrative piece of the puzzle is elicited, rather than told, through a conversation with your witness. And it is a one-way conversation, in that you are asking questions, and the witnesses are giving answers. The key to all of this is to make choices not only about the "how" of the witness' narrative, but also about the story's narrative elements: characters, events, causation, normalization, masterplot and closure.

1. Direct Examination

In 1958 in North Carolina, an African-American man, Elmer Davis, confessed to the rape and murder of a white woman.[5] He was convicted and sentenced to death. His defense attorney had tried to keep the confession out of evidence on the grounds that it was coerced, and appealed the conviction all the way to the Supreme Court.[6]

Let's imagine what might have happened at the suppression hearing on the question of whether the confession should be excluded. Here is a hypothetical transcript—based on language from the actual Supreme Court opinion—of a direct examination of the police lieutenant who had overseen the pre-trial detention of Mr. Davis:

> **Prosecutor:** Lieutenant, who was in charge of overseeing the interrogation of Mr. Davis?
>
> **Witness:** I was.
>
> **Prosecutor:** Is there a Department protocol for interrogation of prisoners?

---

5. This exercise was developed by Carolyn Grose in collaboration initially with Binny Miller from WCL, American University, and ultimately with Peter Knapp at Mitchell Hamline School of Law and is based on Kim Lane Scheppele, *Foreward: Telling Stories*, 87 Mich. L. Rev. 2073, 2086–2097 (1989) (describing two cases that ended up in the U.S. Supreme Court, one involving the rape of a woman, the other involving the allegedly coerced confession of a black man. Scheppele contrasts the appellate court decisions in both cases with the Supreme Court opinions, illustrating points about language and framing as important tools of persuasive storytelling).

6. Davis v. North Carolina, 384 U.S. 737 (1966).

Witness: Yes.

Prosecutor: Please describe that protocol to the judge.

Witness: We limit interrogations to twice daily, once in the morning and once later in the day.

Prosecutor: What procedure did you follow for the interrogation of Mr. Davis?

Witness: We followed that Departmental protocol. I typically interrogated Mr. Davis in the morning, and another officer questioned him later in the day.

Prosecutor: Did that procedure vary?

Witness: No, we followed that procedure the entire time Mr. Davis was in custody, up until the time he confessed.

Based on the facts elicited by this questioning, we can identify the prosecutor's case theory as being that the confession was not coerced, supported by the facts that there was a policy against around-the-clock questioning and that the policy was followed. We might even be persuaded by this narrative. For the moment.

Now here is another hypothetical direct examination at the same hypothetical suppression hearing, but this time conducted by the defense attorney, with the defendant as the witness.

Defense Attorney: Mr. Davis, how long were you in jail before you gave the statement to the police?

Defendant: Sixteen days.

Defense Attorney: Please describe the cell where you were being held.

Defendant: It was a small cell in the back of the jail, with a bed and a chair. There was a little window out into the jail yard.

Defense Attorney: Was there a clock in the cell?

Defendant: No.

Defense Attorney: Did you have a wristwatch?

Defendant: No, they took my watch away from me when they put me in jail.

Defense Attorney: During that sixteen days, how often did the police question you?

Defendant: Pretty much all the time.

Defense Attorney: When you say "pretty much all the time," what do you mean?

Defendant: After I woke up in the morning, one of them would come in and start asking me questions. That would go on all morning and then he'd leave. Then after a while another one would come in and start up all over again.

Defense Attorney: Was it light out while you were being questioned?

Defendant: Sometimes it was.

Defense Attorney: And was it ever dark out while you were being questioned?

Defendant: Sure it was.

Defense Attorney: How long did that kind of questioning go on?

Defendant: Every single day until they got me to sign this statement.

Now what is the case theory, based on what facts? This time, the theory is that the confession was coerced because the defendant felt that he was being subjected to constant interrogation. The facts that support that theory are that he did not know what time it was and that he was questioned while it was light and while it was dark.

The point of these two hypothetical direct examinations is that the facts in both narratives are "true"—there was a protocol observed during the interrogations (twice a day, between 7:30 a.m. and 11:30 p.m.), and the officers in this case followed that protocol; and the defendant's only sense of time was based on the changing light outside his window, and he was questioned while it was light and while it was dark. The prosecutor can therefore argue that the interrogation was "repeated" or "sporadic," and not coerced; therefore, it should be admitted into evidence in the trial. The defense, however, can argue that the interrogation was "constant" and therefore created a kind of duress that resulted in the defendant's confession. Thus coerced, the confession should be suppressed.

Because all the "facts" are "true," the attorneys for both parties have had to make choices about what facts to select to persuade the decision maker that the attorney's particular story is the one to be believed and thus adopted by the court. The exercise demonstrates the lesson we learned way back in Chapter Two, that the "true story"—"what really happened"—is not something objective and static, waiting to be "found" by a good investigative lawyer. On the contrary, "what really happened" is determined by the decision maker's adoption of one or the other of the stories the lawyers have offered. And those stories are, in turn, constructed by the lawyer in consultation with her client with the goal of persuading the decision maker. The law is made by the choices the lawyers make.

This case can also help us identify decisions lawyers must make about when to start their narratives. Let's imagine that we have moved forward in time a bit and are now at the trial. Let's say the judge at the suppression hearing allowed the confession to come in. The same police officer is about to take the stand. When and where should the prosecutor begin the direct examination? How, in other words, should the prosecutor frame the story this witness can tell? As the prosecutor, you probably want to begin with a description of the murder Mr. Davis is alleged to have committed and his subsequent arrest, and the examination should end with his confession. You want to draw a very tight frame around the narrative this witness will tell, and, indeed, the narrative the prosecution tells at this trial is itself a very tightly framed narrative: Davis did this horrible thing. How do we know? Because he told us.

Now let's imagine how Mr. Davis' defense attorney might begin his direct examination of Mr. Davis:

> **Defense Counsel:** Mr. Davis, where did you grow up?
> **Defendant:** Here in Alabama in Jefferson, just five miles from here.
> **Defense Counsel:** Do you remember the first time a policeman ever talked with you?
> **Defendant:** Yes.
> **Defense Counsel:** Tell the jury about that, please.
> **Prosecutor:** Objection, relevance?

Now it is up to the defense attorney to make an argument to the court about why this line of questioning will lead to relevant information. What is the defense attorney's case theory, and how does the defendant's story on direct fit into that case theory? The case theory continues to be that the defendant's confession was coerced (even if the jury doesn't buy this argument, the defense attorney is laying the groundwork here for appealing the judge's ruling at the suppression hearing).

So how is the defendant's first contact with the police relevant? It doesn't take long to get there if we consider the time and place and context in which this narrative unfolds: the narrative of the defendant as a poor black kid in the south at the dawn of the civil rights movement, a young man who is afraid of the police due to frequent and intimidating questioning, provides context and support for the case theory. The background narrative helps the decision maker make the leap to coercion and duress. Again, the lawyer has made choices about how to frame and structure the narrative he is telling to persuade the decision maker to adopt his particular narrative and thus make law that takes that narrative into account.

Experimenting with choices about how to use particular facts, how to frame the examination, what language to use, and what evidence to highlight leads us to recognize that the practice of direct examination is nothing more or less than the practice of telling a persuasive narrative. It is a practice that takes place in a particularized (and often stilted) way, yes, but one that requires intentional and consistent choices to construct a persuasive and compelling narrative for the decision maker. Direct examination, in other words, is not just about asking non-leading questions.

2. Cross-Examination

Now let's look at the other kind of witness-questioning: cross-examining a witness who has already testified in order to check or discredit the witness's testimony, knowledge, or credibility. Cross-examination might not seem like a particularly narrative-based skill, but it is! Like everything else a lawyer does, cross-examination emanates from and leads back to case theory. Aside from asking short, fact-based, leading questions, cross-examination is about making intentional choices about how to use your opponent's facts to help your case.

Effective cross-examination relies on your understanding of your own narrative and the facts it depends on, as well as your opponent's narrative and the facts it depends on. A lawyer's ability to use facts to support her own case, as well as to undermine her opponent's, requires breaking a witness's narrative down into its narrative elements—character, traits, events, setting, causation, normalization, masterplots, and closure—in order to identify inconsistencies or points of confusion. That way, when we question the witness based on those inconsistencies or points of confusion, we do so based on the individual facts of his narrative, rather than based on our own gap-filling or assumptions.[7]

Supportive cross-examination is about using the other side's witnesses to help us tell the decision maker our explanation is the right one. With supportive cross, the advocate is saying "The witness's version of events may be right— but it fits into my narrative better than opposing party's." **Discrediting** cross-examination is about using facts we've found to help tell the decision maker the other side's witnesses don't fit their explanation. With discrediting cross the message is: "The witness's version of events has less probative value than you might have thought." We do this through impeachment.

What do we mean by impeachment? The Federal Rules of Evidence have a whole section on proper impeachment grounds and techniques.[8] And for trials, you will want to tailor your direct and cross-examination to follow those rules. But impeachment has a simpler meaning as well: we often suspect that a witness is not telling the truth. This is nothing fancier than the testimony that makes up his story does not make sense with what we know about the world. Impeachment means that we use what we know about the real world—knowledge gained through constructing our own narrative based on the facts that we have

---

7. *See* Ruth Anne Robbins, et al., Your Client's Story: Persuasive Legal Writing 130–31 (2013) on how to "show not tell" your audience that a witness is not credible or compelling. *See also* Scribendi, *Ten Tips to Help You Avoid Telling Writing*, https://www.scribendi.com/advice/how_to_avoid_telling_writing_in_fiction.en.html.

8. Fed. R. Evid. 607, 608 and 609.

found out there, and anticipating the other side's narrative based on facts we have found out there—to hold the witness accountable for the narrative not matching up, making sense.

Holding accountable means simply that we want the audience—the fact finder—to conclude that because the narrative doesn't match up, this witness's narrative shouldn't be considered a meaningful piece of the other side's puzzle. So to impeach effectively, we need to understand why the narrative doesn't match up.[9]

The great trial lawyer and professor, Michael Tigar, describes four areas of impeachment of the *witness* himself, and four areas of impeachment of the witness's *testimony*. He suggests you can impeach the witness by holding him accountable for the *meaning* of his words—suggesting that he used words that conveyed one impression but which he actually meant in a different sense. You can hold the witness accountable for his *perception*— could he really have seen what he says he saw? You can impeach him based on his *memory*—could he really have a reason or capacity to remember what he says he remembers? And finally, you can hold him accountable for his *veracity* or lack thereof—does he have a reason *not* to be truthful (this is also called bias)?

As for the credibility of *testimony*, this ground for impeachment is similar to normalization from narrative theory: is the witness's narrative consistent with common experience? Is it internally consistent? And is it consistent with other facts established in the matter?[10]

Thus, discrediting cross need not be aimed at proving that a witness is a "total liar" or "completely wrong." The aim may be to show that the witness's narrative is less trustworthy than it first seemed because:

- He said something different before; or
- He behaved in a way that is inconsistent with what we know about him as a person; and/or
- He behaved in a way that is inconsistent with what we know about the world.

Consider this example from the classic movie *My Cousin Vinny*.[11] Here, Vinny Gambino (the defense attorney played by Joe Pesci) undermines the credibility of an alleged eye witness's timeline of the events at issue in a South-

---

9. MICHAEL TIGAR, EXAMINING WITNESSES (1993).

10. *Id.*

11. My Cousin Vinny (1:20:00–1:24:10) (20th Century Fox 1992), https://www.you tube.com/watch?v=h9AqbDtSFNU.

ern criminal trial. Vinny does so by asking questions about the length of time the witness cooked his grits. Using information Vinny had gained by doing some fact-investigation about grits-making, Vinny called into question the witness's whole testimony. Vinny did not seek to make the witness out to be a liar; rather, Vinny just used the Southern cultural information shared by the jurors to had to hold the witness accountable for an inconsistency in his testimony. As you watch the clip, ask yourself:

- What specific facts does Vinny use to impeach or undermine the witness's story?
- Is this cross-examination supportive or discrediting?
- What does Vinny's case theory seem to be?

3. Exhibits

So far in all of these examples and analyses, we have been focusing on using words in specific and particular ways to persuade our audience. What about other tools we might use? Chances are, if you are engaging in a cross or direct examination, you will have the opportunity to at least consider using exhibits. As trial lawyers, we represent a client seeking resolution to a trouble that has disrupted their steady state. We go out in the world and bring back tangible items and narratives from people to prove our case. Most of what we bring back are words, but if we are lucky, we also find tangible residue of the events or other elements of our narrative. Because narratives are more compelling when paired with meaningful pictures, to the extent possible, we try to use those tangible items to illustrate our narrative.

We use exhibits for proof and illustration. As with the questions you ask and the answers you seek, you have choices about what exhibits to use, when to use them, and why. And just as with your choices about words, your choices about exhibits must be made consistent with your case theory, your audience and your context.

Watch another clip from later in the same trial in *My Cousin Vinny* (1:24.29–1:26.37; https://www.youtube.com/watch?v=5gr3jopJmVg) and notice how Vinny uses the photographs to undermine the witness's story about what he had perceived. The questions themselves do not require photographic evidence—the witness could have just testified that he had screens on his windows and trees and bushes in his yard. But notice how two dimensional that recitation of the facts is. That is the "story" of this witness's view from his house. What is the "narrative" of the view from his house? What characters does Vinny evoke in his use of the photographs? What event does he describe? What is the causation, masterplot, normalization emerging from these photographs? And what is the closure? How do the photographic exhibits themselves make the *story* of the witness's view into a *narrative*?

IV. Conclusion

In this chapter, narrative focuses our attention even more closely on audience and context. We explored how the nature of the audience impacts the characteristics of the narrative by forcing the lawyer to make intentional choices about the "what" and "how" of her narrative—whether in direct examination, cross-examination, opening statements or closing arguments. We also suggested that drafting the closing argument FIRST is the best way to prepare for a trial or a hearing because it provides a goal for the attorney to work toward. Once you've drafted your closing argument—with its complete and fleshed-out statement of your case theory—it becomes clear what facts should be included in the opening statement, and what evidence needs to come in on direct and cross-examination. Using the closing argument as a planning tool also helps the lawyer determine how to frame the questions that will elicit the desired response, and when exhibits will help to make the testimonial narrative more compelling and persuasive.

Chapter 11

Written Advocacy

I. Introduction

As we have seen, lawyers are particular kinds of storytellers, influenced by variables unique to their role as tellers of their clients' stories. In that role, as makers of legal arguments, we decide what narrative to tell and how to tell it "guided by some vision of *what matters*."[1] Put another way, in order to figure out what narrative to tell and how to tell it, the lawyer must weigh three substantive factors, the same factors that make up the case theory: the law, the facts and the client's goals.[2] In addition, of course, the lawyer must consider contextual factors, e.g., the audience, the forum, availability of resources, personality of the client, and potential supporting or detracting characters in the narrative. The lawyer must also take into consideration particular cultural norms and values in deciding among different narratives and ways of telling them. Up until now, we have examined narrative and story primarily in the context of oral or verbal communication. But, not surprisingly, these concepts and elements help lawyers practice written advocacy as well.

Narrative theory and storytelling practice works for almost all legal drafting/writing a lawyer does—from appellate briefs to client emails, with all kinds of instruments in between. The connective tissue is that of persuasion: from arguing to a jury to negotiating a contract to filing a form for tax exempt status to drafting a will, lawyers seek to persuade others to act in a way that benefits their clients. What is essential for us as lawyers to understand, therefore, is how to persuade. We have seen throughout this book that a very

---

1. Anthony G. Amsterdam & Jerome Bruner, Minding the Law (2002).
2. *See* Chapter Six.

effective method to learn and practice persuasion is to explore and understand narrative theory and storytelling practice.

Persuasion is all about audience and goals. With each piece of writing you do as a lawyer, you are trying to persuade whoever is reading the document to do something. How you write your narrative, and what narrative you write, is therefore, guided by/dependent on who that person in your audience is, and what it is you are trying to persuade them to do. As with oral advocacy, our goal here is not to take a deep dive into written advocacy but rather to give you some examples of how narrative and story works in written advocacy. Let's go through some kinds of persuasive legal writing you will likely have to do as a lawyer: client letters and transactional documents. You will see as we explore each one of these examples that the same basic narrative principles apply when drafting each one: think about your goal (or your client's goal); think about your audience; and identify the substance and technique (what and how) of your story most likely to persuade. You can use these principles in other written advocacy as well, such as motions.[3] Let's take a look.

II. Client Letters

This might seem like a strange place to start talking about written narrative and persuasion. But in fact, lawyers probably write more client letters than they do any other kind of writing. So it makes sense to think about this very common form of legal writing as an opportunity for persuasion. It requires persuasion of some kind, directed to some audience. Thus the narrative idea helps the lawyer deconstruct and reconstruct the particular task consistent with its goal of persuading; in addition, it helps you see your role as constructor of the narrative that must persuade, and helps you see the choices you have, and how to make those choices intentionally, so as to meet the goal of persuading.

Let's start with a closing letter or email to your client: who is your audience and what are you trying to persuade him/them to do? Your audience here—as with many communications—is manifold. Your client certainly will read this letter, as will perhaps members of his family or community. What are you trying to persuade your client to do? In some cases, if he is a paying client, you are seeking to persuade him to pay any outstanding bill for your services. But are there other goals you may have for this particular audience—whether he

---

3. *See* Chapter Twelve for more on written advocacy in the context of appellate and legislative advocacy.

is a paying client or not? The steady state of your narrative is the lawyer-client relationship; the disruption to that steady state is that the representation is coming to an end. What closure are you and/or the client seeking? You want your client to feel satisfied with your work. You may want him to say good things about your work to members of his community. You also want to consider your client's needs at this point in the representation: you want to communicate clearly that this is the end of the relationship, and here is the work you and the client have done together. So, the letter might need to be persuasive for the lawyer's interests but also communicative for the client's interests.

So how are you going to design your letter, both substantively and visually, to achieve all of these goals? What characters are you going to highlight, with what traits? What events are you going to describe, with what causal connection? What kind of normalization are you fighting against—that you did not accomplish what the client wanted; that your fees are too high; that the whole relationship was a waste of time? Same question for masterplots—the lawyer as "hired gun," unethical, untrustworthy. These are some of the choices you'll need to make when considering your client as your audience, and when considering members of his network as your audience.

But aren't there other audiences as well? How about your senior partner or supervisor? Certainly they will look at your closing letter and accompanying bill or time sheets to see the work you've been doing and how much you are making for the firm, or accomplishing for the company. Of what do you want to persuade this audience? That you are working hard, and an asset to the firm, right? So you'll need to make choices about how to design your closing letter, both substantively and visually, to persuade these audiences as well.

And finally, a decision-making body—such as an administrative law judge, or a bar committee, or the IRS—might look at your letter and final bill or timesheets. Why? What are these audiences looking for? Maybe your firm is involved in a case seeking attorney's fees; or maybe your company is being audited by the IRS; or maybe your fees are being challenged by your client! How are you going to prepare your final client documents—again, both substantively and visually—to achieve your goal of persuading these third-party audiences that you are fair and responsible and accountable for the fees and time you charge?

Obviously, this is a lot to think about for one lousy closing letter and accompanying bill or time sheets. But the more you do ahead of time, the less likely you are to have to confront the challenges that might arise, from any one of these potential audiences. Thinking about the narrative you want to construct for and the story you want each of the folks who will read your client bill to extract as you write goes a long way.

III. Transactional Documents

Let's move to another kind of document: the dreaded legal form document. With the ready availability of all kinds of legal documents on the internet, you might wonder why lawyers need to be involved at all in drafting documents like wills, health care directives, residential leases, articles of incorporation, or applications for federal tax exempt status. The answer is simple: we know how to create these documents in such a way as to persuade whoever reads them to do what the documents ask. Those blank forms available to anyone who has access to the internet are generic narratives designed to apply generally to, let's say, distribution of estate assets. As lawyers, we understand that unlike that blank form on the internet, a will is actually an important tool of advocacy, seeking to persuade some kind of decision maker to act on someone's behalf.

Remember how the chapter started, with reminders to consider your audience, and the context in which a particular legal document will be read. Let's take the documents listed above—wills, health care directives, residential leases, articles of incorporation, or applications for federal tax exempt status. Where will these various documents be read, by whom, and for what purpose. What, in other words, does this document need to persuade someone to do, and who is that someone?

Thus, we imagine bank officers reading powers of attorney and having to decide whether or not to release funds to a particular individual; we imagine health care directives being read by doctors in faraway hospitals, agonizing over the kind of treatment to provide to a comatose patient; we imagine a commercial lease being read by the parties at some point in the future to decide how to resolve a dispute; we imagine IRS agents in cramped offices laboring through stacks of tax documents, wondering whether a particular non-profit organization was connected enough to some public purpose to grant its application for tax exempt status.

Law students and lawyers can generate these scenarios based on what they have come to learn about their clients' lives, the relevant law, and how the world works. Based on this knowledge, they can imagine what narrative they might need to tell, and how they might need to tell it in order to persuade these particular decision makers to act.

Ask yourself how the goals of the particular clients these documents are for inform your drafting choices. This brings your focus back from some future scenario with characters, events, a setting, and a problem seeking closure that we don't yet know, but can imagine, to the here and now of this particular client and his needs and personality, his present problem that may be disrupting his steady state, and his lived present reality.

For example, what if you represented a woman who felt like she had control over very little in her life. She is a homebound elder with diminishing memory and increasing paranoia—that is her steady state. There are various characters in her narrative—an estranged daughter who lives down the road, a daughter who lives far away but with whom she is close, a whole team of social workers she hates, a doctor she trusts completely but to whom she has almost no access. The problem disrupting her steady state is her anxiety about getting her affairs in order. Over several interviews and counseling sessions, you have come to understand that the closure she seeks is for you to create an estate plan and health care directive that anticipates and resolves every possible scenario she and you can imagine.

As her lawyer, you will want to develop a project theory that incorporates the relevant law governing these documents, the important facts of the client's situation, and the client's goals. You know what is required to draft a legally sufficient health care directive—you can actually use a standard form on the internet as a guideline for that! And you know the various characters and events that are important in the client's life. You understand that the client wants to get her affairs in order, but also—and this is perhaps the more important goal— that she wants to feel that she has some control over something in her life.

You will want to draft documents, therefore, that anticipate the normalization your audience—including the client's family and caregivers—might do: she's an old paranoid control freak who doesn't really know what she wants, just wants to control things after she's gone. The health care directive you draft might be significantly longer and more detailed than might be necessary in order to persuade some future doctor to act, but it tells a story on behalf of this client that she feels adequately represents her future needs and wishes. Thus, you, as the lawyer are able to connect drafting these documents with project theory, recognizing that the facts and client goals drive the construction of the narrative document much more than the simple legally sufficient narrative present in the basic health care directive form. You therefore create a more persuasive document, more likely to meet the client's current and future needs.

Both audience and client goals inform the choices lawyers make about what story to tell and how to tell it. By imagining these characters and settings and plots, you move from seeing your jobs in drafting these forms as simply checking boxes and filling in blanks, to constructing stories that accurately reflect your client's goals, and that would be likely to persuade some future decision maker to act in a way that is consistent with those goals.

It is important to recognize that by imagining these future scenarios, lawyers are engaging in gap-filling. As we have seen throughout the book, we all do this, all the time. The key is to do it intentionally, and consistent with your client's goals. When done this way, gap-filling is not only acceptable, but ultimately necessary in order to render a story (in the form of a form) that will persuade some future decision maker.

Inevitably some lawyers do simply download the statutory forms and fill them out with their clients' names and other relevant information. In the face of the critique that these forms don't really tell their clients' story, these lawyers might fall back on the defense that the form has fulfilled the statutory requirement and therefore should be valid. And here is where the difference between legally valid and legally effective lies:

Imagine the scenario in the future when this form needs to be used. Let's say it's a health care directive and the doctor is refusing the treatment that the incapacitated client wants. Of course, someone can take the doctor to court and get an emergency court order, but what happens in the meantime? What if it is a life and death situation? How has the client been served by this health care directive that arguably meets the statutory requirements, but doesn't ultimately persuade the future decision maker?

By having the law define the narrative, you might miss the point of the story you should be telling. As we have seen, legal elements are only one set of elements that make up the narratives lawyers hear, construct and tell. This realization gives lawyers a great deal of power, as you learn to wrestle with the law to have it fit in to your clients' lived realities, rather than funneling your clients' lived realities into what you understand the law to require.

IV. Conclusion

In this chapter, we continue our exploration of audience and context, this time when engaging in written advocacy. Each document we draft as a lawyer has an element of persuasion—even those dreaded legal forms. Thus, narrative is an essential tool for this legal skill. Lawyers have to consider the multiple potential audiences for each document and make intentional choices about both the "what" and "how" of the narrative the document presents. Focusing on the narrative elements of each document—in light of those multiple potential audiences—helps the lawyer create persuasive and effective documents.

Chapter 12

Appellate and Legislative Advocacy

I. Introduction

In this section, we explore two types of legal persuasion that require both oral and written advocacy: appellate advocacy and legislative advocacy. As with the other chapters, we aim in this one to show ways that narrative and storytelling help lawyers perform these basic tasks more effectively.

II. Appellate Advocacy

There are few more iconic images of the lawyer as advocate than that of a lone individual standing behind a podium, looking up at three or more berobed jurists who sit behind a judicial bench. This is appellate advocacy. Or at least the second half of appellate advocacy—the first half is the appellate brief.

Taken together, the appellate brief and the appellate argument cap off a lawyer-client relationship that may have started with an initial client interview and travelled through fact investigation, pre-trial proceedings, negotiations, attempts at settlement, motions to dismiss, more attempts at settlement, a trial, and finally, a notice to appeal. Briefs were prepared, trial record gathered, arguments mooted, until there you are: behind a podium, looking up at your appellate panel, stating your appellate case for the final time. Just as narrative theory and storytelling practice comprised part of the lawyer-client relationship through all the previous steps in this journey, so too, does it help you now. We examine how in this chapter.

A. *Appellate Brief*

As you know, a brief is a persuasive document designed to support an appeal, or a motion, to a decision maker. More than any of the written instruments we have discussed so far, briefs are formal legal documents with very clear formatting and submission rules. Indeed, you have all drafted briefs in some form or another. You know that an appellate brief contains multiple sections, depending, in part, on the forum and court you are practicing in. Most briefs include a table of contents, statement of the case, question presented, summary of argument, statement of facts, argument (including point headings and sub-headings), conclusion and table of authorities. Remember that every one of these parts — including the table of contents — is an opportunity to persuade, one that you would be careless to ignore. The argument section and statement of facts are the most obvious places to use narrative in your brief, but the same principles of persuasion and advocacy apply to the other sections of your brief as well. As you work through your brief, therefore, you want to ask yourself at each section, "can narrative help me here?" And chances are, if the section is one designed to persuade, the answer is "yes."

You know about IRAC or CREAC or TRACC or whichever collection of letters your law school's first year research and writing course uses.[1] And you know that whatever letters guide you, let's take IRAC for instance, the basic idea of your brief is to explain how a legal rule (R) applies (A) to the particular facts of your case in such a way as to lead the appellate decision maker to conclude (C) that your client should prevail on the issue (I) at hand. All of those letters are ways to organize, sequence, and support what amounts to a statement of your case theory regarding each point at issue in the appeal. Take a look at this opening paragraph in a plaintiff's brief's argument section:

TEXT

Defendant's pet fee violates Massachusetts law because a pet fee is not included among the permissible fees in Section 15B(1)(b).

Section 15B(1)(b) includes four permissible fees "at or prior to the commencement" of a tenancy: (1) the first month's rent; (2) the last

---

1. STEFAN H. KRIEGER & RICHARD K. NEUMANN JR., ESSENTIAL LAWYERING SKILLS: INTERVIEWING, COUNSELING, NEGOTIATION, AND PERSUASIVE FACT ANALYSIS (2011).

month's rent; (3) a security deposit; and (4) a lock-change fee. *See* Statute.

To interpret statutes such as Section 15B(1)(b), Massachusetts courts employ the canon of construction *expressio unius est exclusio alterius. See, e.g., Jack v. Jill*, 123 N.E.2d 4, 6 (Mass. 2000). This canon simply means that items that are not included on a list are excluded from the list. Id. at 6.

The pet fee charged by Defendant is not included on the list of permissible fees under Section 15B(1)(b) and is therefore excluded.

As such, Defendant's pet fee is impermissible under Massachusetts law, and summary judgment is warranted.

Based on this paragraph, can you map plaintiff's IRAC? Can you identify his case theory? What law does he rely on to make his argument? What facts? How does that law apply to the facts of his case? To what end? What does the paragraph seem to be asking the decision maker to do, on what grounds? That is the basic structure of legal analysis: the appellant's legal concern as framed and described by the relevant law. Your brief must contain this level of analysis to be minimally legally sufficient.

But you want your brief to be more than just minimally legally sufficient. You want your brief to persuade the decision maker to act on your client's behalf. So go deeper into the question of whether this paragraph is persuasive: What characters are involved in this paragraph? What are their traits? What events drive the narrative forward, with what causation? What attempts at normalization is the narrative fighting against or adopting? Any masterplots? And finally, what closure does the paragraph demand? Does it demand that closure effectively? If so, how; if not, why not?

When you write your own brief, you might start with the first level of analysis—making sure that your paragraphs follow some Issue-Rule-Application-Conclusion structure. But in order to make it persuasive, you need to make sure you have made choices about each of the narrative elements of each part of your narrative. That is how you can use narrative theory and story to strengthen your very formal, and often formulaic argument to the Court about why your client should prevail.

While the universe of legal rules available to this plaintiff's lawyer is limited by the facts of his case, the lawyer made choices about what statute to rely on, and, more important, what portions of the statute to highlight. The same can be said about the facts the lawyer chose to use in explaining why that law should lead the decision maker to the conclusion that the defendant's actions violated the law. A lawyer must make those choices consistent with the universe of fact and law available to her, yes, but also consistent with the narrative elements we have been exploring throughout this book: what characters, events, causation, normalization, masterplot and closure are implicated by the situation under appeal; and how can the lawyer construct a narrative using those elements in the most persuasive and compelling way?

When a lawyer drafts a statement of facts, for example, she does not simply record the known universe of "relevant" facts in an interesting and persuasive way. Indeed, there is no such thing as an absolutely neutral description of the facts.[2] As lawyers, we engage in fact-gathering repeatedly—at initial client interviews, after we've done some legal research, in anticipation of the other side's argument—and then we "pick and choose from available facts to present a picture of what happened"[3] that most accurately reflects our sense of what matters.[4] And the other lawyers involved do exactly the same thing, with exactly the same pool of facts, but emphasizing different details, drawing different inferences, resulting in quite a different picture.[5]

And this goes for the "how" too. The law might define what is relevant (and we say "might" deliberately), but it cannot define "how the relevant facts, in a particular case, are to be expressed."[6] It is up to the lawyer to figure out what words to use, with what emphasis. A lawyer's statement of facts thus "reflects— by its inclusions and exclusions, the emphasis of its sentence construction, and the structures of its argumentation—choices."[7]

As we saw in the earlier chapters on oral and written advocacy, lawyers make choices about the other technical elements of a story as well: when the story should begin and when it should end, how quickly or slowly the action should move, or how fleshed out each character should be. Those choices, too, must be made with attention to the narrative elements of the story, and consistent with the case theory.

---

2. David Luban, *Paternalism and the Legal Profession*, 1981 Wis. L. Rev. 454, 463 (1981); *see also* Kim Lane Scheppele, *Foreword: Telling Stories*, 87 Mich. L. Rev. 2073, 2075 (1989).

3. Richard Delgado, *On Telling Stories in School: A Reply to Farber and Sherry*, 46 Vand. L. Rev. 665, 667 (1993).

4. This is true regardless of the forum or kind of matter—litigation, planning, transactional, mediation, negotiation, etc.

5. Delgado, *supra* note 3.

6. Bernard Jackson, *Narrative Theories and Legal Discourse* in Narrative in Culture: The Uses of Storytelling in the Sciences, Philosophy, and Literature 27 (1994).

7. *Id.*

B. *Appellate Oral Argument*

Like its written counterpart, the brief, appellate oral argument is the most formal kind of oral advocacy. Oral arguments take place after a trial or hearing in order to argue for or against a lower court decision. Leading up to the argument, you have prepared various documents, all designed to persuade your audience to reverse or sustain a lower court decision. The oral argument is your final attempt to persuade that audience. It is literally your last word on the matter.

Let's consider the fundamental questions of oral advocacy we examined in Chapter Ten: who is your audience, what is your context, what story will you tell, and how will you tell it?

In an appellate oral argument, your audience is a panel of or one individual appellate judge(s), sitting behind a desk or judicial bench. You will probably stand behind a podium, or at counsel table. You may not interact with anyone in the courtroom or hearing office other than the judge or judges hearing your case. There are no witnesses. If you are the appellant, you will present your argument first; the appellee (respondent) presents her argument second. The appellant can reserve time for rebuttal following the appellee's argument. It is generally a good idea to do this, so you are sure to get the last word, if you are the one who brought the appeal.

So that's your audience and the physical context of the argument. What is the narrative context of the argument? If you are the appellant, you are claiming that something a decision maker did in a proceeding below was wrong. As the appellee, you are arguing the opposite: that what the decision maker did in the proceeding below was correct. You are trying to persuade, in both cases, that the decision maker in this appeal should take action that benefits your client— either by reversing the earlier decision, or by upholding the earlier decision. What are the narrative elements of this claim? The characters might be the same as those in the underlying action, but would also include the personnel at the earlier trial—the opposing counsel, any witnesses involved, and of course the decision maker herself, i.e., the judge who made the alleged mistake. The events too might include some of the same as those described in the trial, but will also include the trial itself—what happened that you claim caused the problem? And what closure are you seeking—reversal, remand, new trial?

As with all persuasion, your oral argument is built around your case theory. This is different from—though related to—whatever case theory you had at the proceeding below. You need to identify and synthesize the relevant facts for the appeal, which will most certainly include the action that the decision maker below took, and the context in which she took it; the relevant and important law for the appeal, which will include the applicable standard of review, as well as the law governing the underlying action itself; and your client's goal for the appeal, which will be either to uphold or to reverse the earlier decision maker's action. Moreover, you want to include normative theory, not only client-centeredness, but also why is it just, moral, or fair for your client to win.

You will have done all of these things already in your appellate brief. So what is important to do with your limited minutes of oral advocacy? What story do you want to tell, and how do you want to tell it? Oral argument is an opportunity to do three distinct things:

1. Crystallize issues raised in your brief.

This is a unique opportunity in time. You have covered the critical issues in your brief and the other side has staked out its position. In your oral argument, you want to focus the decision maker on one or two things you want him/her/them to do.

2. Answer questions from the decision maker.

While you might be tempted to say "Please don't interrupt me while I'm trying to work,"[8] in fact, you are being given insight into your decision maker's thought process and concerns. What a gift!

3. Appeal to your audience's sense of justice, fairness, morality.

Judges are constrained by the law (some courts less than others, some judges less than others) but will strive to do justice, which means deciding the case in a way that conforms with existing statutory and common law precedent; treats both parties fairly; and leaves the law, and society, in a better place than it was before the decision.

All three of these issues can and should be dealt with in the brief, but the brief is possibly the best place to do statutory and common law precedent. Appellate argument is the best opportunity you have to present a focused narrative that responds to your decision maker's actual, stated concerns, and that exhorts the audience to act in a way that makes the world a better place—and, incidentally, helps your client as well.

It is very valuable to watch actual—as opposed to fictional—appellate arguments as you prepare your own. And it is not hard to do that. Most state

---

8. Thanks to Peter Knapp for this formulation, and also for suggesting the three important functions of an oral argument.

courts have audio and video streaming of their high court oral arguments. These are a great place to watch attorneys and judges at work.

For example, listen to (or read) the oral arguments from the *Obergefell* case in the U.S. Supreme Court.[9] This is the landmark case that ruled, in June 2015, that same-sex couples had the same Federal constitutional right to marry each other as do different-sex couples. The Court heard arguments on the case in April 2015. The arguments are long—almost three hours—and the transcripts are too. But flip through the transcript and consider the arguments in light of the three suggestions above: crystallizing issues in the brief; responding to decision makers' questions; and appealing to the audience's sense of justice, morality, fairness.

Notice how the argument is largely focused on answering questions from the decision makers. There are very few long stretches where one of the attorneys is allowed to proceed on her or his own. Every few lines, one of the Justices asks the attorney either to clarify something raised in the brief, and/or then to argue that point.

Notice also how very few times either attorney—or Justice—refers to precedent or case law by name. What are the attorneys arguing, then, if not the law? Consider this very early exchange between the Appellant's attorney, Mary Bonauto, and the Chief Justice, John Roberts:

> CHIEF JUSTICE ROBERTS: Well, you say join in the institution. The argument on the other side is that they're seeking to redefine the institution. Every definition that I looked up, prior to about a dozen years ago, defined marriage as unity between a man and a woman as husband and wife. Obviously, if you succeed, that core definition will no longer be operable.
> MS. BONAUTO: I hope not, Your Honor, because of what we're really talking about here is a class of people who are, by State laws, excluded from being able to participate in this institution.[10]

Rather than get defensive and argue with the Chief Justice about the core definition of marriage, Bonauto's argument immediately and explicitly appeals to the audience's sense of morality, justice, and fairness. She agrees with Justice

---

9. Obergefell v. Hodges Oral Argument Audio Question 1, Supreme Court of the United States, https://www.supremecourt.gov/oral_arguments/audio/2014/14-556-q1; Obergefell v. Hodges Oral Argument Audio Question 1, Supreme Court of the United States, https://www.supremecourt.gov/oral_arguments/audio/2014/14-556-q2.

10. Obergefell v. Hodges Oral Argument Tr. Question 1 (Apr. 28, 2015) p. 5: 9–19, https://www.supremecourt.gov/oral_arguments/argument_transcripts/2014/14-556q1_l5gm.pdf.

Roberts' core definition, and suggests that marriage, as thus defined, is an exclusive, unfair institution. And it becomes clear from that point that Bonauto wants her audience focused on this issue of fairness and inclusiveness—as opposed to discrimination and exclusion. Consider this exchange between Bonauto and Justice Alito:

> JUSTICE ALITO: You argue in your brief that the primary purpose of the Michigan law limiting marriage to a man and a woman was to demean gay people; is that correct?
>
> MS. BONAUTO: The Michigan statute and amendment certainly went out of their way to say that gay people were in some sense antithetical to the good of society. They wrote that …
>
> JUSTICE ALITO: And did you say in your brief that the primary purpose of that was to demean gay people?
>
> MS. BONAUTO: I think it has that effect, Your Honor. I do. Now, at the same time
>
> JUSTICE ALITO: Is that true just in Michigan or is that true of every other State that has a similar definition of marriage?
>
> MS. BONAUTO: Well, if we're talking about the States that have constitutional amendments, many of them are similar. There are a few States that have just statutes and didn't have amendments, and there's some, of course, that had none of the above. But even if there's not a purpose to demean, I think the common commonality among all of the statutes, whether they were enacted long ago or more recently, is that they encompass moral judgments and stereotypes about gay people.[11]

Justice Alito explicitly asks about something in Bonauto's brief—twice! But instead of referring directly to her brief to explain that point further, she uses the opportunity to crystallize the issue, by focusing not on the specific words of her brief—or of the Michigan statute—but on the underlying issue of fairness and morality. How does she do that? What does she demand the Justices focus on, about these statutes?

A final example from this case, Bonauto was asked by Justice Breyer to answer the question "Why cannot those States at least wait and see whether in fact doing so—denying marriage rights to same-sex couples—in the other States is or is not harmful to marriage?"[12] This is a softball question, coming as it does from one of the liberal members of the Bench, which gives Bonauto the opportunity to remind the Justices of their role in preserving individual

---

11. *Id.* at 8–9.
12. *Id.* at 16.

liberties and upholding the Constitution. She gets interrupted after her initial answer, but manages to return to the matter—which is, after all, the heart of Appellant's argument—to make sure her point is clear: this is a matter of individual freedom, that rests at the heart of the U.S. Constitution:

> MS. BONAUTO: ... In our system, you know, with the Fourteenth Amendment, which again is—sets forth principles that we all are governed by and govern our lives, and you look at examples like coverture. Okay? Even if it was not universal, it was still something that was wide—widespread in this nation for a very, very long time, and that change in marriage was deeply unsettling to people.
>
> Likewise, even if race was not used as a basis for discriminating in every single State as a matter of law by criminal law and constitutional law, it was incredibly pervasive. And again, changing that, as Virginia resisted in the Loving case, resisted and said please, wait and see, 80 percent of the American public was with Virginia on that. But again, it was the question of the individual liberty of the person to do something that was considered a profound change in its time.[13]
>
> ....
>
> Wait and see by itself has never been considered a legitimate justification, a freestanding justification under the Fourteenth Amendment. And what we're talking about here with waiting and seeing is we're talking about we're talking about the Petitioners being denied marriage. And we're talking about a second class status being tried as a matter of the Constitution....[14]

III. Legislative Advocacy[15]

Now we are going to turn to another context for lawyering that employs oral and written advocacy as well: legislative advocacy.[16] Unlike appellate advocacy where we are advocating for a ruling in a particular case with a particular set of

---

13. *Id.* at 16–17.

14. *Id.* at 20.

15. While we focus on legislative advocacy in this section, the process and role of narrative applies to advocacy for new laws, regulations, or rules before such institutions as legislatures, administrative agencies, and regulatory boards.

16. *See e.g.*, Chai Rachel Feldblum, *The Art of Legislative Lawyering and The Six Circles Theory of Advocacy*, 34 McGeorge L. Rev. 785 (2003); Hina Shah, *Notes from The Field: The Role of The Lawyer in Grassroots Policy Advocacy*, 21 Clinical L. Rev. 393 (2015); Marcy

circumstances, in legislative advocacy we are advocating for a new statute to be enacted that would prospectively apply to all relevant situations. Legislative advocacy is often done in a coalition because of the wide-ranging work of persuasion involved. The specific context for much of legislative advocacy is the process of persuading (often called lobbying) legislators to address a policy issue through passing new legislation or stopping proposed legislation.[17] But legislative advocacy also can involve an entire campaign, which includes persuading others to join the coalition as well as the public at large to support the proposed legislation.

Chai Feldblum identifies the following functions involved in legislative advocacy: developing strategy for the entire campaign, managing the lobbying of legislators, legislative lawyering, doing policy research, strategizing for public outreach, and communicating.[18] So what do lawyers do in the role of legislative

---

L. Karin and Robin R. Runge, *Toward Integrated Law Clinics that Train Social Change Advocates*, 17 Clinical L. Rev. 563 (2011).

17. For one state's guide to the legislative process, see The Legislative Process: How a Bill Becomes a Law, Maryland Manual Online, http://msa.maryland.gov/msa/mdmanual/07leg/html/proc.html. Of course, there is also the famous Schoolhouse Rock episode of "I'm Just a Bill." Schoolhouse Rock: America—I'm Just a Bill Music Video, YouTube, https://www.youtube.com/watch?v=FFroMQlKiag. Although the legislative process will vary based on jurisdiction, the rulemaking body, and other variables, a common process involves the following elements that will not necessarily happen in linear fashion: 1. Identifying a problem that can be addressed through new legislation; 2. Understanding the sociopolitical context that will be considered by the legislative body in addressing the problem; 3. Identifying the allies with whom you can work to address the problem through new legislation, including legislators, community groups, stakeholders, and others; 4. Identifying those people and groups that may oppose any proposed legislation; 5. Gathering information and stories concerning the problem and possible resolutions to the problem; 6. Analyzing the problem and proposed resolutions through the lens of the current sociopolitical context as well as arguments from those opposed to possible resolutions; 7. Creating a project theory for the proposed legislation; 8. Drafting the proposed legislation in consultation with legislators, your coalition, and other stakeholders; 9. Meeting with legislators to obtain sponsors and supporters; 10. Possibly meeting with those in the opposition to see if there can be any compromises on the draft to reduce or eradicate their opposition; 11. If the bill gets introduced, during committee hearings on the bill submitting written and oral testimony on the proposed legislation; 12. Through the legislative process meeting with or writing to key legislators requesting their support and answering any questions; 13. Perhaps engaging in a public media campaign through op/ed pieces, letters to the editor, providing information for feature articles, and blog posts, to persuade constituents and their representatives to support the legislation.

18. Feldblum, *supra* note 15, at 791 (Feldblum identifies these functions as part of her "Six Circles Theory of Advocacy" and proposes that there is one person for each of these functions). Hina Shah counters this a bit by explaining that in grassroots campaigns the functions are led by grassroots campaigns, not professional advocates, and multiple

advocacy? Often we are focused on (1) problem-solving and project theory creation, specifically, assessing the problem to be resolved through legislation, researching the problem, proposing solutions and approaches, and creating the project theory; (2) engaging in oral communications, advocacy, and negotiations; and (3) drafting materials, from written legislative testimony to the actual proposed legislation.[19]

Here's an example of legislative lawyering in practice: One state's civil protective order law provided relief for domestic violence, such as stay away orders and no contact orders, for persons in a *family* relationship, but not in a *dating* relationship. As a result, someone in a dating relationship who wanted the protection of a civil protective order could not get it under the law as written. Anti-domestic violence advocates had clients who wanted but were not eligible for a civil protective order because of this definition. A team of student attorneys joined a coalition of other lawyers, organizers and persons who had experienced domestic violence to advocate expansion of the law. The student attorneys researched the protective order law and legislative history in the state, researched the laws in other jurisdictions to see how they defined and addressed dating violence, and worked with people who had experienced dating violence to construct the narratives that would be presented to legislators. Other coalition members conducted outreach to, gathered information from, and negotiated with legislators regarding their support for and concerns about the legislation. The student attorneys worked with the coalition members to construct the project theory for the proposed legislation, coalition members worked with legislative members to prepare the draft bill, and the student attorneys drafted letters to legislators in support of the proposed legislation. And all coalition members, including the student attorneys, provided written and oral testimony in support of the proposed legislation.

Let's now try to break the legislative lawyer's legislative advocacy down into project theory, oral advocacy, and written advocacy, and identify the role of narrative in each segment.

A. *Project Theory*

The building block of your legislative advocacy is your project theory. As we discussed in Chapter Six, your project theory is a storyline based on narrative principles. For instance, a project theory will help you identify the

---

functions may be carried out by one person. Shah, *supra* note 15. Despite these differences, the literature suggests that all of the functions are relevant to legislative advocacy no matter how the functions are staffed or directed.

19. Feldblum, *supra* note 15, at 805.

problem that has disrupted the steady state for which the proposed bill will provide *closure*.[20] The theory will guide your strategic choices by helping to identify the facts and law relevant to the goal of passing the proposed legislation, and to craft those facts and law into a compelling and persuasive narrative. In addition, normative theory focused on the justice aspects of the goal adds to the persuasiveness of the theory.

Using the project theory, you can construct an appropriate narrative for your oral and written advocacy. You can enhance your narratives by showing rather than telling your audience what you want them to do. With permission, you may provide a brief story about one of your clients who has confronted the problem that the bill addresses as a way to illustrate the project theory.

Understanding narrative can also help you construct your project theory with an understanding that your audience may be primed with certain *masterplots* or *causations* that you need to address and discredit. For instance, as Matthew Coles discusses, in litigating for human rights laws for lesbian and gay civil rights in the 1990s, the narrative needed to address and discredit the fallacious masterplot that lesbian and gay men were "more emotionally unstable or more apt to assault children" than straight persons.[21]

Or you may provide a narrative of the evolution of the law, making it a *character* in the narrative, and show how the proposed bill achieves closure to the problem of a gap in the law.

For example, student attorneys working on the proposed legislation to expand the civil protective order law to include persons in a dating relationship, created the following project theory:

> The proposed bill amends the current protective order law to permit persons in dating relationships, including teenagers, to seek a protective order from domestic violence. Studies show that one in four adolescents report verbal, physical, emotional, or sexual abuse from a dating partner each year but they are not eligible for a comprehensive stay away and no contact protective order. Including dating relationships in the protective order statute, as other jurisdictions have done, will permit our state's teens to seek protection from further abuse.

This project theory tells a narrative that involves the problem of teenagers not getting the protection they need from intimate partner violence because of a gap in the law, and offers a solution to that problem—closure—with the proposed bill.

---

20. Robert Bray, SPIN Works! 29 (2002).
21. Bray, *supra* note 20, at 199.

While constructing narratives for your project theory, you will be aided by the cognitive science behind narratives if you ensure that there is *normalization*, that the project theory is internally and externally consistent. Ronald Dworkin describes the law as a "chain novel," where one author writes the first chapter and then passes it to another person who writes the next chapter, and the writing continues from one person to the next, each trying to keep the chapters holding together as a book with shared characters, events, and norms.[22] Each subsequent author is constrained by what comes before in order to ensure consistency. Accordingly, we need to organize the information we gain from all of our coalition members and outreach to legislators and others into a project theory that is consistent with the "chain novel" of the existing law and legislative history so the audience's brain will be open to our communications and not fighting them as random.

B. Oral Advocacy

Using the project theory, you can construct your oral advocacy in support of the proposed legislation. Oral legislative advocacy includes both explanatory and persuasive oral communications and may be made to other coalition members, legislators, stakeholders, the public, and those not in support of the proposal.[23] Explanatory oral communication is used to communicate your project theory and support thereto. As with all communication, your explanatory oral communication must be both clear and concise. Persuasive oral communication is used to convince others to agree with your position, and as such, will be clear and concise and persuasive. And similar to appellate advocacy, because the audience for oral communication may have short attention spans, you will want to construct your narrative in a way to grab the listener's attention and convey effectively the information necessary in a brief period of time.

As we have discussed throughout this book, narrative theory and storytelling practice help lawyers communicate clearly, concisely, and persuasively. Compelling stories help with explanatory and persuasive advocacy by helping an audience pay attention to, understand, and be compelled to fix troubling problems. The idea, then, for oral testimony is not to recite all of your information to the committee but to construct your information into a compelling narrative that will persuade the audience into supporting your proposal. And, part of your oral testimony will be engaging in a dialogue with and answering

---

22. David Ray Papke, Narrative and the Legal Discourse: A Reader in Storytelling and the Law 167 (1991).

23. *Id.* at 813.

questions and concerns raised by your audience. Narrative plays a role in all of this work.

For instance, in providing oral testimony before a legislative committee, a speaker may only have two to three minutes to provide information and persuade the legislators to vote favorably on a bill. The speaker needs to know what matters to the audience, what the audience needs to know, and convey that specific information to the audience.[24] In addition, the speaker needs to listen to what is being said verbally and nonverbally by each audience member and respond accordingly.[25]

Returning to the dating violence bill as an example, student attorneys focused their oral advocacy on stories of teenagers who had been subjected to dating violence and could not seek a protective order. Because the teenagers were uncomfortable testifying, the student attorneys were granted permission to tell their stories. The students also provided information garnered from their legal research of other states' protective order laws and their coverage of dating violence. Learning from the other coalition members who had met with legislators, the student attorneys knew that the legislators were particularly interested in how to define dating. Therefore, they focused only on the dating violence definitions used by other jurisdictions rather than all of the information they garnered from their research.

Finally, how you tell your narrative matters. You will want to find credible witnesses to testify. Experienced legislative lawyers often recommend that the storytellers who are most compelling might be the people who have faced the trouble seeking to be solved in the proposed legislation. As discussed above, such people may not always be available. Whoever is the storyteller, it is important that the spokesperson be believable to the audience and attuned to their concerns.[26]

C. *Written Advocacy*

Written legislative advocacy, like oral advocacy, is grounded in the project theory. Feldblum identifies the following forms of written legislative advocacy: "an options memo for a client, a piece of testimony for a hearing, a set of talking points for staff people, a background memo for coalition members, an

---

24. *Id.*
25. *Id.*
26. *Id.* at 196; The Leadership Conference Education Fund, *Grassroots Campaigns & Advocacy: A Toolkit to Help You Make Change Happen* 19, http://civilrightsdocs.info/pdf/field/toolkit/2015-update/Grassroots-Toolkit-2015-FOR-WEB.pdf.

alert for grassroots activists, an offer of proposed legislative language and committee report language, and comments on proposed regulations." [27] To be effective, written advocacy needs to distill a large amount of research about the problem and potential solutions and convey it concisely and clearly and specifically to the audience to whom it is intended. As with all of your writing, you will want your written advocacy to be easy on the reader and not require her too much to draw her own inferences or struggle to understand the information being conveyed.[28]

Narrative will aid you in the charge of communicating and persuading audience members based on written advocacy. Because legislators are most likely to pass a bill that solves a pressing problem or *trouble* of their constituents, the framing of the problem one seeks to solve, the *closure*, with the proposed legislation is critical to the process of written legislative advocacy.

And written legislative advocacy is an opportunity to consider using narrative in different ways. For instance, when the student attorneys drafted their legislative written testimony on the bill seeking to extend the protective order law to dating violence they utilized three different narratives. First, they discussed a narrative about themselves and their expertise in understanding who was excluded by the protective order law based on the clinic's representation of numerous clients over many years in protective order cases. Second, they obtained permission from their client to share her story of being subjected to dating violence and wanting a stay away order so her ex-boyfriend could not come near her or contact her. The student attorneys shared her specific narrative of being unable to get the relief she wanted because of the gap in the law. And third, they then included the narrative of other states' laws that provided protective order relief for persons subjected to dating violence as potential closures to the problem of dating violence disrupting the steady state of the goal of citizen safety.

IV. Conclusion

This chapter combines the skills and practices discussed in the oral advocacy and written advocacy chapters to address the skills involved in drafting an appellate brief and presenting the arguments contained in the brief during appellate oral argument. Narrative helps lawyers craft a persuasive argument on paper that will be persuasive and compelling to decision makers during the

---

27. *Feldblum, supra* note 15, at 812.
28. *Id.* at 811.

oral argument. This chapter also discussed the three most important things to prepare for during the oral argument—clarifying issues and arguments in the brief, answering questions from the decision maker, and appealing to the audience's sense of justice, fairness and morality. Finally, we explored the functions involved in legislative advocacy, which includes advocating on behalf of, or against, a proposed statute. Legislative advocacy includes problem solving, oral advocacy, negotiation, written advocacy and providing legislative testimony. Constructed narratives, including the project theory, are necessary parts of legislative advocacy.

Index